AF836216

# ORGANIZATIONAL NEEDS ASSESSMENTS

# ORGANIZATIONAL NEEDS ASSESSMENTS

## Design, Facilitation, and Analysis

Samuel B. McClelland

Q

QUORUM BOOKS
Westport, Connecticut • London

**Library of Congress Cataloging-in-Publication Data**

McClelland, Samuel B.
Organizational needs assessments : design, facilitation, and analysis / Samuel B. McClelland.
p. cm.
Includes bibliographical references (p. ) and index.
ISBN 0–89930–950–X (alk. paper)
1. Organizational change. 2. Needs assessment. 3. Human capital.
I. Title
HD58.8.M337 1995
658.4′06—dc20 95–14606

British Library Cataloguing in Publication Data is available.

Copyright © 1995 by Mercedes McClelland

All rights reserved. No portion of this book may be reproduced, by any process or technique, without the express written consent of the publisher.

Library of Congress Catalog Card Number: 95–14606
ISBN: 0–89930–950–X

First published in 1995

Quorum Books, 88 Post Road West, Westport, CT 06881
An imprint of Greenwood Publishing Group, Inc.

Printed in the United States of America

The paper used in this book complies with the Permanent Paper Standard issued by the National Information Standards Organization (Z39.48–1984).

10 9 8 7 6 5 4

To my mother
Leatrice McClelland

And in loving memory of my father
Sam McClelland, Sr.
Who always gave his all and never asked for anything in return

# Contents

# Figures and Tables

## FIGURES

## TABLES

# Acknowledgments

It has been said that no authors ever write books by themselves. This book is certainly no exception. I am indebted to a number of people, many of whom I cannot name individually. I would, however, like to extend my sincere appreciation to a very select group. First, I want to thank my original mentor, John W. McNally, Colonel, USA (ret.), who, some fifteen years ago, challenged me to become involved in HRD as a career. His foresight on HRD emerging from the depths of personnel management and into a preeminence of its own has certainly come true.

Special recognition and very, very special thanks go to two outstanding individuals: Dr. Jack Phillips, who read the entire manuscript and provided extremely valuable insights and detailed suggestions for its improvement; and Ms. Linda Brown, who also read the entire manuscript and provided feedback as to its usefulness as a text in a graduate HRD program. To these persons I am very appreciative and deeply indebted.

I also want to thank several of my colleagues who have read sections of the manuscript and whose individual as well as collective suggestions have served to strengthen it: Dr. Jerry Dibble for his review and critique of the sections dealing with individual interviews and communications; Dr. Stanley J. Smits who reviewed the introduction and first chapter and got me started on the right path; Dr. Robert Elrod for his comprehensive review and down-to-earth recommendations on the section dealing with statistics and data analysis; and last, Dr. Roy Kern who, in addition to critiquing the sections dealing with group dynamics and interpersonal relations, has been a source of inspiration over the many years that it has been my pleasure to know him.

I also wish to acknowledge Dr. John D. Hogan, Dean of the College of Business Administration, and Mr. David R. Forquer, Director of the Center for Executive Education, both of Georgia State University, for providing an environment which made the research and writing of this book possible.

Last, but certainly not least, I want to thank my wife, Mercedes, and my son, Sean Michael, for their love and support. They are real heroes because, without their patience, support, and understanding, this project would never have gotten off the ground.

# Introduction

In today's rapidly changing business environment, organizations have a compelling need to explore what must be done to improve their performance and enhance their competitive positions. As noted author William Tracey observed: "Obviously, organization and group needs are very important; they must be met if the organization is to prosper. . . . The consequences of failing to meet these needs are far-reaching and can be disastrous for any enterprise—poor morale, low productivity, declining profits, and high turnover with its associated high costs."[1]

This book has been written with one principal purpose in mind: to present an applications-oriented framework within which various needs assessment theories can be practically applied. In taking this approach, the concept of defining organizational as well as individual needs is explored and presented in a "systems" format by stressing the mechanics of assessment project design, facilitation, and data analysis.

This book is directed at two broad audiences: (1) training, Human Resource Development (HRD), and Organization Development (OD) practitioners and consultants who are in need of an information resource on designing and conducting organizational needs assessments; and (2) students who are preparing themselves for a career in HRD or OD so they can enter the profession with a fundamental understanding of what needs assessments are and how they are designed and implemented.

The book is divided into five parts. Part I focuses on the emerging importance of HRD and the importance of its role in furthering the organization's business goals and strategies. Chapter 1 presents a brief overview of human performance and its relationship to organizational and individual productivity. It defines the strategic and integrative role that the human resource department plays in identifying organizational and individual needs. A brief history of the origins of needs assessments is presented along with perspectives on their overall importance to organizational success. The concept of the needs assessment as the first step to identifying barriers to increasing organizational and individual performance is discussed along with an overview of how *needs* and *wants* can sometimes congruently emerge. Different sources of background information, useful for understanding the organization's culture and operational environment, are presented along with a brief discussion on the terminology used throughout the remaining chapters.

Chapter 2 defines the reasons why organizations conduct needs assessments and illustrates different types and approaches. It summarizes the advantages and disadvantages to using commercially available standardized assessment instruments and emphasizes the advantages, long-term cost-effectiveness, and utility in developing the ability to design custom needs assessment systems. The roles of external consultants as experts in the customization process are discussed along with details relating to needs assessment planning. The chapter concludes with the presentation of a systems model for needs assessment design, facilitation, and analysis.

Part II details the fundamental tasks necessary to design a comprehensive needs assessment system. Chapter 3 discusses the need to define and establish assessment goals and presents various goal-setting processes and alternatives. An overview of organizational policy considerations and how they can affect assessment planning is included. Factors that are useful for identifying assessment group populations are presented along with details on how to identify and select assessment project resource staff. The value in selecting and using internal consultants—particularly as subject matter experts (SMEs)—is also presented with emphasis placed on the importance of using external consultants. Chapter 3 contains guidelines on managing external consultant relationships in a mutually beneficial "win/win" context and concludes with a detailed overview of assessment project budgeting procedures by presenting various ways for calculating project costs.

Chapter 4 presents detailed information on needs assessment data-gathering methods. The differences between narrative (qualitative) and numerical (quantitative) data are discussed along with their advantages and disadvantages. Four types of data-gathering methods are detailed: survey questionnaires, individual interviews, focus groups, and on-site observations. In addition, recommendations and examples are presented on how these methods are used either individually or in an aggregate manner. Other types of data-gathering methods such as telephone surveys, electronic mail (e-mail), and satellite or distance conferencing are discussed, as are their advantages and disadvantages. Chapter 4 also provides guidelines for deciding which data-gathering methods to use. It includes a detailed table of decision factors useful for identifying an appropriate mix of data-gathering methods. Aggregate data-collection methods are discussed, as are their major advantages and disadvantages.

Part III focuses on the mechanics of needs assessment implementation, facilitation, and control. Chapter 5 addresses the basics of pretesting the assessment and summarizes various sampling procedures. It stresses the importance of pretest results as a way of predicting how the needs assessment will perform once it is formally implemented. Logistical considerations such as the correlation between questionnaire length and response rates and the scheduling of interviews, focus groups, and on-site observations are detailed. Emphasis is placed on the necessity to review the project plan by developing project time lines and conducting a comprehensive review and update of budgetary information. Chapter 5 concludes by emphasizing the necessity of gaining senior management's approval and support of the assessment before formally announcing it to the organization's employees.

Chapter 6 emphasizes organization and control of the needs assessment by presenting techniques on how to resolve interview, focus group, and on-site observation scheduling conflicts. Methods for estimating survey questionnaire response rates along with techniques for handling nonresponses are also presented as part of the organizing and control process. Decision factors related to the use of computers for processing needs assessment data along with various types of software programs are also discussed, as is the importance of establishing a central data receiving point to maintain consistency in the data entry process. Chapter 6 concludes with an overview of the dangers of preliminary biasing brought about through early exposure to emerging data patterns.

Part IV explores various statistical techniques used for analyzing and evaluating needs assessment data. Chapter 7 presents statistical methods commonly used in needs assessment data analysis. It includes a variety of examples of how these techniques and tests can be applied and concludes with an explanation of how statistically based information is analyzed, summarized, presented, and ultimately interpreted.

Chapter 8 details procedures for formulating recommendations derived from a comprehensive summary and analysis of information produced through aggregate data-gathering methods. It highlights the mechanics for comparing and contrasting both quantitative and qualitative data sets and includes commentary on how to treat qualitatively based peripheral information. Methods for formulating intervention recommendations and activities—along with their associated levels of risk—are also provided. A comprehensive discussion on the preparation of the final report to management along with techniques that can be used to enhance the report presentation is included. Chapter 8 concludes with suggestions for conducting a postassessment project summary and review and emphasizes the importance of such a review as a reference for future assessment projects.

Part V examines the utility of needs assessments in developing training programs. It also explores their value as front-end diagnostic tools for implementing organizational change, reengineering and restructuring efforts, Total Quality Management (TQM), Strategic Management Development

(SMD), and other performance improvement programs. Chapter 9 presents a framework by which training programs can be developed from needs that were identified through a comprehensive assessment process. This framework includes the writing of instructional goals and objectives derived from the assessment outcome(s), techniques for appraising employee learning capacities, and methods for developing an instructional strategy, sequencing of the course content, developing instructional materials and an accompanying lesson plan, selecting instructors, designing effective evaluation systems, pretesting, and monitoring and evaluating the training's long-term effectiveness. It concludes with techniques for preparing a composite evaluation and report of the training's effectiveness for presentation to management.

Chapter 10 illustrates the utility and value of needs assessment data in improving organizational and individual performance, in facilitating organizational change, in designing and implementing TQM programs, and in designing SMD efforts. The concept of change as both a challenge and as an opportunity is discussed along with how OD is used to initiate change resulting in organizational transformation. The similarities and differences between OD and needs assessments along with methods for assessing the organization's readiness to accept and undergo change are also presented. Chapter 10 provides information on how needs assessment data can be used for designing and implementing TQM programs and includes a discussion of the value of needs assessment data in designing and establishing an SMD effort. It concludes by outlining the utility of organizational needs assessments as a front-end process useful in organizational reengineering, in designing employee involvement programs, and for diagnosing performance improvement obstacles which can be addressed through effective Employee Assistance Programs (EAPs).

Chapter 11 contains a case study that was drawn from an actual needs assessment. It illustrates how different events can affect assessment design, facilitation, and analysis and how outcomes can and will vary. The chapter concludes with a number of discussion questions that are relevant not only to the case as it is presented but also to what can be realistically expected during an organizational needs assessment project.

Finally, the appendixes contain useful examples of actual assessment budgeting and reconciliation forms, an organizational climate survey, a sample needs assessment interview script, a sample focus group moderator script, sample job and task analysis forms, and an exhibit of the results of an actual needs assessment project.

Because there are no absolute or universally recognized needs assessment models, the methods and approaches presented throughout this book may not be appropriate under all conditions and circumstances. Without doubt, there exist many successful needs assessment models. However, the fundamental components of planning, data gathering, analysis, summarization, and the formulation of recommendations are germane to organizational needs assessments irrespective of the approach taken.

The scope of this book is centered on conducting systematic needs assessments in large organizations. That does not mean that it is not applicable to smaller ones as well. The concepts, methods, and techniques presented are fundamental to conducting successful systematic needs assessments regardless of the organization's size. What differentiates small from large assessments is the complexity and the number of variables that influence their outcomes. Generally speaking, the larger the organization, the more complex the assessment will be. Also, the level of detail in the presentation of assessment results and recommendations to management is usually considerably less where smaller organizations are concerned. Overall, however, the underlying components of assessment design, facilitation, and analysis are the same.

One final note: Becoming a good needs analyst requires time, patience, and practice, all of which adds up to experience. One cannot get experience without experimentation. Therefore, the best advice that can be given to those who are interested in developing their organizational needs assessment skills is to not be afraid to experiment. Study what has worked well and, more specifically, why. Learn from mistakes, share experiences with others, and, most of all, be creative in your approach.

It is my sincere hope that this book will in some way contribute to furthering the development of successful needs assessment models on both a professional and an academic level.

## NOTE

1. W. R. Tracey, *Designing Training and Development Systems*, rev. ed. (New York: AMACOM, 1984).

PART I

# The Role of Human Resource Development in Diagnosing Organizational and Individual Needs

CHAPTER 1

# Needs Assessments in Human Resource Development

Human Resource Development (HRD) has emerged as an important and exciting field. Once regarded simply as training and considered part of the personnel function, over the last decade it has evolved into a discipline and profession unique to itself. As the field has grown in popularity and significance, more emphasis has been placed on its role and importance in identifying individual and organizational needs.

## STRATEGIC IMPLICATIONS FOR HUMAN RESOURCE DEVELOPMENT

In today's globally competitive environment, it is unrealistic to believe that the successful management of an organization can be accomplished without trained and experienced personnel. It is also unrealistic to believe that an organization can ignore the forces of change. The last twenty-five years or so have had dramatic effects on the way organizations are structured and, more important, how they operate. This is perhaps nowhere more prevalent than in today's globally competitive environment. Globalized competition has forced widespread organizational restructuring and downsizing. This has resulted in acute shortages in many organizations' human resource base.[1] The implications of this are tremendous. Because they can no longer afford the luxury of hiring managers into areas of functional specialty, organizations now find that they must prepare their employees to take on broader and more generalized responsibilities. In response to this challenge, many creative approaches to addressing organizational and individual needs have emerged. Many organizations have found that they must now work with limited resources while simultaneously trying to anticipate constantly changing conditions. Within this dimension, the role of HRD has changed from being primarily a training-based endeavor to that of being a key facilitator in implementing organizations' business and competitive strategies.

The need to become proactively involved in strategy formulation and implementation signals a departure from the traditional role of HRD. Most notably, the mind-set of many HRD professionals is changing to focus on the corporate vision by emphasizing growth, organizational renewal, and progressive transformation. In order to accomplish this, however, the HRD function itself must take on broader levels of responsibility by moving from a tactical to a long-range view of its role in the strategy formulation process. It must become actively engaged in activities designed to augment the organization's business strategy. In this role, HRD must direct its efforts toward strategy interpretation and the enhancement of human performance as a means for developing potential to improve organizational performance, efficiency, and productivity.

## Human Performance and Organizational Productivity

HRD has traditionally been concerned with increasing human performance and, as such, with enhancing employee performance through a variety of applied learning processes. There is, however, a sometimes dubious relationship between employees who are supposedly performing at peak or maximum levels and the return (in terms of profits, cost savings, improvements in quality and service, etc.) the organization actually receives. Historically, HRD has emphasized that organizations are made up of people, all of whom have different personalities, backgrounds, and experiences and differing sets of needs, wants, and expectations.[2] In essence, it is comprised of individuals. Yet, even though HRD has contributed to increasing levels of individual performance, this has not always translated into increased levels of organizational performance and productivity.

To more fully understand the relationship between individual and organizational performance, it is necessary to first explore factors which have considerable influence on employee performance. Some of these are the following:

1. An understanding of how workers view themselves
2. How this view contributes to the overall work effort
3. The type of job, activity, or function employees perform in the organizational setting
4. The physical environment in which these functions or activities take place

Each of these can have a positive or a negative effect on organizational performance. Factors such as pay and incentive systems, delegation of responsibility with the level of authority necessary to ensure the responsibilities are adequately met, and a broadening of career advancement opportunities are but a few examples.

In a macroorganizational sense, individual performance goals should be realistically established and periodically reviewed to make certain they are synchronous with the organization's goals and business strategies. Goals should be designed to foster individual and group participation. They should stress achievement and contribute directly to furthering organizational success. In concert with this, HRD policies should be designed to complement organizational policies by focusing on the job of increasing individual effectiveness within the organizational structure.[3] Through proper design and execution, HRD policies can and will have a significant impact on both individual and organizational performance.

### The Role of the Human Resource Development Department

In today's complex business world, HRD's role in supporting organizational functions has undergone dramatic transformation. As more organizations have undergone downsizing, restructuring, and decentralization efforts, traditional hierarchical structures have been flattened to the point where decision making and profit–loss responsibilities have been pushed lower and lower throughout all levels. Therefore, in the current business environment, the role of the HRD department may be better defined as follows:

1. To establish HRD standards and policies commensurate with organizational standards and policies
2. To develop systems and processes for assessing organizational needs
3. To set the direction for HRD efforts to support the organization's business strategy
4. To conduct ongoing monitoring and analysis of line and staff functions, formulate recommendations for interventions, and report these to appropriate management personnel
5. To design, conduct, evaluate, and analyze all training and developmental activities including benefits, returns on investment, and cost justifications

In order to successfully implement this more strategic role, it is imperative that the HRD department be staffed with trained, knowledgeable, and competent professionals. It therefore becomes the responsibility of senior management to ensure that these individuals are carefully recruited, selected, evaluated, and provided with the necessary resources and authority. HRD must have ultimate responsibility for ensuring that all of its activities are contributing to furthering the organization's strategy and competitive position by positively impacting human as well as organizational performance. One way in which this can be accomplished is by conducting assessments that are designed to identify individual and organizational needs. From these, interventions (e.g., training) can be developed to provide employees with the knowledge, skills, and abilities (KSAs) that will allow them to perform at significantly higher levels.

## SOME HISTORY

Assessments have long been used in the fields of psychology, social science, and education to gather feedback for purposes of applied as well as clinical research. Although it is difficult to accurately define, the origins of needs assessments can be traced back to the Frederick W. Taylor era of scientific management. His views were based upon (1) the scientific method of job design (which was accomplished through data gathering), (2) the teaching or development of employees as a means of improving individual and, hence, organizational performance, (3) the joining of employees and work methods so that jobs could be more carefully designed, and (4) the necessity to bring management and workers closer together in a form of mutual dependency and cooperation.[4] This led to the emergence of new approaches to the problems of defining worker training needs. One of the earliest of these was the formation of an advisory service known as Training Within Industry (TWI). Originated by the National Defense Advisory Commission in August 1940, its purpose was to train people for work in defense-related industries to replace men who were being conscripted into the armed services.[5] One of its first actions was to establish the Job Instruction Training Program whose primary objective was to develop systems that enabled new workers to become trained and fully productive as quickly as possible, thereby maintaining and eventually increasing America's wartime industrial manufacturing capacity.

During late 1940 and early 1941, as replacement workers were hired in increasing numbers, it soon became evident that there was a wide discrepancy or gap in the KSAs these new hires were bringing to the job. The ability to be able to adequately determine the competency levels of new employees and then develop appropriate training to get them fully operational necessitated that a diagnostic approach be designed and implemented. Knowing that skill or knowledge gaps would vary widely between individuals, a systematic approach incorporating different diagnostic methods would be needed. In response to this, a combined-methods approach was devised. Based on the understanding that the output of skilled and semiskilled workers varies widely and is dependent on the type of work to be performed (e.g., office or administrative work, service or manufacturing work, or supervisory/management tasks), it incorporated the use of selected diagnostic methods that were related to the position(s) in question. For example, if individuals were being considered for a manufacturing job that required a certain skill to operate a piece of machinery, the type of diagnostic approach or instrument used would have to measure the individuals' present skill level as well as their potential ability. The methods most widely used to assess these were the following:

1. *Productivity and performance measures*: Also known as operational audits, this approach was used to measure present output (and hence present skill level) and then compare it to desired or preferred performance levels. The difference between the two would be used an an indicator of what skills workers needed to acquire in order to perform satisfactorily.
2. *Observations*: Taken by skilled workers who were familiar with certain work processes, it emphasized work methods and behaviors related to the job and the work environment and whether the person(s) either selected or under consideration to fill the vacancy had the potential to perform the job-related tasks.
3. *Surveys, interviews, and simulations*: This method included written questionnaires, individual and group interviews, and critical-incident situational simulations to predict how individuals may react and how they would otherwise perform in certain situations.

The original work of the TWI contributed greatly to introducing and understanding the concepts of needs assessment design, facilitation, and analysis. Although it has long since gone out of existence, the methods the TWI originated are still in widespread use today. However, these have undergone considerable change and refinement.

One of the first major efforts to define, change, and redefine organizational needs categorized needs assessments into three interrelated components: organizational analysis, operational (or task) analysis, and person analysis.[6] This led to other significant efforts which involved the categorizing of needs assessment methods in an effort to expand on the specific techniques for gathering training-related data.[7] Most notable among these were advancements that were made during the 1950s which integrated management concepts with the behavioral sciences.[8] Many of these methods contributed to forming the basis for the various types of needs assessment models in use today.

## THE NEED TO ASSESS NEEDS

Many times needs are obvious. For example, in order to sustain life, human beings need oxygen and water. We also have other needs, many of which are rooted in our culture, our societal values, and in our expected norms of behavior. In order to fully understand the requirements of these needs, we look to peers and to peer groups and to what our society as a whole believes are acceptable forms of conduct and behavior. In addition, we look within ourselves to determine what we feel we need (or want) in order to make our lives more meaningful and what our conscience tells us is morally as well as ethically correct. As a society, we constantly assess our physical environment to find out what is needed to better our standard of living. We assess our needs both individually and collectively.

Organizations are essentially microcosms of the larger society in which they function. As such, they share the same needs, wants, and desires, albeit on a smaller scale. They are in a state of continual evolution and change. Fundamentally, organizations have a prevailing need to continually assess and reassess their positions, values, policies, goals, and mission. They assess and reassess their employees and their customers in an ongoing effort to achieve maximum performance. Like members in an individual society, organizations in the private sector have the principal responsibility to provide returns to their shareholders, while public organizations have the principal responsibility to make judicious use of taxpayers' monies to provide better and more cost-effective services. In order to accomplish their missions, organizations require both internal as well as external information so that they can make informed decisions concerning the efficient use of their resources. Information on marketing data, demographics, consumer profiles, pending government regulations, and employment and environmental laws are all examples of an organization's external data needs. Additionally, in order to fulfill their mission through strategic use of their human resources, organizations need to collect internal information on their operational environments, their employees' morale, the effect that social, political, and economic change has on their operational environment, communication systems, management styles, performance and productivity levels, and so on. Critically important information such as this can be obtained through properly designed needs assessment systems. However, more often than not, many types of intervention programs (e.g., training, organizational change, restructuring, work redesign, changes in compensation structures, workforce reductions, etc.) are implemented without the organization first undertaking a comprehensive needs assessment. The result is misdirected activity that consumes precious funds while producing little in the way of tangible, bottom-line results.

## REASONS FOR CONDUCTING NEEDS ASSESSMENTS

Needs assessments produce both quantitative (numerical) and qualitative (text or narrative) data. Information such as this can be useful for calling management's attention to needs that exist within the organization. Further, needs assessments can identify what activities as well as resources will be required in order to see that these needs are met. Since management does not usually favor investing scarce resources in activities that have not been proven to be necessary or that provide little in the way of return on investment (ROI), using needs assessment data will, among other things, assist in providing justification for funds to support needs assessment processes. With increasing pressure being applied on HRD managers to associate and justify costs with returns, assessments can identify areas where strategies and resources designed to address individual as well as organizational needs can be more effectively applied.

Organizational needs assessments are designed and implemented for many reasons, some of which are the following:

1. To gain insight into employee morale and attitudinal issues which, if left unattended, can inhibit individual as well as organizational performance
2. To identify gaps or deficiencies in KSAs
3. As a means for formulating objectives for training or other intervention strategies
4. As a means for identifying other forms or types of organizational problems and/or opportunities
5. To obtain feedback on the organization's operations, its systems, and on its internal as well as its external environment

As far as justifying resources to management is concerned, needs assessments provide data that can contribute to answering the following questions:

1. Is there a problem with organizational or individual performance?
2. Are there problems related to organizational or individual productivity?
3. Are there skills and knowledge gaps or deficiencies?
4. Are there problems with the organizational structure?
5. Are there communication problems?
6. How are external conditions (e.g., markets, competition, economic, and regulatory) affecting the organization?
7. What do the organization's shareholders and customers think?
8. Does the organization suspect that problems on either a micro or macro level (or both; e.g., departmental or organization-wide) will affect desired performance levels?
9. How important or urgent are these problems?
10. What interventions are needed (e.g., training, process consultation, counseling, structural or policy changes or revisions, etc.)?

To the HRD professional, organizational problems can be viewed to represent opportunity. In fact, an important first step to identifying organizational needs is made by adopting the position that problems should be viewed as opportunities for improvement.

## THE NEEDS ASSESSMENT AS THE FIRST STEP

In the early part of the twentieth century, needs assessment methods were first used to pinpoint knowledge and skills deficiencies of newly hired workers. Today, their use has evolved much further. In the contemporary organization, various types of needs assessment methods are used for effective workforce planning. Thus, a needs assessment can be defined as a composition of analytical methods comprised of various diagnostic instruments and procedures whose purpose is to investigate performance deficiencies (the obvious as well as the not so obvious) and to pinpoint areas where an intervention strategy may be developed and applied to correct the deficiency or fill the knowledge gap.

As the sophistication of needs assessment methods and their importance to the HRD field have increased, many myths have also evolved about what a needs assessment actually is, what it involves, and what it is supposed to do.

Myth I: Needs analysis and needs assessments are the same thing. Although many argue that the difference between the terms assessment and analysis is a matter of semantics, the fact is, a needs analysis is a part of the overall needs assessment process.[9] Needs analysis is a stage within a needs assessment where data are evaluated, thus providing the basis from which subsequent recommendations regarding intervention activities are made.

Myth II: Needs assessments focus only on training needs and are predisposed to recommend training as a solution. This is a widely held belief. Many times training is indeed recommended, but not always. Other intervention strategies such as employee coaching and counseling, job rotation, process consultation, organizational restructuring, reengineering, and redesigning employee compensation systems are also frequently recommended as a result of an analysis of the data collected via the organizational needs assessment process.

Myth III: Employee or organizational surveys are needs assessments. Employee or organizational survey methods can be part of an assessment process, but they usually do not constitute a complete needs assessment of and by themselves.

Most needs assessments are directed at organizational systems and the KSAs employees use to accomplish tasks. Specifically, they are aimed at the organizational structure within which these tasks are carried out. Depending on their scope and overall intent, assessments vary in complexity and length. With the overriding goal being to increase organizational performance and, ultimately, the output of quality goods and/or services, needs assessments become the first step in a chain of intervention processes and activities (see Figure 1.1).

Needs assessments are used to gather data on individual needs within the organization's framework. Although primarily directed toward the individual (micro level), they emphasize the individual's contributions to improving organizational performance. This increase translates to total organizational output or, rather, to the amount of goods and/or services the organization provides to the marketplace and to the general public at large (macro level). This output is expressed in economic terms as the gross national product (GNP). The GNP represents the collective value of these goods and services which

**Figure 1.1**
Needs Assessments and Their Relationship to the Levels of Input(s), Output(s), and Value(s)

Micro Level:
Individual Employee Contribution
to Organizational Performance and
Productivity (Input)

▼
▼
▼

Macro Level:
Goods and/or Services Produced by
the Organization and Provided to the
Marketplace(s) (Output)

▼
▼
▼

Gross National Product (GNP):
Collective and Cumulative Value
of Goods/Services Produced

▼
▼
▼

Societal Value (SV):
The Value Which Society, as a
Whole, Derives from the Collective
Output of Organizational Goods/
Services

ultimately translates into Societal Value (SV) or the benefits and values provided to the society as a whole.

## Defining Needs versus Wants

One aspect of the needs assessment process that presents a conflict to HRD analysts is the necessity to separate employee and organizational needs from wants. In a strict sense, needs can be defined as a gap or deficiency between current and/or desired skill levels. Alternatively, wants can be defined as those things which employees (and organizations) feel would be beneficial, even nice, but which, when viewed realistically, do little to contribute to filling a KSA gap or deficiency. That is not to say that wants are of little value or serve no particular purpose. Quite the opposite is true. Addressing wants can be an excellent way to increase employee morale and provide greater degrees of incentive and motivation toward satisfying existing needs or even those that will, at some future point in time, become prevalent. For example, consider an organization whose current financial data suggest that performance and productivity are at acceptable levels (or even slightly above). Profitability is good and the prospects for output at the individual as well as organizational levels is expected to be above average. The results of a needs assessment revealed that many employees felt productivity could be improved through the publication of a monthly newsletter highlighting individual contributions and achievements. Is this actually a need? Should management give serious consideration to the publication of the newsletter? Will it really impact the bottom line, improve profitability, and raise individual as well as organizational performance? Perhaps . . . perhaps not. But when the costs associated with producing such a newsletter are weighed against the possibility of stagnant or decreased employee morale and productivity, the want can certainly become justified.

Needs and wants can sometimes emerge congruently. Many times the needs of one individual or group in the organization can also be the wants of another individual or group, and vice versa. For example, consider the following scenario: A company is about to install new data base software on its existing computer system. The old software is slow, difficult to learn, and requires substantial maintenance, programming, end-user input time, and updating. Needs identified through an assessment process showed that the new software must be faster, more flexible, user friendly, and should require less maintenance and updating. Alternatively, the end users, many of whom are computer literate, want the new software to be easy to learn. Management feels that the overriding decision factor should be the initial expense incurred in converting existing data from the old to the new data base. After an extensive search based on the defined needs criteria, a new software program is chosen. It is versatile, it runs faster on the company's existing equipment, and it is more flexible, thereby giving the company greater control over its applications. It is also easier to use, thus reducing the amount of training and retraining that would otherwise be necessary with another type of data base program. In this example, the needs of management and the information systems personnel (e.g., increased versatility and flexibility, greater control, and cost-effectiveness) and the wants of the end user (e.g., ease of use) have both been met. In essence, the needs of one group matched the wants of the other. When properly considered, needs and wants can sometimes be met simultaneously through an effective needs assessment process. The end result can be very positive.

## BACKGROUND INFORMATION

Background information is important in the needs assessment process. Information such as the organization's history, its position in its respective marketplace, its mission and business strategy, its management and employees, and so on is important and useful for understanding the organization's culture, its operational environment, its business objectives and strategies, and its competitive positioning. Background information like this is necessary in order to better understand how and in what context the organization functions.

Background information can be obtained from a variety of sources. Some of these are annual reports, company personnel records, internal audits (although, for proprietary reasons, these may be classified as confidential), news or press releases about new products or services, records and results from past training courses, articles in business journals, customers as well as suppliers, and, of course, information from any needs assessments that were previously conducted.

## A WORD ON TERMINOLOGY

Like other disciplines and professions, HRD has terminology that is unique to itself. There are many different words and terms that are used to describe different aspects of the profession and the variety of topics it encompasses. Unfortunately, many of these words and terms are not universally applied nor recognized as meaning the same thing to everyone. For example, in the finance and accounting professions, the term *balance sheet* refers to a financial document which reflects an organization's financial status. It is a term that financial analysts and accountants agree upon because it means the same thing to both professions. Alternatively, in HRD, the terms *needs assessment* and *needs analysis*, as discussed earlier, can mean the same thing to some people, while to others a needs analysis is but a part of a needs assessment process.

Terminology can thus serve to distract and confuse as much as it can serve to clarify. The problem with HRD terminology is that many terms are often used interchangeably. In the interest of clarification, considerable effort has been made to recognize that some of the terms used throughout this book will mean different things to different readers. Therefore, some terms will be presented as being interchangeable (e.g., the words "program" and "course" are used in Chapter 9 to describe a classroom training activity).

## SUMMARY

HRD has emerged into a preeminence of its own. Once viewed simply as training that was conducted under the auspices of the personnel department, it is now viewed as a means for assisting the organization in developing and implementing its business and competitive strategies. The last quarter century has produced dramatic changes in the way organizations are structured. This has produced a need to modify the organization to better respond to changing economic conditions.

One of the most important strategic roles for HRD is to refocus on the long-term development of human resources through an anticipatory and proactive position. This requires continual involvement in the formulation of organizational strategy and the development of effective HRD policies designed to continually improve and enhance individual and, thus, organizational performance. By focusing on the individual's contribution to the organizational effort, HRD seeks to understand how workers view themselves, how they view the job they perform, and how they view the environment in which they perform their job or function. To accomplish this, it is necessary to make certain that policies designed to foster improved performance are in place, continually monitored, and revised to reflect current operational and market conditions. HRD must take the lead in researching and establishing performance standards and goals and should actively engage in policy formulation. In order to fulfill these roles, it is imperative that the HRD department be adequately funded and staffed with trained and experienced professionals.

The first step to diagnosing organizational deficiencies and gaps in employee KSAs lies in assessing the organization, its structure, and the individuals it employs. This is accomplished through the implementation of needs assessment systems. These include various types of data-gathering methods that are directed at investigating organizational systems and the people who work within them. They can be focused on individual or group participation or they can be directed at total organizational systems, including operational environments and cultures. In undertaking a needs assessment, needs must be analyzed and viewed differently from wants. Needs are defined as a gap between current and desired skill or knowledge levels, while wants are defined as those things that would be nice to have but that may not necessarily contribute to furthering individual and organizational performance. Wants, however, should not be entirely dismissed as being noncontributory to furthering the goals of the organization. Many times wants and needs represent the same things to different groups. If viewed objectively, both individual as well as organizational needs and wants can be met simultaneously.

The data obtained from a well-planned needs assessment can be useful in developing interventions (including training-based activities) designed to address as well as overcome gaps in employee KSAs. Furthermore, they can provide information that is useful for implementing organizational change strategies.

## NOTES

1. S. Fisher, "Cutting Costs or Rebuilding Business?" *European Management Journal*, Vol. 11, No. 1, 1993, pp. 74–79.
2. E. Smith, *The Productivity Manual* (Houston: Gulf Publishing, 1990).

3. J. Berry, "Linking Management Development to Business Strategies," *Training and Development Journal*, Vol. 44, No. 8, pp. 20–22.
4. F. Taylor, *The Principles of Scientific Management* (New York: Harper and Row, 1911).
5. V. Miller, "The History of Training," in *Training and Development Handbook: A Guide to Human Resource Development*, 3rd ed., R. Craig, ed. (New York: McGraw-Hill, 1987), pp. 3–18.
6. W. McGehee and P. Thayer, *Training in Business and Industry* (New York: Wiley & Sons, 1961).
7. M. Moore and P. Dutton, "Training Needs Analysis: Review and Critique," *Academy of Management Review*, Vol. 3, No. 3, pp. 532–545.
8. D. McGregor, *The Human Side of Enterprise* (New York: McGraw-Hill, 1960); R. Likert, *New Patterns of Management* (New York: McGraw-Hill, 1961); V. Vroom, *Work and Motivation* (New York: Wiley & Sons, 1964).
9. R. Kaufman, "Auditing Your Needs Assessments," *Training and Development*, Vol. 48, No. 2, pp. 22–23.

CHAPTER 2

# Preparing for a Needs Assessment

This is the first stage of a systematic approach to designing and conducting organizational needs assessments.

## GENERALIZED TYPES OF NEEDS ASSESSMENTS

Although there are no universally accepted standards for needs assessment design and application, the following are some generalized assessment types that are in widespread use.

### Competency/Skills

These usually consist of survey, interview, and observation methods. They are used to identify skill or competency deficiencies by comparing current performance levels to predetermined standards. A popular use is screening applicants for technical or manufacturing positions, particularly where the job requires the use of automation or other types of specialized equipment and technology. It is also widely used to identify training needs and is generally applied at the individual (micro) level.

### Knowledge/Experience

These focus on the individual's professional, educational, and experiential background. They are used to identify and equate current knowledge or experience levels, to apply the results to standard or desired levels, and to estimate an individual's potential to acquire additional knowledge or experience. The ultimate goal is to provide employees with KSAs that will allow them to perform to the established standard or, preferably, to surpass it.[1] Assessments of this type are frequently used to determine an individual's ability to assume a more challenging position of increasing responsibility where analytical, problem-solving, and decision-making qualities are required.

### Behavioral

Also known in the psychological profession as behavioristic assessments, this type emphasizes the diagnosis of undesirable behavioral traits and patterns in relation to the context and the environment in which they are displayed.[2] Behavioral assessments are predicated on the assumption that the behavior being observed is the result of previous learning and experiences. The objective of this approach is to determine what particular behavioral patterns work best in given situations and whether the individual being observed has personality characteristics that are compatible with the requirements of the position(s) under question. Tests, interviews, and observations of employees' reactions under controlled situational simulations are the prevalent diagnostic methods used in behavioral assessments and are usually conducted by two or more trained specialists.

### Attitudinal/Morale

This type is primarily used to explore the effect of employee attitudes and morale on individual as well as group performance. It is generally initiated through a variety of different data-gathering methods, such as questionnaires, observations, and interviews. It is useful for planning and implementing large-scale organizational change and is widely used as a team-building intervention.[3] It is also used to identify training needs with emphasis on team building, leadership, and goal setting.

### Organizational Climate

This type of assessment is designed to focus primarily on the physical work environment—specifically, on how it affects the psychological and emotional state of the employee and, further, what effect this has on morale. It is based on the theory that employee perceptions and feelings (emotional states) have the greatest impact on performance (and ultimately, on productive output). It seeks feedback on goal, job, and task clarity, on the dynamics (challenges) of the job(s), and on the levels of trust employees have in management's ability to set policy and make rational decisions. Overall, it seeks to determine or to otherwise measure the degree of harmony present in working relationships.[4] The methods used in this approach include surveys, interviews, focus groups, and observations. It is also widely used to identify training needs and as an indicator for other intervention strategies, such as team building, process consultation, and employee coaching and counseling.

### Cultural

This approach is used to investigate the organization's environment and how it affects employee performance and productivity. It evaluates how well organizational policy is established and how well the organization's internal relations are managed (both interpersonal as well as interdepartmental). It also examines the organization's level of acceptance and readiness to change by evaluating what impact its policies and rules have on its operations. Specifically, a cultural assessment is concerned with what effect the organization's culture has on employee morale and, likewise, performance levels.[5] Although, in theory, it closely resembles the organizational climate assessment, it emphasizes a macro view of the organization as a whole rather than as separate work units. Cultural assessments are widely used as OD interventions for identifying and diagnosing barriers to change but have been criticized when used in large, geographically diverse, and decentralized organizations because of the possibility of introducing dysfunctionality between the various organizational units. Their most valuable use is for highlighting attitudinal and cultural differences between organizational units that have significant operational autonomy.

### Leadership

Leadership assessments are very popular and widely used. These are geared toward diagnosing individual leadership styles. They provide input in the form of suggestions (based on applied research) on how to improve one's ability to influence and motivate others toward task and goal accomplishment.[6] Depending on its intent and scope, it generally defines the development of leadership styles as patterns of behavior that were either learned or acquired. Leadership assessments are also useful for identifying the conditions or circumstances that a person's particular style would best be suited for. They may emphasize building on identified strengths as a means for defeating or otherwise correcting behavioral shortcomings. Leadership assessments are very popular and widely used as a training-needs indicator because they produce data that are especially applicable for designing executive and management training and development programs.

### Benchmarking

Although not considered as a formal type of needs assessment per se, benchmarking has become popular and is also widely used. Defined as the continuous process of measuring the quality of the organization's products, services, and management practices against acknowledged leading competitors, benchmarking seeks to explore and identify areas for improvement.[7] Until recently, benchmarking has not received a great deal of application in the HRD field. It is, however, very useful as an indicator for intervention methods that are directed at and contribute to raising individual employee as well as organizational performance standards.

### Operational Audit

Sometimes referred to as a managerial audit, this type of assessment examines the organization's structure, plans, objectives, and how efficiently it uses its human and material resources. Similar in some respects to benchmarking, it is usually conducted by external consultants who evaluate the organization's financial status, earnings, production efficiencies, and managerial control systems. Points are assigned to whatever criteria and categories the operational audit is designed to include. The results are compared to previous years' performance and also to the results of competitors. An operational audit provides valuable information on the organization's current operational condition.

### Job and Task Analyses

Job and task analyses are very similar in that each attempts to define what employees need to do to perform at consistent levels. Where they differ is in the dimensions and in the criteria each examines.

A job analysis takes a macro look at a job from two distinct views: functionality and required KSAs. Through functionality, the job analysis attempts to determine what the worker actually does, what clusters of duties and tasks are included in the job, and the overall nature of the work. KSAs include the knowledge, skills, and abilities the job requires of its incumbent. Data are then collected and analyzed to identify any deficiencies or inconsistencies that exist in the job function itself and, further, what deficiencies or knowledge gaps exist within the person who presently occupies the position being investigated. From this information, a variety of outcomes are possible:

1. Job descriptions can be more accurately developed.
2. A job can be redesigned, if necessary, to more appropriately fit into the organizational or departmental framework.
3. The outcome can provide a basis for the design of accurate performance evaluation criteria.
4. The outcome can provide detailed information upon which decisions regarding compensation levels can be made.

5. The outcome can be used as a basis for designing a job-applicant screening tool.
6. The outcome can be used to document and justify job classifications to satisfy equal employment opportunity (EEO) or other statutory guidelines.
7. The outcome can provide the basis for determining training needs or some other intervention strategy.

An example of a job analysis form is included in Appendix F.

A task analysis seeks to define a job on a micro level by detailing each task that a particular job requires. Further, it seeks to define subtasks that, when broken down to a detailed level, identify groups of individual functions that are necessary for the job to be successfully carried out. It also seeks to define standards against which performance levels can be compared.

A task analysis consists of six basic steps. They are the following:

1. The identification of the major components and outputs of a particular job (this is usually obtained through a comprehensive job analysis)
2. The use of various data-collection methods to record the job's main tasks
3. The breaking down of tasks into individual steps and, further, breaking these into separate subtasks
4. The validation of all tasks and subtasks as being genuine elements of the job
5. The preparation of a list of all the tasks required to successfully do the job
6. The preparation of a task analysis report for management and incumbent employees to review, verify, and confirm

Any discrepancies that arise in the verification and confirmation processes provide the basis for further investigation. Many times these discrepancies can indicate gaps between identical jobs. An example of a task analysis form is provided in Appendix G.

Task analysis is popular and widely used for determining needs—specifically, needs that are training based. A task analysis produces hard data leading to measurable and meaningful results. These can be quantifiably linked as outputs resulting from specific training (input). A task analysis is also useful for isolating and identifying skills that are required to complete each task.

Many experts maintain that task analysis and needs assessments are similar. Indeed, each requires data gathering, each is dependent on input and measurable output, and each requires substantive and quantifiable analysis. However, a needs assessment is used mainly to identify needs on a more macro level, while a task analysis is used to analyze what will be required so that each identified need can be satisfied. Therefore, in this context, a task analysis can be viewed as a component of a needs assessment system.

Task analysis is not a stratified or standardized technique. Rather, it is a generalized term that can incorporate a variety of methods. Two of the more common ones are task inventories and the stimulus–response approach.

*Task Inventories.* Task inventories are statements that describe work activities in specific areas. They are used to specify actual job tasks. This involves organizing tasks in order of importance or frequency and then detailing and sequencing the steps within each task. Task inventories are useful for exploring the relationships between jobs and their associated tasks and what is required (level of output) for successful completion and performance.

*Stimulus–Response Approach.* The stimulus–response approach to task analysis identifies both the stimulus and the response to each task requirement. The stimulus is the requirement of each job, and the response is the appropriate performance of that particular job. For example, assume that the task was to operate a personal computer.

| Stimulus | Response |
|---|---|
| 1. Computer is inactive. | 1. User turns computer on. |
| 2. Computer is active but there are no visual cues on the monitor indicating that it is functioning. | 2. User turns computer monitor on. |
| 3. The computer requires input. | 3. User types commands on terminal keyboard (input). |

A successful task analysis usually incorporates *algorithms* or activity flowcharts. These are used to itemize all components of a particular task and to visually arrange and sequence them in order of importance so that the task can be successfully completed.

Both job and task analyses employ virtually all types of data-gathering methods. The most widely used are interviews and on-site observations involving job incumbents, other employees with whom the incumbents interact, and the incumbents' supervisors or managers. Table 2.1 illustrates a needs assessment model which presents both task and job relationships. The data produced are analyzed, and any gaps or deficiencies in KSAs form the basis for exploring interventions or other corrective activities and strategies (e.g., job redesign, training, etc.).

### Assessment Centers

Assessment centers represent a specialized approach to assessing organizational needs. They are used to estimate or approximate current as well as future employee development needs. The primary use of assessment centers has been to identify individuals who have the capacity and potential to assume broader and more challenging job responsibilities. The assessment center method involves processes where individuals are put through a series of diagnostic tests and simulations. The goal is to determine their levels of suitability in regard to a particular position or their capacity to assume higher levels of responsibility. A wide variety of observations and measurement

**Table 2.1**
A Needs Assessment Model Using Task and Job Analysis Methods

| | | |
|---|---|---|
| Step 1 | Sequentially arrange which tasks should be learned | Identify which competencies and/or behaviors are required and acceptable to job performance |
| Step 2 | Determine levels or standards of performance relating to the task | Determine minimum qualifications and preferences related to experiential learning, pre-requisite skill levels, and formal educational requirements |
| Step 3 | Develop testing instruments to measure performance against standard | Develop testing instruments to measure performance and evaluative instruments and/or procedures to ascertain other requirements |
| Step 4 | Formulate instructional strategies to address performance gap | Formulate instructional strategies to address job discrepancies |

methods are used by teams of trained specialists and experienced managers who observe and record the participants' behavior and reactions. Once all of the diagnostic measurements are completed, the data are integrated, analyzed, and rated. Predictions about employees' future potential are then made. As a result, strategies for placing them in specific positions are devised.

Assessment centers have become popular for diagnosing and developing human resource potential. Many organizations such as AT&T, IBM, and GE have used assessment centers for analyzing and predicting performance levels and for facilitating individual growth, capacity, and potential. However, there has also been much criticism of the assessment center approach. The most influential argument against their use is their cost. They are expensive to establish, professionally staff, and maintain.

It should be noted that these descriptions represent some of the most popular types and generalized approaches for assessing organizational needs. In addition, there are various processes that integrate two or more of these generalized approaches. However, due to the volatility of dealing with behavior and personalities, caution should be used when attempting any type of behaviorally based assessment. These should be conducted only by trained professionals.

Each of the aforementioned assessment types can be conducted at various organizational levels (e.g., executive, middle management, first-line, professional, technical, administrative, etc.). There are some differences at these levels not so much in the actual assessment type, but rather in how it is designed and, particularly, in how it is implemented. For example, if part of the assessment included individual interviews, timing and scheduling would be more important at the senior levels because of time constraints. Also, the structure and tone of any interviews that are directed at the senior levels would need to be focused more at the organization in general as opposed to addressing specific functions. Likewise, if interviews were conducted at the first levels of the organization, questions would not necessarily be directed at broad organizational issues such as strategy and policy formulation but would tend to focus more on specific functions. Various types of data-gathering methods, along with their similarities and differences, are presented in detail in Chapter 4.

There are essentially two ways of undertaking and implementing a needs assessment: (1) purchase and use commercially available assessment instruments and (2) develop the ability to custom design needs assessment systems (including any and all data-collection instruments). Customizing assessments requires a fundamental understanding of how assessment systems are designed and structured and what technologies (e.g., computers, software, etc.) are available. It also requires an in-depth understanding of data collection and analysis procedures. However, before continuing with a comprehensive discussion of the development of custom needs assessment systems, it would be useful to first examine the advantages as well as the disadvantages in using commercially available instruments.

## COMMENTS ON USING COMMERCIALLY AVAILABLE ASSESSMENT INSTRUMENTS

Rapid growth in the HRD field has spawned equally rapid growth in subsegments of the industry. One of the most notable areas where this has occurred is in the consulting field. There has been a dramatic increase in the number of consulting organizations that publish assessment instruments and offer needs assessment services. In fact, a cursory review of HRD industry sources reveals that there are at present more than 150 vendors and providers of needs assessment instruments in the United States alone.[8] The types of commercial instruments available cover all areas, from OD to training, from culture to organizational analysis, from leadership to team building, and virtually all other areas in between. These include everything from simple self-scoring survey questionnaires to expensive computer-based data analysis systems. This gives a very good indication of the demand for HRD and organizational assessment instruments and services. There are many advantages to using commercially available assessment instruments. Some of them are the following:

1. *Standardization*: Many assessment instruments have been developed and refined over time. Because they have been (presumably) used consistently, their validity is considered by some to be significant.
2. *Customization*: Many instruments provide for a certain degree of customization in that they contain questions or employ open formats which provide flexibility. Some permit users to insert their own questions as long as they are written in a specific style or format. Some provide generalized formats that are intended to cover a broad range of applications, while others allow a greater degree of independence because they permit users to write their own questions as long as they comply with a specific style and structure.
3. *Cost*: Most standardized instruments are relatively inexpensive to acquire when compared to the more costly alternative of designing your own. This feature is particularly attractive to many HRD managers.
4. *Ease of use*: The majority of standardized instruments require little, if any, training or experience to administer and to analyze the data they produce. Many are provided with computer-based grading and scoring instructions which ease the analysis and interpretation process.

There are, however, significant disadvantages to using standardized assessment instruments. Most notably, they are the following:

1. The reliability of many standardized, commercially packaged assessment instruments is questionable. Reliability is very important, especially when the results are used to make intervention recommendations and cost justifications. An instrument's reliability is determined mainly by the number of times it has been consistently administered. Generally speaking, the more the instrument has been used to produce uniform and stable results, the higher its reliability can be said to be. However, if over time it has produced wide data fluctuations or if there have been significant discrepancies in the number of times it has been used, the reliability level will be low. Likewise, if the instrument is relatively new or is a redesign of an older version, its reliability will also be low until such a time when it has been administered consistently and begins to produce stable and uniform results.
2. Some assessment instruments claim to be useful as cross-purpose diagnostic tools, implying that they are suitable for a variety of measurement applications. For example, some are advertised as being applicable for gathering feedback on everything from employee attitudes to determining executive training and development needs. These types of instruments represent a sort of "one size fits all" approach in that they are based on similarity rather than on differentiation or uniqueness, thereby causing some to question their suitability for any specialized purposes.
3. Many standardized instruments are not objective or comprehensive enough to meet an organization's specific needs. Most are designed to provide immediate results, meaning they are focused on producing data for short-term analysis and contribute little in the way of producing information that has any strategic or long-term value.
4. No matter how "customizable" or adaptable an instrument is claimed to be, it is highly unlikely that it can be modified to the extent that it will fulfill all the HRD analysts' (or the organizations') requirements. Unless it was written by someone who was or is intimately familiar with the particular organization it is to be ad-

ministered to, it will ostensibly contain a high degree of generalized criteria that will make its fit for a particular or specific purpose awkward at best. The results produced under such circumstances will subsequently require a broad interpretation and analysis of the data and will not contain much in the way of organizational specifics.

The alternative to using standardized instruments (and approaches) is to develop the ability to design unique, customized needs assessments; in effect, to be able to develop organizationally specific needs assessment systems.

## ADVANTAGES OF CUSTOM-DESIGNED NEEDS ASSESSMENT SYSTEMS

Acquiring the knowledge and experience necessary to design custom needs assessment systems is both challenging and rewarding. It can also be frustrating and somewhat intimidating, particularly if one is starting from the beginning and has no knowledge or experience in data gathering, statistical analysis, and evaluation methods. To become a good assessment designer and analyst does not require a substantial background in research, statistics, or other analytical methods. It does, however, require the ability to seek rational solutions to what sometimes appear to be irrational problems.

There are definite advantages to developing the skills and abilities needed to design custom needs assessments, not the least of which is having the capability to gather feedback that is unique to one's own organization. By developing the ability to assess needs through a variety of custom methods designed to work within the existing organizational structure and culture, the organization adds another capability to its asset base.[9] Because this activity is normally centered in the HRD department, developing this ability will also add value in that HRD personnel will make significant contributions to furthering organizational goals.

Some of the principal advantages to developing the ability to design customized needs assessment capabilities are the following:

1. They are a readily available reference resource that can provide detailed and comprehensive feedback on the organization's structure, operations, and culture, and, more specifically, on how these can be changed to further enhance performance and productivity.
2. They have reference value because they allow continual monitoring of organizational systems and their effectiveness.
3. They highlight areas for improvement by indicating where funds can and should be allocated to further improve individual as well as organizational performance.
4. They identify potential problem areas by generating feedback not only on how well existing systems are functioning but also by highlighting potential performance improvement obstacles.

5. Over time they become more cost-effective because it is generally less expensive to develop in-house assessment expertise than it is to hire external consultants or to continually purchase commercial instruments on a case-by-case basis.
6. They are a means for keeping proprietary information private and safeguarding confidential organizational issues and plans.
7. They provide a means for controlling assessment project costs.

## PLANNING FOR THE CUSTOM ASSESSMENT

Planning is a way of identifying and solving problems before they arise. It is also a way of discovering and taking advantage of long-term opportunities. As such, some basic rules in relation to assessment planning are the following: (1) it should be a concerted and organized effort; (2) it must be centered on establishing and communicating goals; and (3) it must center on raising awareness of and promoting acceptance for change.[10]

Planning for any project involves time and preparation, especially if the plan also includes information on costs and the use of other resources. Planning for a customized needs assessment project involves, among other things, establishing goals for the assessment, identifying resources, establishing a project plan or time line, identifying the sample assessment population, determining which mix of data-gathering methods to use, establishing administrative and logistical requirements, establishing budgetary and other cost data, and securing senior management's approval, support, and participation.

Planning, in its purest sense, attempts to answer the following questions: (1) Where have we been? (2) Where are we now? (3) Where do we want or need to go? and (4) How do we get there?[11]

One begins planning for a needs assessment by answering the first question—in essence, by looking at the organization's policies, goals, and business strategies.

The second question prompts examination of the organization's culture and structure and the behaviors and attitudes of its employees. These are areas where needs assessments are most directly focused. Beginning with the current culture, the HRD analyst or consultant will attempt to link employee attitudes and levels of trust and confidence in management's abilities with the current operational environment and competitive positioning of the company. Further, in examining the organization's mission, goals, and objectives, one can get a good understanding of how the organization goes about conducting its business within its operational environment and how well it utilizes its resources (both human as well as material). Additionally, by examining the company's policies, information on how well these are contributing to growth and profitability can be obtained. Business policies and strategies can also give a good indication of how well the organization has positioned itself within its respective marketplace(s).

The third and fourth questions provide answers as to why an assessment is being undertaken. Each is concerned with conditions as they now exist and what needs to be changed to improve organizational performance. Areas such as growth, market share, and long-term profitability are frequently examined.

The answers to these questions provide preliminary needs assessment data. They are the basic ingredients necessary to design a customized needs assessment system.

## A "SYSTEMS" APPROACH TO NEEDS ASSESSMENTS

Many experts advocate a logical and sequential approach to conducting needs assessments. In particular, they take a systems-view of the assessment by stressing process as well as logic in both its design and its implementation.

A system is a group of interacting components designed to operate as a whole.[12] In needs assessment terminology there are essentially two types of systems: closed and open. A closed system is comprised of elements that operate in a hierarchical order (e.g., X must be initiated before Y, which must precede Z, and so on) because each preceding element has properties that subsequent ones will require. An automobile is an example of a closed system; it requires gasoline or fuel (X) in order for its engine to be started (Y) so that it can be driven (Z). In an open system, however, elements have greater degrees of flexibility because many can operate independently and do not necessarily require properties from the others (e.g., Z can be initiated without needing anything from either X or Y).[13] Both types, however, require input in order to produce output.[14]

Needs assessment input is information that has been generated through a variety of data-gathering methods. This input is analyzed through various processes. It provides a means for drawing conclusions and making intervention recommendations.[15] It forms the basis for designing and implementing different kinds of organizational interventions or changes. In systems jargon, these are referred to as output. Figure 2.1 is a model of a systems-oriented needs assessment. Although it is hierarchical in nature (e.g., events have precedent relationships), the types of assessments and data-gathering methods shown have open-systems properties in that each can be used as a stand alone method or as part of a variety of aggregate correlational options.

The model represents a framework for initiating a systematic needs assessment. The tasks as outlined provide the basis for conducting a systemic and systematic assessment that will be discussed throughout subsequent chapters of this book. Even though they are presented in a sequenced order, many varieties and alternatives are possible. Therefore, while sequence is important, particularly for purposes of illustration, reference, and discussion, the model is not a static representation that is meant to be interpreted literally.

**Figure 2.1**
"Systems" Model for Designing and Conducting Organizational Needs Assessments

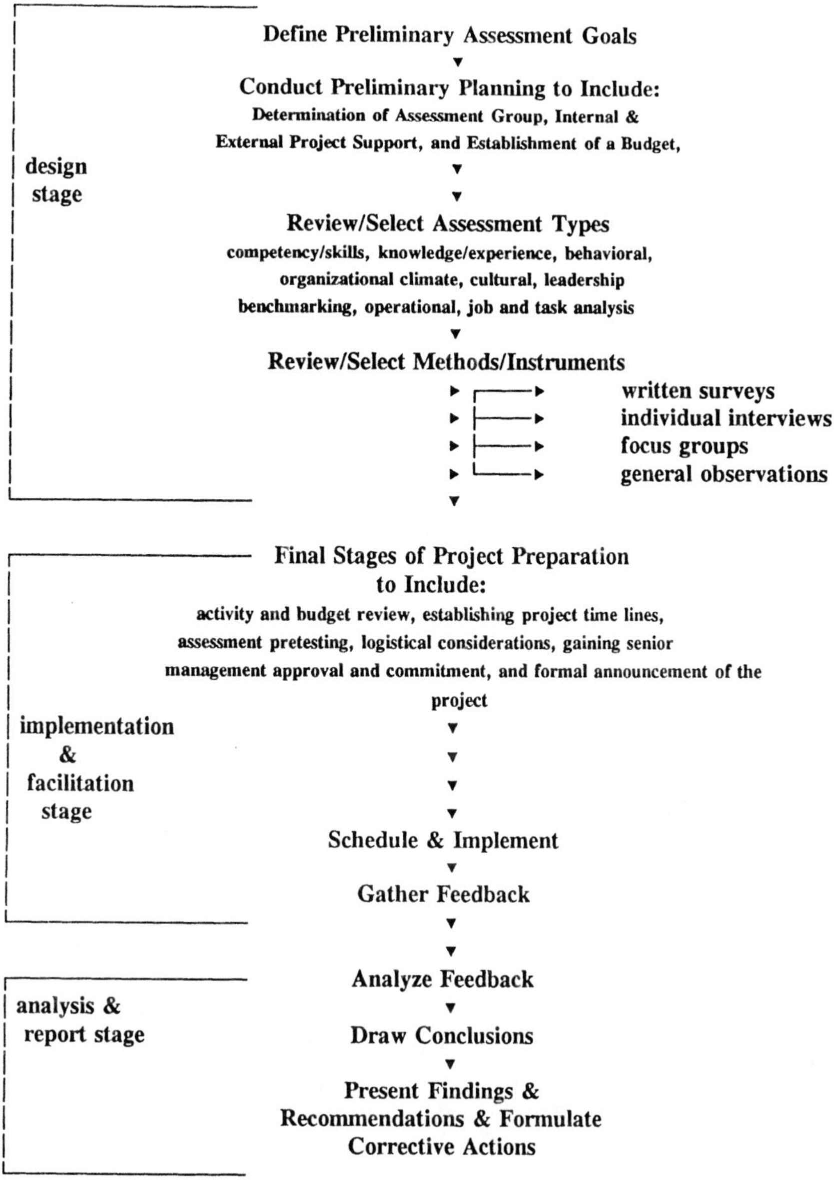


*Source:* Adapted from Samuel B. McClelland, "Training Needs Assessment: An 'Open-Systems' Application," *Journal of European Industrial Training*, Vol. 17, No. 1, 1993, pp. 12–17. Reprinted with permission from MCB University Press.

Since each assessment project is unique, some tasks will require significantly more emphasis than others. These can, and often do, occur in a sequence that differs from the model that is presented here.

Needs assessments are used to diagnose organizational needs. Their outcomes represent an opportunity for developing solutions to both routine and nonroutine problems. Needs assessments and methods come in many different forms. The most widely recognized types are (1) competency/skills, (2) knowledge/experience, (3) behavioral, (4) attitudinal/morale, (5) organizational climate, (6) cultural, (7) leadership, (8) benchmarking, (9) operational audits, (10) job and (11) task analysis, and (12) assessment centers.

With over 150 vendors producing assessment instruments in the United States alone, it is tempting to use a modification of a standardized instrument in an effort to save both time and money. There are advantages to using standardized assessment instruments, some of which are established levels of validity, (presumed) reliability, and ease of use. There are also significant disadvantages. Many are marketed or offered as cross-purpose diagnostic instruments and propose a sort of "one size fits all" approach. Many do not incorporate the flexibility that is required to produce organizationally specific data upon which valid recommendations and intervention activities can be based. Alternatively, there are significant advantages to being able to develop custom needs assessments that are uniquely suited to a particular organization's culture, social environment, systems, and personnel. Some of these are the following: (1) custom assessments will yield organizationally specific information that can be useful as a readily available reference source; (2) they introduce as well as maintain the means for continual monitoring of organizational needs and problems; (3) they highlight areas where improvement is necessary or is otherwise desirable by (4) pinpointing problem or potential problem areas; (5) they can be more cost-effective over the long-term once the basic investment in developing assessment skills and methods has been made; (6) they are a means for maintaining confidentiality; and (7) they permit the organization to maintain control over the handling of both sensitive information as well as costs.

Planning is the fundamental step in an organizational needs assessment. The planning stage enables the HRD analyst or consultant to itemize the basic elements necessary to design a customized and process-oriented needs assessment system.

Experts have long advocated a systems approach to designing and conducting needs assessments. This can be in the form of either a closed or an open system (or a combination of both). Closed systems are mostly hierarchical because tasks that lie further along in the process rely on the activation of previous ones in order to function properly. Alternatively, open systems are comprised of elements that are relatively independent of others because they can be activated without any precedent activity. A systems approach to needs assessments allows the designer or HRD analyst maximum flexibility while emphasizing a logical sequence and format.

## NOTES

1. W. Borg and M. Gall, *Educational Research: An Introduction*, 4th ed. (New York: Longman, 1983).
2. V. Vroom, *Work and Motivation* (New York: Wiley & Sons, 1964).
3. C. Sweets, "Role of Employment Communications," in *ASPA Handbook of Personnel and Industrial Relations*, D. Yoder and H. Heneman, Jr., eds. Bureau of National Affairs, Washington, D.C., 1979, pp. 395–396.
4. Ibid.
5. H. Park and J. Harrison, "Enhancing Managerial Cross-Cultural Awareness and Sensitivity: Transactional Analysis Revisited," *Journal of Management Development*, Vol. 12, No. 3, pp. 20–29.
6. D. Langdon, "The Individual Management Development Program," *Training and Development Journal*, Vol. 36, No. 3, pp. 78–82.
7. D. Ford, "Benchmarking HRD," *Training and Development*, Vol. 47, No. 6, 1993, pp. 37–41.
8. *ASTD Buyer's Guide and Consultant Directory*, 1994.
9. R. Sahl, "Company Specific Employee Attitude Surveys," *Personnel Journal*, Vol. 69, No. 5, pp. 46–51.
10. H. Koontz and C. O'Donnell, *Principles of Management: An Analysis of Managerial Functions*, 4th ed. (New York: McGraw-Hill, 1968).
11. L. Rue and L. Byars, *Management: Theory and Application*, rev. ed. (Homewood, Ill.: Richard D. Irwin, 1980).
12. S. McClelland, "Training Needs Assessment: An 'Open-Systems' Application," *Journal of European Industrial Training*, Vol. 17, No. 1, pp. 12–17.
13. S. McClelland, "A Systems Approach to Needs Assessment," *Training and Development*, Vol. 46, No. 8, pp. 51–53.
14. Ibid., p. 51.
15. G. Rummler, "Determining Needs," in *Training and Development Handbook: A Guide to Human Resource Development*, R. Craig, ed. (New York: McGraw-Hill, 1987), pp. 217–247.

PART II

# Fundamentals of Needs Assessment Design

CHAPTER 3

# Preliminary Assessment Components

## ORGANIZATIONAL POLICY CONSIDERATIONS

The design of successful needs assessment systems requires one to first gain a fundamental understanding of the organization's policies and how these can serve to either facilitate or hinder the design and implementation process. The investigative nature of a needs assessment can sometimes place it at odds with existing organizational policies. For example, in the course of conducting a needs assessment, access to personal data may be restricted by policies that are designed to safeguard confidential information. Situations like this will require that exceptions to such policies be obtained prior to initiating the needs assessment.

The word *policy* means different things to different people. To some it represents rules that are established by management to govern the behavior of the organization's employees. To others it represents principles that guide the organization's actions toward attainment of its business objectives. In many respects, both interpretations are correct: Policies are generally formulated by senior management in consultation with lower-level managers and are meant to establish guidelines and rules within which the organization conducts its business.[1] Policies are designed to provide general business, ethical, and behavioral guidelines at all departmental levels. Rules, on the other hand, are drawn from policies and are meant to guide individual employee actions.[2]

When conducting needs assessments, intentional as well as unintentional violations of policies and rules can occur. This is sometimes due to a lack of knowledge about certain policies and rules being in effect. A needs analyst can easily and unintentionally violate a standing policy or rule. As part of the assessment process, the analyst can gain access to confidential information (e.g., work processes, financial information, special projects, and so on). Thus, care must be taken to ensure that proprietary information remains just that. Access to data and other records containing sensitive information should be scrupulously safeguarded. For example, assume an organization has a policy of not releasing information concerning ongoing research and development projects. During the course of a needs assessment interview, an analyst receives proprietary information from a technician who is working on a confidential project. The feedback the analyst received was peripheral to the focus and scope of the interview and just happened to come up coincidentally in the normal flow of conversation. Was a policy or rule violated? Technically, yes; however, since the analyst and the technician are employees of the same company, the breach of policy occurred within ethical boundaries and was, therefore, contained. The responsibility to maintain confidentiality about the project information, however, remains in the domain of the analyst. In the interest of maintaining high ethical standards, it is important that policies and rules be adhered to so as to avoid breaches of confidentiality and conflicts of interest.

## ESTABLISHING PRELIMINARY ASSESSMENT GOALS

The first formalized step in planning for a needs assessment is to identify its goals or objectives. These represent the reasons for undertaking the assessment and have three important attributes: (1) goals establish a projected outcome; (2) they direct all assessment activities toward the projected outcome; and (3) they provide a directive for accomplishing individual needs assessment tasks.

Because there is no real indication of what the assessment outcome will be, it is necessary to first establish preliminary goals. These direct attention to the needs assessment process and become the catalyst for moving the project forward.[3] Formulating preliminary goals also provides an opportunity to reframe and restate them as the project moves along. Having this ability is important, because as the assessment progresses, its preliminary goals are likely to change. For example, at the beginning of an assessment, it may not be prudent to set a goal of 100 percent employee participation. The chances of this occurring are relatively low. Rather, preliminary goals should focus on the assessments effects. These can be classified into three types: predetermined, measured/observed, or desired. Effects provide indications of causality, or rather, they become the reason or reasons for initiating the needs assessment.[4] In this sense, preliminary goals serve as a means for determining what needs to be done to address the cause that produced (or has the potential to produce) the effect.

A predetermined effect is the most probable outcome of an event or situation. For example, if a company was about to replace outdated equipment with newer computerized machinery, it would be logical to assume that the operators of the old equipment would need to be trained to run the new equipment. Failure to provide training on how to operate the new equipment could have potentially disastrous results (e.g., a collapse of productivity, safety concerns, etc.). In a situation like this, the identification of predetermined effects is important because it will be necessary to take proactive steps to offset them. Thus, the preliminary goal in this example would be to retrain employees on how to operate the new equipment.

Alternatively, a measured or observed effect is the result of a problem or situation that has already occurred (e.g., an increase in absenteeism). Subsequent actions taken to offset this are reactive because they are initiated after the problem has already appeared. For example, in order to take steps to reduce absenteeism, one must determine why it increased in the first place. Thus, determining the cause for the increase becomes the preliminary goal.

Inevitably, organizations will, at some point, need to improve the quality of their products or services. This desire, as such, has neither a predetermined nor a measured effect, yet it represents a broadly defined goal: to improve quality. When framed as the question, "What needs to be done to improve quality?", the need becomes the goal. Subsequently, a needs assessment would be conducted, and, if the results indicated that training (or some other intervention) were necessary, corrective steps would then need to be taken. The importance of establishing preliminary goals cannot be overemphasized. Regardless of whether a goal's effect is predetermined, measured, or desired, it should be subjectively devised, stated in realistic terms, and be attainable. Table 3.1 illustrates the preliminary goal-setting process and includes examples of predetermined, measured, observed, and desired effects.

### Forecasting Needs

Another method used for setting preliminary assessment goals is known as *forecasting*. Although it is less precise than the effect method described earlier, it represents a way to predict employee and organizational needs. Sometimes known as workforce planning, forecasting can be defined as a formalized means to predict what should (or needs to) be done with regard to the organization's human resources so that the organization can attain its business objective. This method has had limited success in smaller organizations that by virtue of their size have attained higher degrees of flexibility resulting from internal cross-training and job rotational programs. In many smaller organizations, efforts like these have produced a work force where most employees have out of necessity developed a familiarity with many of the jobs and tasks.

**Table 3.1**
**Effects that Drive Needs Assessment Preliminary Goal Determination**

| Predetermined, Measured, Observed, or Desired Effect | Preliminary Goal Determination/Causality | Possible Assessment Type/Approach | Organizational Level Assessed |
|---|---|---|---|
| 1. Improve quality (desired effect) | Design methods or approaches to improve quality | Operational, Competency/Skills, Knowledge/Experience, Benchmarking, TQM | All levels |
| 2. High rate of absenteeism (measured effect) | Identify reason/cause | Behavioral, Attitudinal/Morale, Organizational Climate, Cultural | Level where effect(s) is/are measured |
| 3. Poor employee morale (observed effect) | Identify reason/cause | Attitudinal/Morale, Organizational Climate, Cultural | Level where effect(s) is/are observed |
| 4. Managerial decision making is inconsistent (observed/ measured effect) | Identify inhibitors to managerial decision making | Leadership, Cultural, Attitudinal/Morale | Management, Executive levels |
| 5. High cost of goods sold (predetermined effect) | Identify reasons | Operational, Benchmarking | All levels |

Alternatively, in larger organizations, forecasting personnel needs first requires that the analyst gain a fundamental understanding of supply and demand factors. In effect, the goal of forecasting is to estimate the number of employees the organization will need to meet its business objectives and then estimate how many trained employees will be available over time. If the forecast indicates that the need for financial analysis skills will be greater than the need for systems programmers, HRD efforts would be focused on sharpening the financial skills of managers and employees. One popular technique used to forecast personnel needs is *trend analysis*, a technique that is well known in the economics and finance disciplines.[5] In trend analysis, information on personnel needs is collected over a period of time. This provides a basis for examining emerging trends in personnel requirements in order to meet as well as to maintain adequate staffing levels. For example, if an analysis of personnel needs indicated a steady growth pattern in both staffing and training requirements for a particular position, the assumption under trend analysis would be that this would continue. In response, the HRD department would prepare for an increase in the number of training activities related to this particular position, although in reality this increase may only be incremental. The use of trend analysis could lead to the design of training programs for newly hired personnel and a retraining of current employees to assume broader roles and responsibilities. While the theory behind trend analysis appears sound, its use in HRD has been criticized because it is not a precise means of work force planning. For instance, in the example just given, staffing levels are subject to a variety of influences such as economic conditions, sales volumes, management policies, and advancements in technology, all of which will affect personnel requirement trend patterns. Consequently, it has not been viewed as a reliable way for assessing employee or organizational needs, particularly over the longer term.

Another approach to forecasting needs is done by knowledgeable line and staff personnel who come together to compare notes based on individual observations of the organization's needs. Borrowed from a forecasting model developed by the RAND Corporation and known as the Delphi technique,[6] it involves the anonymous collection of written information (in this case on observed needs) from several individuals, then letting all involved read what the others have written. Each observer is then permitted to revise his or her own needs forecast. A major benefit to using the Delphi technique repeatedly is that it prompts each person to revise his or her own forecasts until repetitious similarities begin to emerge. The key to using this technique successfully lies more in the variety of inputs as opposed to their frequency. Some major criticisms of the Delphi technique are that (1) the process of managing and controlling it becomes cumbersome, particularly where a significant number of individuals are involved, and (2) the length of time it can take to reach any type of consensus may offset its usefulness.

### Alternative Means for Determining Goals

There are a variety of other methods that can be used to set needs assessment goals. Three of these are deductive and inductive reasoning, the more rigorous scientific approach, and intuitive reasoning.

Reasoning is essentially the formulation of a hypothesis or a belief that is based on intuition. Needs analysts generally frown on using an intuitive approach because the theory or hypothesis is often predicated on past experiences, many of which are not documented. Thus, quantifiable data tend to be scarce. For example, an analyst may deduce that a certain data-gathering method (e.g., focus groups) will not produce substantive feedback because the structure of the company is highly compartmentalized and encourages individual effort and not group interaction. In knowing this, the analyst deduces that focus groups, which require considerable group interaction, would not be particularly useful. Known as deductive reasoning, it attempts to link theory with observation.

Alternatively, the opposite of deductive reasoning often is used. Known as inductive reasoning, this approach takes what is considered to be obvious and concludes that because it is obvious the hypothesis must be true. For example,

| | |
|---|---|
| Deductive reasoning | All organizations employ people.<br>Training is needed in all organizations.<br>Therefore, all people need training. |
| Inductive reasoning | All organizations employ people.<br>Therefore, all organizations conduct training. |

Inductive reasoning can perhaps be best described as reaching a conclusion by observing and generalizing from individual examples to universality. In order to be confident of an inductive conclusion, however, the analyst must observe all examples. Therefore, in order to reach absolute conclusions through inductive reasoning, the group to which those conclusions apply must be small enough to be observable. The example given does not meet this criterion.

The scientific approach is based on two assumptions: (1) that reality (or truth) is derived from observation and (2) that all variables observed conform to lawful relationships. In needs assessments, scientific inquiry focuses on the relationship between and measurement of variables that can, and often do, assume different values. The systems approach to assessment design, facilitation, and analysis is more analogous to and representative of the scientific approach because (1) it seeks to define the problem (effect); (2) it establishes a goal or goals; (3) it identifies the most appropriate data-gathering methods to use to address causality (the causes of the problem); (4) it provides feedback on a variety of variables and values related to the cause(s); and (5) through the analysis and the formulation of recommendations, it seeks to address causality in a more efficient and cost-effective manner.

Another approach to setting needs assessment goals is through intuitive reasoning. Although less stringent than the scientific approach, intuitive reasoning is nonetheless one of the most frequently used types of needs assessment goal-setting methods. It requires analysts to rely on their own intuition about what they feel the organization's needs really are. Intuitive reasoning is grounded in experience and requires intimate familiarity with the organization's culture.

Needs analysts will often find that prior to the implementation of a needs assessment they will have consciously or subconsciously formulated a theory or hypothesis about its outcome. Whether this was formed through deductive, inductive, scientific, or intuitive reasoning is of little importance. What is important is to take steps to ensure that the selection of the data-gathering methods to be used in the needs assessment was made with the understanding that they are the best choices possible for gathering feedback on needs within the context of the organization's culture.

## DETERMINING THE ASSESSMENT GROUP COMPOSITION

Once the preliminary goals have been established, the next logical step is to identify the assessment population. These individuals can be influential when choosing what type of assessment methods to use. Generally, an assessment population would include all persons who either displayed or were part of the observed cause or measured effect that drove the preliminary goal-setting process. However, many times an assessment is implemented only to a target or sample group of individuals without any consideration having been given to other segments within the organization who influence the performance of the group scheduled to undergo the assessment. For example, consider a case involving a cellular telecommunications company that was formed in the mid-1980s. Even though the company was new, it was comprised of individuals who collectively had many years of experience in both the local and the long-distance telecommunications industry. The emerging cellular phone market unleashed brutal competition. In order to position itself as quickly as possible, the company was structured into three major operating units: marketing and sales, operations, and finance. In an all-out effort to capture market share, considerable emphasis was placed on and resources given to the marketing and sales group. However, as the president of the newly formed company observed, there was also a significant amount of conflict arising between the sales and the finance divisions. Most of the conflict, it seemed, stemmed from poor interdepartmental communications and interpersonal relations. Thinking that this was an opportunity to explore and investigate the causes of the conflict and also to establish a comprehensive internal employee-development program, the president initiated a needs assessment. Outside consultants were hired to work with the director of human resources and an assessment directed at the sales and finance groups was conducted.

Although the president's initial reaction was to provide training or some type of intervention specifically for the sales and finance groups, the results of the assessment indicated that the main source of the differences was not between those two groups at all but, rather, was stemming from the operations group that was charged with delivering and installing equipment that the sales department was selling. Moreover, because of the large volume of installation, connection, and maintenance work, operations had not been able to keep up with some of the administrative requirements that finance needed in order to establish customer accounts. In order to gain a clearer understanding of the effects (problems) present within these three groups, another assessment was conducted (at additional time and expense). This assessment included the operations group so that the feedback obtained from them could be integrated into the data obtained from the first assessment.

The point here is simple: Had the assessment been directed at all three groups instead of at just the two that were thought to be the causes of the problems, the company could have saved time and money while simultaneously gathering information that would have enabled them to establish a more substantial HRD effort. Even though causality (and effect) had been determined, consideration should have been extended to and included all the individuals or groups of individuals who were or possibly could have been contributors to the effects. It should also be noted that simply calling attention to a problem may in itself provide a solution.[7] Known as the *Hawthorne* or the *Halo* effect (after the famous Hawthorne studies), this phenomenon illustrates that results, whether correctly or incorrectly interpreted, can be obtained simply by the introduction of an intervention (in the previous example the intervention was the design and implementation of the first needs assessment).

One common misconception about assessment group composition is the supposition that it involves only the organization's employees. Adopting this view negates the opportunity to look beyond the organization's borders. Studies have shown that a great deal of valuable information about an organization's needs can be obtained by including its customers as well as its suppliers in the assessment process. For example, many fast-food chains regularly assess their customers on how well their food was prepared, how long it took to receive it, how they were treated by the restaurant's personnel, and so on. Answers to these seemingly innocent questions can uncover a wealth of information, not only on possible training needs, but also on what improvements may need to be made (if any) to existing programs, work methods, and processes.

## IDENTIFYING PROJECT RESOURCES (STAFF)

Once the assessment population has been identified, the next step is to identify those individuals, internal as well as external, who will play principal roles in the implementation of the assessment. Normally, this would include all resources necessary for the design, implementation, and analysis phases and should also include any individuals who are necessary to administratively support the project. At this point, some thought must be given as to whether the assessment will be managed by an internal person who has the necessary knowledge and expertise, whether it will include the use of computers, whether any information-systems expertise will be required (e.g., programmers), whether internal resources such as subject matter experts (SMEs) will be needed, and, in particular, who will be providing the necessary logistical and administrative support (e.g., clerks, secretaries, administrative assistants, etc.). In short, this is the stage where the assessment project team is formed. The following is a list of individuals who are normally included in a needs assessment project team. A brief description of their duties is also provided.

*HRD Manager*: In many organizations such individuals are also the director or even the vice president of human resources. Whatever their title, they are ultimately in charge of and responsible for any and all HRD programs and projects. They are usually charged with providing control oversight, have overall budgetary responsibility, and are instrumental in the preparation and delivery of the final report (including any recommendations) to senior management.

*HRD Analyst*: These people usually report to the HRD director or manager. They have the specific responsibility for the design and implementation of the assessment project. This includes data analysis and evaluation, the formulation of recommendations, and the drafting of a report containing all of the findings. HRD analysts usually serve as the principal administrator and/or coordinator (i.e., the "Team Leader") for the assessment project team.

*Consultant*: The role of consultants, whether they are external or internal, is to provide expert feedback on all phases of the assessment. Because they are (presumed) neutral in that they are not normally influenced by internal organizational politics, external consultants are usually retained for their expertise in designing data-gathering instruments. Consultants are also used to conduct individual interviews as well as focus groups. They report to the HRD analyst in an advisory role and usually do not have any direct line responsibilities or authority other than those specified.

*Administrative Assistant*: These people also report to the HRD analyst. Their primary role is to take charge of all administrative tasks (e.g., duplication, dissemination, and collection of survey questionnaires, scheduling interviews and focus groups [if used], and preparation of the final reports). They also are usually assigned the task of tracking and recording incoming data (often requiring the use of a computer).

*Subject Matter Expert (SME)*: SMEs also report to the HRD analyst. Their principal role is to conduct any on-site observations that may be required in the data-gathering phase. SMEs are usually employees of the organization and are selected based on their knowledge of the jobs, systems, operations, and behaviors to be observed within the assessment population.[8] SMEs can also be external consultants who specialize in certain areas.

*Others*: Examples of other individuals who may be needed in an assessment project are the following: (1) Information Systems Specialists or programmers whose role may be to recommend software or to design computer programs to be used in the data recording, compilation, and statistical analysis phases. They may also be used in collecting data via electronic mail (e-mail) or for any other tasks requiring their particular expertise. (2) Focus Group Leaders whose principal role is to conduct needs assessments focus groups. Figure 3.1 contains an example of a typical needs assessment project team.

## USING INTERNAL CONSULTANTS

Many times, one of the least used resources for designing needs assessment projects is the organization's own personnel. One reason for this is that in some manager's minds, truly expert advice can be obtained only from outside of the company.[9] Obviously, this is simply not true. Organizations are

**Figure 3.1**
Needs Assessment Project Team

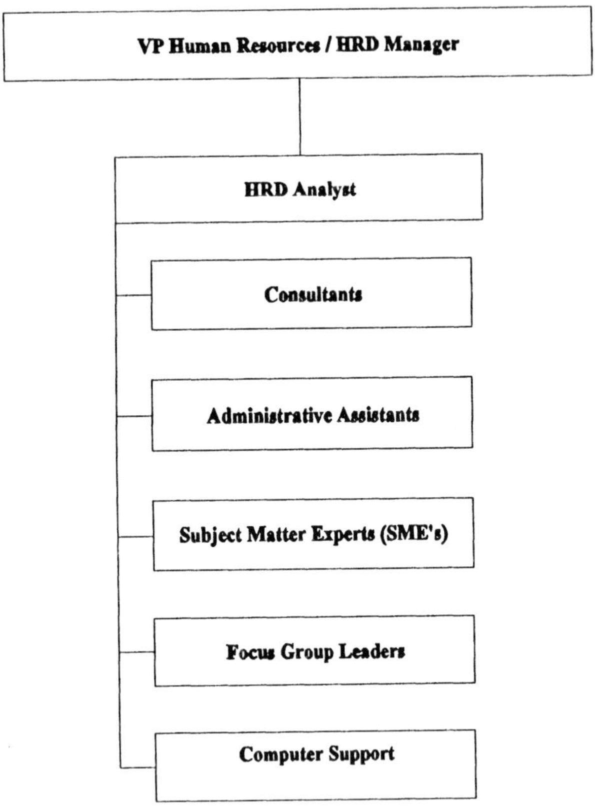


made up of individuals who by virtue of their knowledge and/or experience have considerable expertise in areas which may be valuable in the needs assessment process. Known as internal consultants, they can be useful for identifying what new skills are needed by the work force for solving work- or process-related problems, and, in general, for intuitively identifying needs. Many larger organizations employ individuals solely for the knowledge or expertise they bring to this aspect of HRD. In this respect, these individuals are much like external consultants. The major difference is that they are employees of the organization, whereas external consultants are hired or are usually retained on a project-to-project basis.

Because they work within the organizational structure and are generally familiar with its systems, policies, and processes, internal consultants such as SMEs are useful for identifying barriers to improving organizational performance. To illustrate, take the case of a company whose policies stipulate that any purchase over a certain amount must be made through the purchasing department and be put out on a bid, a process that under certain circumstances can require considerable time. While these policies are designed primarily as cost-control measures, they can, at times, hinder efficiency. For example, assume that a machine broke down and that the part needed to fix it cost $105.00. Employees know who stocks the part and could have the component installed within a couple of hours. However, the company has a purchasing policy that states that all purchases in excess of $100.00 must be bid through the purchasing department, thus prohibiting the employees from directly contacting the vendor. As internal consultants, employees who are familiar with barriers such as these can provide valuable input for rewriting policies or for identifying areas where otherwise well-intentioned policies and rules can actually obstruct performance gains.

## USING EXTERNAL CONSULTANTS

Consultants or externally based experts can play an important role when the organization is only beginning to develop internal expertise and has not yet acquired the skills necessary to develop customized and organizationally unique assessment approaches. Using external consultants has specific advantages. First, an outside consultant will introduce a certain degree of neutrality and impartiality into the assessment project by providing an outsider's view. The fact that they are (or should be) relatively immune to normal organizational politics adds to the probability that an outside consultant cannot be influenced by internal politics. Also, external consultants do not normally harbor any preconceived notions about the outcome of the assessment before it has even begun.

Some of the disadvantages to using external consultants are that (1) external expertise costs more on a project-by-project basis than developing internal expertise does; (2) HRD personnel may feel that they may lose control of the project; and (3) management may have reservations about opening the organization up to external scrutiny and examination, particularly where sensitive areas and issues are concerned.

The role of external consultants can either be broad (such as providing input and assistance across the entire spectrum of the project) or it can be very specific (such as providing assistance in relation to a particular project phase). Their principal purpose, however, should be to provide expert guidance (facilitation) in making valid and justifiable recommendations by providing input into solving organizational problems. In particular, they should play an important role in analyzing data, in drawing conclusions, and in impartially facilitating the overall assessment process.

The use of external HRD consultants (e.g., individuals hired from outside of the organization) is increasing.[10] Because of this, it is important to evaluate external consultants thoroughly so that the organization can be confident it is retaining the talent it needs (in this case, to provide expert input and guidance as a member of the needs assessment project team).

One of the principal roles of external consultants is to provide expert advice and guidance on designated phases of the project. This can range from participation in the design of survey questionnaire items, to devising, writing, and conducting interviews, to organizing and moderating focus groups, and, in certain instances, to assuming the role of SMEs. However, in order for the organization to make an educated choice about which consultants to hire, it must first carefully evaluate potential candidates. Specifically, it should look for consultants who

1. Are able to provide references or a client listing for whom they have provided like or similar services.
2. Can provide a list of projects that are similar to the one for which they are being considered. (Most notably, this list should emphasize what results were produced and not merely indicate their participation.)
3. Have a resumé of closely related work experiences indicating that they are specialists in the fields for which they are being considered.
4. Are in demand. Good consultants are usually very busy and will have several projects going on simultaneously. This can also be a disadvantage in that the consultants may be engaged in so many projects that they do not have the time to dedicate to the details of the project for which they are being considered. Ideally, a balance between the amount of time consultants spend on different projects must be struck. Higher demand is also a reflection of the consultants' esteem and reputation.
5. Are professional and have excellent human relations and interpersonal skills. They should be excellent communicators, be articulate, and have a thorough knowledge of the project's goals. Specifically, they should be able to quickly grasp what their role will (and will not) be. Above all, they should have consistent work habits, be accessible and punctual for meetings and appointments, and be flexible.
6. Charge realistic and reasonable fees. The more effective consultants will be in higher demand and therefore command higher fees. Generally, the more specific a client can be in defining the consultant's role, the more specific consultants should be in proposing a fee for any services to be provided.
7. Ask intelligent questions about the project for which they are being considered. Ideally, candidates should have already done some background research about the client organization and have specific questions about the role(s) they will play. Moreover, experienced consultants should be able to ask intelligent questions about the goals of the assessment project and what kinds of results they (the consultants) will be expected to produce.

### Defining External Consultant Roles

External consultants can be of considerable value in the design, facilitation, and analysis of needs assessments. Overall, however, their principal role as part of the assessment team should be that of a specialist. External consultants should not be used to perform routine tasks because doing so would violate the primary reason for hiring them in the first place; that is, they are hired because the expertise they bring with them is not available internally. Insofar as the needs assessment project itself is concerned, external consultants can make a significant contribution and add value by injecting a high degree of objectivity and bringing new perspectives to the project. The first step, however, is to find the right person with the necessary experience and qualifications.

*External Consultants as Expert Problem Solvers.* Known also as the lead or principal consultant (especially when more than one is retained as part of the assessment project team), these individuals' primary role is to provide advice and guidance to the person who has overall charge of the project (e.g., the HRD analyst, the training director or manager, etc.). Because they are retained primarily for their knowledge and experience in solving both routine as well as nonroutine problems, primary consultants provide guidance in the design, facilitation, and data analysis phases. This requires that they have excellent problem-solving skills and be intimately knowledgeable about the mechanics of needs assessment design. This includes but is not necessarily limited to establishing goals, deciding which type of assessment approach and accompanying data-gathering methods are the most appropriate to use for a given needs assessment population, helping to identify internal resources to enlist as part of the project team, assisting in the design of survey questionnaires, interview scripts, focus group, and general observation procedures, performing job and task analyses, and assisting in the development of a project chronology or time line model. In addition, they can also provide insight and, if required, oversight of the implementation of the assessment.

The individual chosen as the principal or lead consultant must have extensive experience in needs assessment design, implementation, facilitation, and analysis. Specifically, the person who is ultimately selected to fulfill this role should have

1. A proven track record of successful needs assessment projects conducted for a variety of organizations.
2. A genuine desire to participate as a member of the assessment project team, or to lead if required.
3. A demonstrated ability to solve routine as well as nonroutine problems.
4. The ability to forecast potential problems and advise team members on the ways and means to properly manage them.
5. The confidence and experience necessary to gain the trust and cooperation of other team members.
6. Expertise in dealing with behaviorally challenging or emotionally charged groups in building consensus from sometimes ambiguous and diverse opinions and viewpoints.
7. A personal goal of introducing and maintaining objectivity into the project team; this is particularly important as the project moves into the data analysis stage(s).

The relationship between the staff and the principal consultant is a very important one.[11] In particular, these individuals must be able to interact on a professional basis, share a common vision of the project and its benefits, be able to communicate openly and candidly, and have clearly defined lines of authority and responsibility. After finding the ideal expert, it is not uncommon for the person in charge of the project to relinquish most or all control. Although in most instances this is not done intentionally, it is imperative that any decision-making authority remain with the staff project leader. That is not to say, however, that the lead consultant should not be given a certain degree of autonomy. Indeed, the very nature and essence of the consultant's role requires that a considerable degree of latitude be extended. Thus, the division of labor or division of authority and responsibility must be clearly articulated, understood, and agreed to by both parties at the project's onset.

*External Consultants as Interviewers.* Another role external consultants are frequently called on to play is that of interviewer (interviews as a data-gathering method are discussed in detail in Chapter 4). Besides requiring absolute objectivity, it is imperative that the person chosen for this role have excellent verbal as well as nonverbal communication skills. The ideal candidate should have considerable interviewing experience in script preparation as well as in actual interviewing and be well versed in dealing with situations involving sensitive personal information. The candidate must also be knowledgeable and skilled in reading and interpreting respondents' body language.

Using consultants to conduct individual interviews has advantages as well as disadvantages. The advantages are that potential interviewees may be more truthful and candid in their responses when interviewed by an outsider whom they view as neutral and nonthreatening. In thinking the consultant may not be familiar with all of the particulars surrounding certain issues, an interviewee may be more inclined to offer additional information. This greatly enriches the data yield and can lead to substantive problem identification which heretofore may have gone unnoticed to other members of the project team.

Alternatively, using external consultants as interviewers has the potential to produce exactly the opposite effects: Because the consultants are "outsiders," interviewees may be reluctant to open up to them. This could actually impede the feedback process. Such reluctance could stem from a fear of sharing organizational and/or personally sensitive information with a stranger, or it could originate from mistrust, suspicion, or fear of retaliation from management whom respondents may believe is using an outsider to obtain feedback which may not have been accessible to fellow employees. This reverse psychological effect can produce potentially disastrous results.

Although there is no way to completely eliminate or otherwise offset these disadvantages, they can, in part, be managed in two ways. First, consultants being considered as potential interviewers should have the ability to quickly instill confidence and build rapport with any respondent. This means that they should be able to present themselves in a congenial and nonthreatening manner. In order to substantiate these qualities, it is good policy to subject potential candidates to interview simulations and to observe how they handle and react to behaviorally charged situations. Second, interviewees should receive advance notification of the interview along with information on who will be conducting it. This can help to offset any potential disadvantages or problems. Also, assurances that information divulged during the interview process will remain confidential can help to offset the reverse psychological effect.

*External Consultants as Focus Group Moderators.* Because the moderator is the central person in the needs assessment focus group method (focus groups are also discussed in detail in Chapter 4), it is extremely important that he or she be experienced in dealing with issues involving group dynamics. Moderators must be able to adapt to and direct the energies of the group towards goal attainment. They must also maintain control of participant interaction. Since all group activities involve expressing opinions in interpersonally dynamic situations, moderators must not only be skilled in focus group communication processes, they must also have experience in group facilitation. Many organizations do not have individuals who possess the degrees of experience or knowledge necessary to conduct productive focus group sessions. Therefore, help is frequently sought from external moderators and consultants.[12] Focus group facilitation has in recent years become both popular and profitable. Because of this, a number of people (experienced as well as inexperienced) have been attracted to the profession. Given the degree of interpersonal dynamics involved, and since there is no licensing or formalized accreditation for focus group moderators, retaining an expert requires very careful consideration.[13] Because the required experience does not generally exist within most organizations, retaining an outside moderator is usually preferable because they are generally not susceptible to internal organizational pressures and politics and are, therefore, considered to be more objective in their views and approach.

When interviewing candidates for an external moderator position, there are a number of factors that merit consideration. Such individuals should

1. Have considerable experience in conducting focus group sessions.
2. Be able to provide references regarding past assignments.
3. Be able to demonstrate an ability to maintain control of a group without leading them (this may require conducting trial group simulations).
4. Be able to utilize group-facilitation techniques such as word projection and association and, further, have the ability to move the group from conceptualization to closure in a structured and orderly manner.
5. Be people-oriented, articulate, and have a pleasing and congenial attitude. They should be patient, enthusiastic, and have a high energy level. Overall, they must be excellent problem identifiers and solvers.

External moderators can play a valuable role in maximizing group participation by extracting candid, frank, and open responses from the group members.[14] However, since they will have access to a considerable amount of potentially sensitive information, it is always a good idea to interview a number of potential candidates. This should be done before making a final selection. Qualifying interviews will provide opportunities to establish levels of trust and confidence in the moderator's abilities.

*External Consultants as SMEs.* Although SMEs are generally recruited internally, external consultants are sometimes called on to fulfill this role as well. They are usually brought in to observe and to provide objective feedback in areas where the organization feels that the value of using an external SME outweighs the value of using an internal one. For example, organizations will routinely use external SMEs to conduct operationally based time, motion, and benchmarking studies because of their familiarity with specific work methods and because of their knowledge of the processes that other organizations are using.

External SMEs should be experts in their respective fields and should have acquired considerable knowledge through their association and/or employment with a variety of other organizations. Many will have acquired their knowledge and experience as employees and managers in other companies. External SMEs can possess a wealth of industry-specific information about new work methods, processes, and technologies that can add considerable value to a needs assessment project, particularly one that is aimed at updating skills and/or technical competencies. Many SMEs also conduct various types of skills training courses and seminars as a core part of their consulting services.

Some guidelines for qualifying external SMEs are the following:

1. They should be experts in narrowly defined areas such as project management, time and motion studies, manufacturing and production methods, technology acquisition and implementation, and the like.
2. They should have amassed considerable knowledge and experience in a particular area and spent a considerable amount of time within a given industry or profession.
3. They should have compiled a track record of successful client relationships, having worked on a wide variety of projects.
4. They should have developed keen observation, analytical, communication, and human relations skills.

External SMEs should be evaluated on their familiarity with the tasks and/or processes they will be observing and commenting on. They should be able to blend unobtrusively into a given environment where their observations will be conducted, and they should be able to provide objective feedback that is supported by and through work-related experiences.

One principal disadvantage to using external consultants as SMEs is that organizations may have equally qualified personnel on staff. Under such conditions, the act of bringing an outsider into a work setting where a qualified staff member is present could lead to expertise conflict. In those situations where it is either necessary or even desirable to retain an outside SME for placement in an area where internal expertise exists, the individual chosen for the role should make a point of identifying those expert employees and enlisting their input and assistance. Under these circumstances, taking a proactive approach can offset potentially disruptive situations before they have a chance to occur.

### Evaluating an External Consultant's Proposal

Professional consultants should be required to submit a complete proposal that reflects a thorough understanding of the assessment project. Specifically, it should outline what their roles will be and what measurable outcomes they will produce. The proposal should be neatly and thoughtfully prepared, focus on results, and include time frames, a progress chronology, costs, deliverables, and billing information.[15] In particular, the organization should consider the following when evaluating a consultant's proposal:

1. Who will actually provide the services? Is it the consultant with whom contact has been made or is the consultant just serving as the "point" person who will hand off the detail work to another and perhaps less qualified individual?
2. Is the proposal written in clear and concise terms and does it reflect a clear understanding of the scope of the project?
3. Does it reflect a clear understanding of the consultant's role(s)?
4. Does it specify deliverables (e.g., custom survey questionnaires)?
5. Does it contain a guarantee of confidentiality by specifying that all of the information the consultant has access to during the course of the project will remain client proprietary?
6. Does the proposal contain a noncompetition clause that prevents the consultant from doing similar work for a competitor immediately after the closure of the project?
7. Does the proposal clearly state what will be done and how the results can be measured?
8. Are costs clearly defined? (Fees specified should include all costs such as time, travel, and any and all per diem expenses.)
9. Does it contain an appropriate chronology or time schedule?

Another major factor to consider when selecting and retaining external consultants is determining how well they fit into the assessment project team. Although this is largely a personality issue, experience has shown that if consultants cannot interact both professionally as well as socially with other team members, their usefulness, and consequently the value of their services, will be considerably diminished.

### Managing External Consultant Relationships

Consultants and organizations must develop and nurture ongoing professional relationships. Where consultants are concerned, this is mandatory because their ongoing contact with clients is their livelihood. Without clients, consultants are spending valuable time selling their services in a marketplace already crowded with professionals and novices alike. Alternatively, organizations, having invested considerable time and monies in finding the right consultant that meets their needs, also have a vested interest in maintaining the relationship. Thus the client–consultant relationship is based on mutuality: Each has a need for the other.

Paramount to the success of this relationship is the necessity to manage it correctly. This requires that high levels of trust be established between the parties.[16] Reaching this point requires an in-depth understanding of each other's needs and, in particular, the roles each will play in fostering and improving the relationship. These roles can range from being the implementor of high-scale intervention strategies (e.g., coach, partner), to intermediate-scale intervention strategies (e.g., counselor), to low-scale intervention strategies (e.g., facilitator, observer, advisor).[17]

From the organization's perspective, there are several guidelines for successfully managing the client–consultant relationship. First, the consultants' role and what is expected of them should be clearly defined. This should be written in as detailed a manner as possible. Second, fees that are reasonable to both parties should be openly negotiated. Third, by holding regular debriefing and evaluation sessions with the consultants, the organization will help to determine the consultants' level of progress and performance. Fourth, the organization must be open to critical and constructive feedback from the consultants. Fifth, the consultants must be able to adapt to the organization's culture and normative values.

In periods where the organization does not have consultants actively working on an assessment project, the effort expended by both parties to remain in contact eliminates the need to reintroduce one another when the need to hire external expertise arises again. Maintaining the social side of the relationship is very important. If the organization knows it will be needing ongoing assistance, it should consider placing the consultants on a retainer. This is good for the organization because it gives them a means for controlling costs while simultaneously providing accessibility to the consultants' expertise on relatively short notice. Alternatively, this type of agreement is also beneficial for the consultants because it provides a steady source of income and enables them to gain additional experience and familiarity with the organization's structure, culture, norms, values, personnel, and operational environment. From a more strategic perspective, nurturing this relationship can greatly reduce the amount of time it would otherwise take to get new or future assessment projects up and on-line.

Since most needs assessment projects are not normally ongoing, it may seem to make little sense to keep consultants on a retainer. This may or may not be so. From an activity perspective, it may seem costly, yet from a performance perspective, it makes good sense because it is usually more efficient to enlist expert advice from consultants who have ongoing familiarity with the organization and the various types of assessment projects it has undertaken than it is to negotiate new contracts and bring the consultants back up the learning curve after a period of absence. Thus, the benefits associated with retaining external consultants are in developing and maintaining familiarity with the organization's culture and operations and short notice access to what may be critically needed expertise.

## NEEDS ASSESSMENT PROJECT BUDGETING

Human Resource Accounting (HRA) is a specialized field that originated as a way to assist managers in planning and controlling the use of human resources within their organizations.[18] It seeks to account for all aspects involving human endeavors toward the attainment of organizational objectives and, further, to measure results in terms of profit and loss.[19]

Accounting (budgeting) for costs is a central factor in organizational needs assessment planning. Many of the techniques in use today evolved from concerted research in the HRA field. Consequently, many of the budgeting and costing methods subsequently discussed in this section are modifications and, to a degree, distillations of established HRA methods.

The needs assessment budget is an integral component of a systematic needs assessment. Not only is it used as a means for recording and comparing costs, it is also valuable in the planning process. As with any budget, most costs begin as estimates. They will not, therefore, be as accurate as one would normally like them to be. However, as more experience is gained in developing needs assessment budgetary information, the more accurate these front-end cost estimates will become.

There are many ways to budget for a needs assessment. Many HRD professionals have their own models, methods, and approaches. Due to the number of variables involved, there is no one recommended method to follow. There are, however, some general items which should be included in any needs assessment budgeting process.

Certain budgets may include only direct costs (such as materials and supplies), while others are developed to reflect overhead costs (e.g., portions of salaries, benefits, and other expenses). Since management's questioning of the ROI for HRD programs has become more frequent in recent years, many professionals are now including not only the costs associated with the assessment's design, facilitation, and analysis, but they are also including estimated costs associated with researching and developing intervention activities. This is actually a more realistic method of accounting and provides for estimates of the real costs normally associated with this type of project.

Some items included in a comprehensive needs assessment budget are overhead expenses (which are based on portions of the salaries of all employees involved), any consultant fees, material costs (such as paper, envelopes, computer time, and software), mailing and postage costs, meeting room rental (for conducting individual interviews or focus groups), any audio-visual equipment rentals or acquisitions, and any travel and per diem expenses related to the design and implementation of the assessment. These are usually considered to be developmental costs.[20]

One aspect of developing an assessment budget that presents problems for many HRD personnel lies in estimating or otherwise calculating the amount of time that individual employees spend on the project. This problem is compounded further in translating the calculated time (in numbers of hours and days) into dollar amounts. Over the years, many creative ways of handling this problem have been devised; however, one of the simplest and most direct ways to figure time costs for both salaried (exempt) and hourly (nonexempt) employees is illustrated as follows:

For salaried employees

1. Figure the employee's total salary including benefits (e.g., $40,000.00).
2. Estimate the total number of hours annually worked (e.g., 40 hours per week × 52 weeks per year = 2,080 hours per year—note that this figure assumes and includes paid leave and/or vacation time).
3. Divide the annual compensation by the total number of hours worked (e.g., $40,000 ÷ 2,080 = $19.23 per hour).

For nonexempt or hourly paid employees

1. Figure pay per hour (e.g., $8.00 per hour).
2. Estimate the total number of hours per week this employee would work on the project (e.g., 40 hours).
3. Multiply the per-hour pay times the number of hours per week times the number of weeks (e.g., assuming the project was to take four weeks to complete, the cost would be $8.00 × 40 × 4 = $1,280.00).

Note that this figure does not include any overtime hours. Any overtime worked would be charged at the applicable overtime rate (e.g., overtime is paid at time plus one-half [$8.00 plus $4.00 = $12.00 per hour overtime]). In order to contain costs, overtime should be used only where it is considered to be absolutely necessary and should require the HRD manager's approval.

When figuring portions of either salaried (exempt) or hourly (nonexempt) employees, the total amount of the time they are actively working on the project also has to be calculated. In accounting terms, this method of costing is known as a determinant of individual contribution.[21] For example, it is unlikely that the vice president of human resources or the HRD director or manager would allocate 100 percent of their available time to a project (although, depending on its size, scope, and complexity, this has happened). For illustrative purposes, assume that an assessment is being contemplated and that it has an estimated time span of eight weeks. The amount of time the HRD director will spend on the project during that period is estimated to be 20 percent. Assuming the director's salary is $60,000 per annum, the amount of the director's time and associated costs to be charged to the project would be calculated as follows:

Director's salary: $60,000

Hourly cost: ($60,000 ÷ 52 weeks) = $1,153.85/40-hour week = $28.85 per hour

Time allocated to project: 20 percent of 8 weeks = 64 hours (8 weeks × 40 hours = 320 × 0.20 = 64)

Cost of director's time charged to project: $1,846.40 (64 hours × $28.85 per hour)

The same type of calculations can be applied for any hourly nonexempt employee. For example:

Hourly cost: $8.00 per hour

Time allocated to project: 75 percent of 8 weeks = 240 hours (8 weeks × 40 hours = 320 × 0.75 = 240)

Cost of hourly, nonexempt employee's time charged to project: $1,920.00 (240 hours × $8.00 per hour)

For budget estimating purposes, there are essentially two ways for estimating needs assessment project costs. One is to figure only those costs directly associated with the assessment (such as those examples already given). While this reflects estimates of direct costs, it does not give a clear picture of the overall total costs. Another method, though far from precise, does provide a more realistic overview of the estimated costs that are likely to be incurred. This alternative method also includes indirect costs, some examples of which are the following:

1. Costs related to the time it takes members of the assessment sample population to complete any written surveys
2. Costs related to the time it takes members of the sample assessment population to participate in any individual interviews
3. Costs related to the time it takes members of the sample assessment population to participate as members of a focus group
4. Additional expenses such as travel and per diem for members of the assessment sample population and HRD staff
5. SME costs, which, if employees are used, are computed on the basis of their salary or hourly rates

Of these, the costs associated with the time it takes to complete a survey questionnaire are variable, meaning that (1) it is impossible to calculate exact times for everyone involved; (2) it is unlikely that everyone who receives a questionnaire will actually complete and return it; and (3) not all of the potential respondents who have been selected to participate will either be able or willing to do so. Costs like these can only be estimated because they vary with the number of respondents scheduled to participate. Therefore, all costs should be considered to be estimates, with those relating to the time it takes respondents to complete and return survey questionnaires as being the ones that are the least probable to state with any degree of certainty.

One way in which costs that are associated with questionnaire completion times can be more realistically estimated is to run a series of trial tests on the survey instrument. At some point, an average figure of the time it takes to complete the questionnaire can be determined. To illustrate, assume a survey questionnaire was distributed to a group of 120 hourly employees, many of whom are at different pay levels. One way to average the costs related to the time it takes to complete a survey questionnaire is to (1) get information on the highest and the (2) lowest hourly pay rates, (3) average the rates together, (4) estimate the time it takes to complete the survey (thirty minutes), (5) calculate the total average costs, (6) estimate the number of surveys that are expected to be completed and returned (75 percent), and then (7) calculate the total averaged cost. For example:

| | |
|---|---|
| 1. Highest hourly rate | $20.00 per hour |
| 2. Lowest hourly rate | $12.00 per hour |
| 3. Averaged rate | $16.00 per hour |
| 4. Estimated time to complete survey | 30 minutes |
| 5. Average cost per survey | $8.00 ($16.00 per hour [average] × 0.5 = $8.00) |
| 6. Estimated number to be completed and returned | 90 (120 × 0.75) |
| 7. 90 estimated returns at $8.00 per return | $720.00, which is the estimated total cost for hourly employees to complete and return the survey questionnaire |

Alternatively, the same method to calculate averaged costs can be applied to exempt, salaried workers as well. For example, assume twenty salaried employees:

| | |
|---|---|
| 1. Highest salary | $80,000 (including benefits) |
| 2. Lowest salary | $12,000 (including benefits) |
| 3a. Highest salary calculated hourly | 52 forty-hour weeks = 2,080 hours<br>$80,000/2,080 = $38.46 per hour |

| | |
|---|---|
| 3b. Lowest salary calculated hourly | \$12,000/2,080 = \$5.77 per hour |
| 3c. Averaged salary per-hour cost | \$16.35 [(\$38.46 – \$5.77) ÷ 2] |
| 4. Estimated time to complete survey | 30 minutes |
| 5. Average cost per survey | \$8.18 (\$16.35 ÷ 0.5) |
| 6. Estimated number of surveys to be completed and returned | 15 (20 × 0.75) |
| 7. 15 estimated returns at \$8.18 per completion | \$122.70 estimated total cost for salaried employees to complete survey |

Averaged estimates can also be used to calculate costs related to employee participation in all of the other data-gathering methods used (e.g., individual interviews, focus groups, s groups, observations, etc.).

Averaged costs will vary, sometimes considerably, due to events that normally arise during the assessment and which are beyond anyone's control. For this reason, once the assessment has been formally implemented, it is important for the project team to maintain as accurate an account of the times associated with employee participation as possible. These times can then be translated into actual costs which are then reconciled against the estimated costs. The result are costs that were actually incurred. An example of a budget form illustrating direct and indirect cost estimates is shown in Figure 3.2. A reconciliation form that compares the estimated with the actual costs incurred is shown in Figure 3.3. Examples of completed forms used in an actual needs assessment are provided in Appendixes A and B.

## SUMMARY

Policies establish guidelines by which the organization conducts its business. Rules, on the other hand, are drawn from policies and are meant to guide employee actions. A fundamental part of needs assessment planning is developing an understanding of how an organization's policies and rules can either facilitate or hinder the needs assessment process. Because needs assessment data-gathering methods are investigative in nature, policies and rules can sometimes be unintentionally violated through normal data-gathering procedures. Therefore, one must first gain an understanding of what organizational policies and rules are in place and, further, attempt to determine if any of these can or will be violated during the conduct of the assessment.

The first formal step in the needs assessment planning stage is to establish goals. Preliminary goals reflect predetermined, measured/observed, or desired effects. A predetermined effect is the most probable outcome of an event before it has taken place; a measured and observed effect is the result of something that has already occurred; and a desired effect is likewise a wanted or a needed outcome.

**Figure 3.2**
Needs Assessment Estimated Budget Form

Needs Assessment Estimated Budget Form

Project Name: Number of Salaried Employees: Number of Hourly employees:
Duration:
Overview:
Expense Itemization:

**HRD Department**

| | | | | | |
|---|---|---|---|---|---|
| Name ______ | Title ______ | % of time allocated ____ | salary: ____ | hourly rate: ____ | ttl. est. cost: ____ |
| Name ______ | Title ______ | % of time allocated ____ | salary: ____ | hourly rate: ____ | ttl. est. cost: ____ |
| Name ______ | Title ______ | % of time allocated ____ | salary: ____ | hourly rate: ____ | ttl. est. cost: ____ |
| Name ______ | Title ______ | % of time allocated ____ | salary: ____ | hourly rate: ____ | ttl. est. cost: ____ |
| Name ______ | Title ______ | % of time allocated ____ | salary: ____ | hourly rate: ____ | ttl. est. cost: ____ |

**Consultant**

| | | | |
|---|---|---|---|
| Name ______ | Hours ______ | @______ per hour | ttl. est. cost: ____ |
| Name ______ | Hours ______ | @______ per hour | ttl. est. cost: ____ |

**Data Gathering Costs**

| Method | Est. time to complete | Est. # Employees Participating | Total |
|---|---|---|---|
| 1. ______ | ____hr. ____min. | ____ salary ____ hourly | ____ |
| 2. ______ | ____hr. ____min. | ____ salary ____ hourly | ____ |
| 3. ______ | ____hr. ____min. | ____ salary ____ hourly | ____ |
| 4. ______ | ____hr. ____min. | ____ salary ____ hourly | ____ |

**Calculations: Hourly Employees**

| | Highest rate | Lowest Rate | Average Est. time to complete | avg.cost to complete | est. no. employees participating | cost |
|---|---|---|---|---|---|---|
| 1. | | | | | | |
| 2. | | | | | | |
| 3. | | | | | | |
| 4. | | | | | | |

**Calculations: Salaried Employees**

1. ______
2. ______
3. ______
4. ______

**Other Costs: (itemize)**

1. ______
2. ______
3. ______
4. ______

TOTAL ESTIMATED PROJECT COSTS: ______

**Figure 3.3**
Needs Assessment Budget Reconciliation Form

## Needs Assessment Budget Reconciliation Form

Project Name:________________ Number of Salaried Employees:________ Number of Hourly Employees:________
Duration estimated:________ Actual Duration:________ (Under)/over:________
Expense Summary:

**HRD Department**

Name:____________ Title:__________ % of time allocated____ actual time____ est.cost:________ actual cost:________ (under)/over:____
Name:____________ Title:__________ % of time allocated____ actual time____ est.cost:________ actual cost:________ (under)/over:____
Name:____________ Title:__________ % of time allocated____ actual time____ est.cost:________ actual cost:________ (under)/over:____
Name:____________ Title:__________ % of time allocated____ actual time____ est.cost:________ actual cost:________ (under)/over:____

**Consultant**

Name:____________ Hours:__________ @________ per hour est. cost:________ actual cost:________ (under)/over:____
Name:____________ Hours:__________ @________ per hour est. cost:________ actual cost:________ (under)/over:____

---

| **Data Gathering Costs** Method | est. time to complete | actual time | est.no. employees participating | actual no. participating | est.total | actual total | (under)/over |
|---|---|---|---|---|---|---|---|
| 1.____ | ____ | ____ | ____ | ____ | ____ | ____ | ____ |
| 2.____ | ____ | ____ | ____ | ____ | ____ | ____ | ____ |
| 3.____ | ____ | ____ | ____ | ____ | ____ | ____ | ____ |
| 4.____ | ____ | ____ | ____ | ____ | ____ | ____ | ____ |
| **Calculations: Hourly Employees** | | | | | | | |
| 1.____ | ____ | ____ | ____ | ____ | ____ | ____ | ____ |
| 2.____ | ____ | ____ | ____ | ____ | ____ | ____ | ____ |
| 3.____ | ____ | ____ | ____ | ____ | ____ | ____ | ____ |
| 4.____ | ____ | ____ | ____ | ____ | ____ | ____ | ____ |
| **Calculations: Salaried Employees** | | | | | | | |
| 1.____ | ____ | ____ | ____ | ____ | ____ | ____ | ____ |
| 2.____ | ____ | ____ | ____ | ____ | ____ | ____ | ____ |
| 3.____ | ____ | ____ | ____ | ____ | ____ | ____ | ____ |
| 4.____ | ____ | ____ | ____ | ____ | ____ | ____ | ____ |

**Other Costs:**

1.______________________________ estimated:________ actual:________ (under)/over:________
2.______________________________ estimated:________ actual:________ (under)/over:________
3.______________________________ estimated:________ actual:________ (under)/over:________
4.______________________________ estimated:________ actual:________ (under)/over:________

TOTAL ACTUAL COSTS: ________

TOTAL ESTIMATED PROJECT COSTS:____________ ACTUAL PROJECT COSTS: ____________ (UNDER)/OVER:________

Forecasting is another method that is used for setting goals. Because it is less precise, it has been limited to use in smaller organizations that have more flexible work structures. An effective method for forecasting assessment goals is based on the Delphi technique. This requires a group of employees to compare notes based on their individual observations. The outcomes are then shared anonymously with other members of the group, thus allowing individuals to revise their own needs forecast until a similarity of needs (goals) emerges.

The assessment sample group must include all individuals or groups of individuals who are either part of or have contributed to the effects that were used to establish the preliminary goals. Assessment populations can also include individuals from outside the organization, such as customers, as well as the organization's vendors and suppliers.

Another important step is to identify individuals who will be part of the assessment project team. This usually includes the HRD director or manager, the HRD analyst, administrative assistants, internal or external consultants, SMEs, focus group leaders, and any information systems staff, particularly if any part of the assessment is to include the use of computers for tabulating responses and for performing statistical tests on collected data.

Internal consultants are a valuable but often overlooked resource. This is due mainly to the existence of a mind-set in many organizations that says the kinds of expertise required can only be enlisted from outside of the company's ranks.

External consultants can provide significant value because they bring objectivity as well as specialized knowledge, experience, and skills to an assessment project. The role of external consultants—most notably, that of the lead or principal consultant—is to provide expert guidance and advice on various phases of the project. This input is normally drawn from experience they have had with similar organizations and with similar projects. They can play an important role in the design and delivery of custom needs assessments. Though there may be disadvantages to using them (such as higher costs and internal resistance from management), the advantages are that they are immune from organizational politics and therefore bring higher degrees of objectivity to the project experiences.

External consultants can be retained to provide a variety of services. They can be retained as expert problem solvers, as interviewers or focus group moderators, and, under certain circumstances, they may be hired to fill the role of SME as well. External consultants should be excellent communicators. They should be particularly adept in dealing with issues of diversity. They must also have excellent human relations skills. The consultant's proposal should clearly state who will actually provide the services specified, the scope of these services, and what the costs will be. The proposal should contain guarantees of confidentiality, meaning that all organizationally specific information the consultants acquire as part of their work remains client proprietary. It should also contain a noncompetition clause prohibiting the consultant from accepting similar work with a competitor within a reasonable amount of time after the project has formally concluded. Last, a well-rounded proposal should contain a project chronology and a detailed description of the consultant's role and related activities.

The necessity to establish a solid and trusting relationship between the consultants and the client organization is of paramount importance. How well this relationship is managed reflects how well the consultants and the organization interact on a professional as well as a social basis. Once this relationship has been established, it is usually a good idea for the organization to place the consultants on a retainer whereby they will have access to these persons' expertise on an ongoing basis.

Needs assessment budgets should include all costs directly and indirectly associated with the design, facilitation, and analysis phases of the assessment. This includes all salary or compensation expenses based on the amount of time it takes each individual to participate throughout the duration of the project. The budget should also contain estimates for supplies and materials, computer time and usage, and mailing costs, along with estimated expenses for meeting space and any travel and per-diem costs.

## NOTES

1. J. Gibson, J. Ivancevich, and J. Donnelly, Jr., *Organizations: Behavior, Structure, Processes*, 6th ed. (Plano, Tex.: Business Publications, Inc., 1988).
2. Ibid., p. 595.
3. S. McClelland, "Training Needs Assessment: An 'Open-Systems' Application," *Journal of European Industrial Training*, Vol. 17, No. 1, pp. 12–17.
4. L. James, S. Muliak, and J. Brett, *Causal Analysis: Assumptions, Models, and Data* (Newbury Park, Calif.: Sage Publications, 1982).
5. Bureau of Business Practice, *BPP Training Director's Handbook* (Waterford, Conn.: Prentice Hall, 1989).
6. W. Borg and M. Gall, *Educational Research: An Introduction*, 4th ed. (New York: Longman, 1983).
7. E. Hawthorne, *Evaluating Employee Training Programs: A Research-Based Guide for Human Resource Managers* (Westport, Conn.: Quorum Books, 1987).
8. D. Gayeski, L. Wood, and J. Ford, "Getting Inside an Expert's Brain," *Training and Development*, Vol. 48, No. 8, 1992, pp. 106–110.
9. S. Parry and W. Ouweneel, "Consultants," in *Training and Development Handbook: A Guide to Human Resource Development*, 3rd ed., R. Craig, ed. (New York: McGraw-Hill, 1987), p. 813.
10. J. Phillips, *Handbook of Training Evaluation and Measurement Methods*, 2nd ed. (Houston: Gulf Publishing, 1991).
11. H. Shenson, *How to Select and Manage Consultants* (Lexington, Mass.: Lexington Books, 1990).
12. T. Greenbaum, *The Practical Handbook and Guide to Focus Group Research* (New York: The Free Press, 1990).
13. T. Greenbaum, "Do You Have the Right Moderator for Your Focus Groups?" *Bank Marketing*, Vol. 23, No. 1, p. 43.
14. S. Erkut and J. Fields, "Focus Groups to the Rescue," *Training and Development Journal*, Vol. 41, No. 10, pp. 74–76.
15. Parry and Ouweneel, p. 815.

16. D. Champion, D. Kiel, and J. McLendon, "Choosing a Consulting Role," *Training and Development Journal*, Vol. 44, No. 2, pp. 66–69.

17. Ibid.

18. E. Flamholtz, *Human Resource Accounting*, 2nd ed. (San Francisco: Jossey-Bass, 1985).

19. Ibid., p. 135.

20. Ibid., pp. 173–176.

21. Shenson.

CHAPTER 4

# An Overview of Needs Assessment Data-Gathering Methods

## GATHERING DATA

Once the preliminary goals and plans (including the budget and the identification of the sample population) have been considered, the next step in the design and development of a systematic needs assessment is to select the type or types of data-gathering methods to be used.

As noted in Chapter 1, organizations undertake surveys for a variety of purposes. They may have a need (or desire) to obtain feedback on their environment (internal as well as external), to gather information about their structures, cultures, or operational frameworks, or to get feedback from employees about what can or needs to be done to improve efficiency and performance. This kind of feedback often highlights areas where some sort of intervention is either necessary or desirable. A needs assessment can produce a cadre of information about organizational as well as individual employee needs. It can also produce data that are related to other issues which the organization may have not heretofore considered.

The methods by which data are gathered can and do have considerable impact on their quality (and subsequently on the analysis and evaluation from which results and recommendations are made). The ways and means used to gather data can bias or influence the outcome of the assessment project. Data can be manipulated in a number of ways to serve a variety of purposes (e.g., from supporting a particular hypothesis to dispelling a long-held belief). Moreover, how they are collected and interpreted profoundly impacts the results. Because of this, it is important to gain a fundamental understanding of the basics of data gathering and, moreover, of what effects the various data-gathering methods can produce.

In the needs assessment data-gathering process, it is mandatory to maintain as high a degree of objectivity as possible. To be objective, one must take safeguards to dispel any preconceived notions about the intent or content of the feedback that would otherwise cause one to intentionally select a method or methods that would increase the probability that such feedback would actually be received. For example, assume that an analyst, based on informal conversations with various employees, theorizes that there is a morale problem between a group of individuals and a particular supervisor. In order to prove this, the analyst knows that face-to-face interview questions could be based on those employees' interaction with the supervisor. Yet, by basing interview questions in such a manner, the analyst would increase the probability of proving that his or her theory about morale being an issue between certain individuals and the supervisor is true. Armed with this information, the analyst selects the interview method and "scripts" it, knowing that the feedback received will support his or her theory. This is known as intentional biasing.

Biasing can also occur unintentionally. For example, in conducting an assessment directed at identifying the technical training needs of a group of machine operators, an analyst constructs a survey questionnaire with an introductory heading that states the following: "Since your jobs have changed it is obvious that new skills will be needed in order for you to perform effectively." Maybe their jobs have not changed that much and, certainly, at the starting point in any data-gathering process, nothing is obvious. If it were, then for what purpose is the assessment being conducted?

Although it may seem a bit premature to discuss data analysis at this point (this is presented in greater detail in Chapters 7 and 8), the outcomes that will eventually be provided are to a considerable extent influenced by the design and content of the selected data-gathering method(s) and accompanying instrument(s).[1]

### Data Summaries and Analyses

A commonly used technique is to statistically arrange and summarize the data that have been collected. There are three primary types of summaries in which statistical manipulations are applied. They are the following:

1. Descriptive summaries which involve the reduction of data into dimensions that normally address "what" and/or "where" questions. An example of this would be "What qualities do you look for in a leader?" This question could require a narrative (written statement) or the selection of an answer that was drawn from a set of predefined responses.
2. Explanatory analysis which is concerned mainly with "why" questions such as "Why do you feel that certain organizational policies are unfair?" This type of question format will normally require a narrative response.

3. Predictive analysis, which is used with any "what if" questions. For example, "If this new system were purchased, what benefits do you believe the company would realize?" Again, this type of question format will normally require a narrative response unless a predetermined set of possible choices (answers) is provided.

## QUANTITATIVE AND QUALITATIVE DATA TYPES

The data generated from a needs assessment consist basically of two types: *quantitative* and *qualitative*. Quantitative data are derived from assessment methods that normally involve numerical tabulation and computation. These include virtually all types of feedback that can be numerically ordered, ranked, summarized, or otherwise counted. Quantitative data are generated from observations of work processes (e.g., number of units produced, number of phone calls answered in any given period of time, etc.), from questionnaire feedback (e.g., "Rank your preference in descending order from the following list of options."), or from interview formats (e.g., "Which two of the following four methods would you prefer to use?"). They are the simplest to organize, tabulate, and analyze. One caveat is that raw quantitative data do not contain information that may be relevant because of the limited range of answers or choices available to the respondent. For example, consider the following question: Which of the following do you believe are important topics in this training program? Please rank your answers in *descending* order of importance.

___ Communication Skills

___ Leadership Skills

___ Motivational Techniques

___ Decision-Making Techniques

The range of available choices has been predetermined by the individual(s) responsible for composing the question. It presupposes that the respondent will interpret the question in the same manner in which the designer wrote it. To the respondent, it suggests that this range includes all possible choices that have been determined (by someone) to be valid. However, it is very probable that many individuals will consider other topics that are not listed to be of equal or greater importance. Because the respondent does not see what they consider to be important enough to be included under this listing, some may choose not to answer the question at all, or they may choose to write in their own responses. While requiring individuals to answer within a limited range that has a numerically based sequence does provide for a simple way to tabulate the responses, it also illustrates some of the constraints and restrictions of using only quantitatively based data—particularly in forced-choice and closed-ended question formats. Additional details on constructing and writing questions like these are presented later in this chapter.

Qualitative or narrative data usually take the form of a statement in which respondents are asked to provide input in their own words. As mentioned earlier, this type of data generally contains more in-depth information regarding respondents' reactions or feelings toward a particular subject and is very useful for obtaining feedback that is broader and has a greater degree of depth. Qualitative questions are commonly referred to as being open-ended in that there is no predetermination of the response by the writer or analyst. Qualitative information can add an extra dimension to quantitative data because numbers alone often do not give the sufficient level of detail that is sometimes necessary for making value-based decisions or judgments.[2]

Alternatively, analyzing qualitative data is more time consuming because it presents choices that are not normally present with quantitative data sets. First, qualitative feedback may be difficult to read, particularly if the respondent's handwriting is not clear. Second, the respondent, though well intentioned, may not have written an appropriate response to the query (this can also indicate grammatical problems which are discussed later in this chapter). Third, qualitative feedback is highly subjective to the respondent's interpretation of the question being posed.[3]

On average, most needs assessment professionals recommend a combination of both quantitative and qualitative feedback because of the advantages each possesses. Depending on a number of other variables that will be covered later in this chapter, using a combination of both types will yield a greater in-depth feedback that is necessary to provide a balanced summation upon which future recommendations (e.g., training or other types of interventions) can be made.

## NEEDS ASSESSMENT DATA-GATHERING METHODS

There are basically four principal methods for gathering needs assessment research data: (1) survey questionnaires, (2) individual interviews, (3) focus groups, and (4) on-site observations. Each method, as outlined in Figure 2.1, is part of an "open-systems" approach to assessing organizational needs (i.e., each method can be used independently or in conjunction with any of the others). Many, if not all, will produce substantial in-depth feedback when used in concert with one or more of the other methods. Knowing how and when to use which method(s) in what types of situations or organizational settings to obtain what types of feedback gives the analyst a wide range of custom needs assessment design options. Each of the methods can be applied to any of the assessment approaches outlined in Chapter 2 (e.g., behavioral, attitudinal, organizational climate, cultural, etc.). What must be understood, however, is what each method involves and how it is used in a systematic needs assessment. Table 4.1 illustrates data-gathering methods that are commonly used in organizational needs assessments.

## SURVEY QUESTIONNAIRES

Survey questionnaires are the most popular and widely used data-gathering method. They are used to gather feedback on virtually everything ranging from demographic data (e.g., the U.S. census) to consumer behavior. They are also cost-effective, particularly if the assessment population is situated in geographically diverse locations.

**Table 4.1**
Types of Needs Assessments and Accompanying Data-Gathering Methods

| Assessment Type | Commonly Used Data-Gathering Methods |
|---|---|
| Competency/Skills | Questionnaires, Interviews, Focus Groups, On-Site Observations |
| Knowledge/Experience | Questionnaires, Interviews, On-Site Observations |
| Behavioral | Interviews, Questionnaires, On-Site Observations |
| Attitudinal/Morale | Questionnaires, Interviews, On-Site Observations |
| Organizational Climate | Questionnaires, Interviews, Focus Groups, On-Site Observations |
| Cultural | Questionnaires, Interviews |
| Leadership | Questionnaires, Interviews |
| Benchmarking | Questionnaires, Interviews, Focus Groups, On-Site Observations |
| Operational | Questionnaires, Interviews, Focus Groups, On-Site Observations |
| Job/Task Analysis | Questionnaires, Interviews, Focus Groups, On-Site Observations |

In organizational needs assessments there are five primary steps in survey questionnaire construction. They are the following: (1) defining its content, (2) writing the actual survey items (questions), (3) pretesting, (4) developing the final instrument, and (5) gaining management's approval of the instrument before formally implementing (distributing) it. This section is concerned with steps 1 and 2. Steps 3, 4, and 5 are discussed in detail in Chapter 5.

### Survey Questionnaire Content

The content of the survey, or rather, the type, format, and focus of the questions it contains, is directly linked to the type of assessment being conducted (see Chapter 2). Thus, the construction of the items in a survey questionnaire should be directed at obtaining feedback that is needed by the type of assessment being planned.

The first task in survey questionnaire construction is to identify as extensively as possible the range of dimensions that are to be used when writing the actual survey questions.[4] These include but are not necessarily limited to interviews and discussions with job incumbents, personnel performance documentation, and results from previous assessments (if any). An additional source of information that is rich in content but is greatly underutilized is literature searches and reviews on topics, methods, and approaches that are directly related to the current needs assessment project. To illustrate, assume a survey questionnaire is being designed to query employees about what competencies and skills they feel they need to develop in order to improve their performance levels. The type of needs assessment most likely to be used to obtain feedback in this instance would be the competency/skills type. Therefore, it is important for the analyst or writer to have some insight into what competencies and skills are required of employees so that the questions developed for the questionnaire would be relevant to employees' jobs and present as well as desired performance levels. Alternatively, if an organization wanted to investigate its efficiency levels and chose to undertake an operational audit, the analyst would need to devise questions that are designed to obtain feedback on the organization's structure, operational plans and objectives, and on how well it maximizes the efficient use of its human as well as its material resources.

### Writing Question Items

Writing intelligent, concise, and readable survey questions requires both rigor and common sense. One of many concerns the writer has to deal with are grammatical issues. It is imperative that any and all steps are taken to ensure that the questions will be interpreted as they are meant to be. One way this can be done is to write in short, simple, and declarative sentences using everyday, common language. Also, using jargon that is common or related to specific jobs or functions which respondents are familiar with can also help to insure clarity. The importance of writing questions clearly and concisely cannot be overemphasized.[5]

Questions that are written to provide demographic feedback or, rather, personalized descriptive information, are almost certain to be included in any survey questionnaire. The problem with requiring too much demographic information is that it can cause respondents to become suspicious about the intent of the survey, particularly if it is not conducted anonymously (i.e., respondents are required to identify themselves). This can negatively affect response rates and can also raise questions about respondents' candidness.

*Respondent Anonymity.* The question of respondent anonymity poses many problems, not the least of which is how to follow up and contact nonrespondents. Some studies suggest that response rates are higher when individuals are required to identify themselves.[6] However, this has also raised counter-concerns about the truthfulness of their responses.[7] Since there are no universally accepted solutions to the problems raised by the anonymity question, the following guidelines are useful:

1. If the survey questionnaire contains questions eliciting substantial demographic or sensitive information (e.g., levels of drug use in the workplace, issues related to sexual harassment, etc.), anonymity should be guaranteed.
2. If a high response rate is required, steps should be taken to balance or otherwise limit the amount of demographic or sensitive information so that a satisfactory response level can be obtained.

*Coding.* A popular method that is used to obtain greater response rates in anonymous questionnaires is known as coding. Coding requires the writer to develop a list containing the names of all individuals included in the survey population and then to assign a "code" to each name. Each survey is then encoded with the respondent's assigned code and sent out. Once the deadline for questionnaire return has passed, a record of the missing code numbers is then generated and compared to the master list which is held in confidence. From this, the analyst can identify and attempt to contact those individuals who have not responded.

The main advantage to using questionnaire coding is that it gives the analyst the opportunity to increase the number of responses, thereby creating a larger data set. The main disadvantage is that using codes can raise respondent suspicion levels because, having been told that there was no interest or need in identifying them with their answers, employees may become wary when they see some type of coding appear on the questionnaire. This can have very negative consequences because (1) fearing retaliation, respondents may not answer the questions truthfully; and (2) knowing that someone has access to their identities through the codes assigned, they may become wary of the intent and purpose of the questionnaire.

If anonymity is stated and/or guaranteed and a coding system is used, potential respondents must be informed of what the code represents and why it is being used. Depending on the climate and level of trust prevalent in the organization, taking this approach usually produces a higher response rate, although questions regarding respondent truthfulness still remain.

*Question Formatting.* Choosing an appropriate format is also an important factor in constructing survey questionnaires. Three basic formats are commonly used: closed-ended or forced-choice, open-ended, and a combination of the two.

Closed-ended formats are much easier to tabulate because respondents are required to choose their answer from a predetermined set. Yes/No formats consist of questions requiring a yes or no answer (e.g., Would training in how to conduct performance appraisals be of benefit to you in your present position? Yes/No [circle your response]). True/False formats require an answer of true or false (e.g., I have complete confidence in management's ability to lead this organization. True/False [circle your response]). *Note*: Care must be taken when using closed-ended formats so that the two options given (e.g., yes or no, true or false) are the only choices appropriate for the way in which the question is posed.

Multiple-choice formats require respondents to choose from a given set of options. An example of a multiple-choice question is as follows:

Which of the following best describes your position? (circle one)

a. Executive level management (sets policy, plans strategy)
b. Mid-level management (oversees policy and strategy implementation)
c. First-level management (implements policy and strategy)

Multiple-choice formats have an inherent disadvantage because the writer may have unknowingly failed to include all possible options that are relevant to the group to whom the questionnaire is being administered. This could cause some respondents—particularly those whose position or level is not indicated—to leave the question unanswered. In order to overcome this, it is always preferable to include a separate option labeled *Other*, which allows individuals to write in a separate qualitatively based response.

Another type of closed-ended format is known as ranked order or ranked choice. An example of this would be the following:

Please rank, in ascending order of importance, the day on which you prefer training to be conducted:

___Monday ___Tuesday ___Wednesday ___Thursday ___Friday

Since this is actually a multiple-choice format, the *Other* option should be included here as well for those individuals who may respond with a different answer like "Saturdays," "evenings," "mornings," and so on.

A popular type of closed-ended question is known as a rating scale, an example of which is the following:

I would rate my competency in using this equipment as being

| excellent | good | average | below average | poor |
|---|---|---|---|---|
| 5 | 4 | 3 | 2 | 1 |
| | | | | |

Also commonly referred to as scaled questions (one popular type is the Likert Scale, named after its developer, Rensis Likert), questions such as this should be written to establish a direct link between the scale (e.g., "excellent," "good," "average," etc.) and the subject matter being rated (e.g., "my competency in using this equipment").

A major advantage in using rating scales is that they establish a correlation between qualitative and quantitative feedback because they present an uncomplicated way to assign numerical values to answers.

Open-ended question formats require a respondent to provide a written or a narrative answer, often in the form of a statement. Also known as a "fill-in-the-blank" question, an example of this would be the following:

I believe that training would benefit this organization because

________________________________________

________________________________________

________________________________________

________________________________________.

There are one principal advantage and two principal disadvantages to using the open-ended format. The advantage is that qualitative or narrative feedback provides a substantially higher degree of substantive information. Allowing respondents to provide statements in their own words raises the quality and sometimes the usefulness of the information and goes far beyond the more restrained and somewhat sterile answers provided through the closed-ended question format. The major disadvantages are these: (1) Qualitative feedback can be difficult to clarify, particularly if the question was not well written (e.g., it could have caused misinterpretation by the respondent); and (2) written answers can sometimes be hard to read, thereby making recording and the subsequent analysis of the response more difficult.

In an effort to obtain both quantitative as well as narrative or qualitative feedback, professional survey designers will often use a combination of closed-ended and open-ended response formats. An example of a combination format would be the following:

I would rate the working environment of this organization as

| excellent | good | average | below average | poor |
|---|---|---|---|---|
| 5 | 4 | 3 | 2 | 1 |
| | | | | |

Please give a brief explanation of your response:

______________________________________________________________

______________________________________________________________.

*Readability.* Another important consideration lies in determining the readability level of the questionnaire. Readability refers to the equivalent scholastic grade level an individual would need to be at or have surpassed in order to read and understand the questions. In determining readability levels, factors such as sentence structure, length, word usage, and so on are considered. Keeping questions simple and straightforward, as mentioned earlier, keeps the readability requirement level low and will generally increase the likelihood that response levels will be higher because respondents will not have to first spend time deciphering or otherwise interpreting the question.[8]

*Positively and Negatively Worded Questions.* A popular means for minimizing response bias is to write questions in both a positively as well as a negatively worded context. The intent is to score answers to negatively worded questions in reverse order. For example, the statement "I do not like the new pay system because . . ." elicits a respondent to indicate why individuals do not like the pay system, regardless of whether they actually like it. Writing in this manner presupposes the intent of the question. The underlying theory for using this format is based on the assumption that people tend to respond in a positive sense. This assumes that a respondent would answer the sample question as not applicable or would otherwise write in a response contrary to the way in which the question was worded. In reality, however, this has not been proven to always be true. The most common result obtained is respondent confusion.[9] Unless the question's focus is generally accepted as being either positive or negative by the survey population at large, the use of positively and negatively worded questions should be avoided.

*Questionnaire Length.* Although it is desirable to obtain as much feedback as possible, care should be taken to not make the questionnaire excessively long. If this is not possible, it may be advisable to break it up into sections, then carefully analyze each section as to its relevance and importance in determining causality. Other considerations regarding questionnaire length are (1) the number of qualitative or open-ended questions used, (2) the time it takes to complete it, and (3) whether the survey is to be completed using company or personal time. If it is to be completed on personal time, it is almost certain that the response rate will be lower and the level of quality feedback diminished—particularly if the questionnaire is unduly long.

One overriding consideration associated with the writing of survey questionnaires has already been addressed earlier in this chapter, albeit on somewhat of a different dimension. That consideration is objectivity. As this applies specifically to questionnaire composition, extreme care must be taken to avoid writing biased or otherwise leading questions that elicit a certain kind of response.[10] Although this would tend to increase response outcome and predictability, it also has the potential to skew the results. Neutrality is paramount in constructing and writing survey questionnaire items. An actual example of a needs assessment survey questionnaire is included in Appendix C.

## INTERVIEWS

Interviews are well recognized data-gathering methods that are regularly used in virtually all types of needs assessments (see Table 4.1). Specifically, interviews involve the collection of feedback through direct and verbal interaction between individuals. Unlike the questionnaire process, it is interpersonally dynamic because the interchange between interviewers and interviewees is immediate. This permits interviewers to follow through or clarify points that are not immediately clear. It also provides a way to obtain peripheral information that may be linked directly or indirectly to the cause(s) and effect(s) that were used to establish the assessment goals (see Chapter 2).

Interviews are mainly used to provide in-depth narrative feedback. In a systematic needs assessment, interviews can be used (1) to correlate the content of a survey questionnaire; (2) as a stand-alone method for producing data for subsequent analysis; or (3) in conjunction with another data-gathering method(s) (as illustrated in Table 4.1) for correlating and validating data obtained through the other method(s).

### Advantages and Disadvantages

Using individual interviews has advantages as well as disadvantages. Perhaps its greatest advantage lies in its adaptability. Well-trained and experienced interviewers can retrieve more qualitative data through an interview than can be obtained from virtually any other data-gathering method. Also, the quality and depth of the narrative information obtained through a well-planned interview process will be far superior to that obtained by any of the other methods. On a more personal level, interviews can provide a truer picture of opinions as well as feelings.

In contrast, interviews have a number of disadvantages. First, they are one of the most costly types of needs assessment data-gathering methods to use, particularly for obtaining feedback from a geographically diverse population.[11] For example, the logistical costs to interview fifty people in three different locations can be considerable. Another disadvantage is that because it is easier to ask questions than to administer, tabulate, and score survey questionnaires, interviews are often misused to collect quantitative data that could be collected more efficiently through another method (e.g., through survey questionnaires). That is not to say that the collection of quantitative data cannot or should not be part of the interview process; however, considering the costs involved, quantitative data can be obtained less expensively and, depending on the skills of the interviewer, more accurately by using the survey questionnaire data-collection method.

Another important limitation of interviews lies in the approach that is used. Many of its strengths (e.g., adaptability, human interaction, etc.) allow for varying degrees of subjective biasing on behalf of interviewers. For example, eagerness by respondents to answer all questions, antagonism that always has the possibility of arising between interviewers and interviewees, or intentional biasing by interviewers in asking or otherwise framing questions to obtain a desired type of response are all examples of subjective biasing. Known more predominantly in the research profession as *response effect error*, this can best be defined as the difference between the answer given by the respondent and the true answer. To illustrate, assume interviewees were asked how they felt about training being conducted on personal time, perhaps during evenings or weekends. Out of fear of retaliation from their supervisor, the respondents may say that it would be fine with them, when, in reality, they reject the idea completely.

Another form of response effect error lies with the predisposition of the interviewers. The interviewers' attitudes, how they phrase questions, and whether they allow their own opinions to influence or otherwise take precedence over what they actually hear from interviewees profoundly affects the quality and the objectivity of data produced through the interview method.

A third type of response effect error is rooted in the mechanics of the interview process. Some procedural abnormalities that can produce response effect errors are (1) whether coercion is used to gain a respondent's cooperation, (2) the actual length of the interview, which can affect both parties, and (3) the physical location where the interview is conducted.

The following guidelines are provided as a way of safeguarding against response effect errors:

1. Interviews should be conducted in a nonthreatening manner. A formal business-like approach tempered with cordiality toward the respondent will generally produce an atmosphere of mutual trust, respect, and cooperation.
2. Interviewers should attempt to eliminate or at least suppress any personal bias or predispositions regarding the intent and content of the interview (although under certain conditions, such as those instances where the interviewer has strongly held personal beliefs, this may be difficult to do). Every effort to eliminate interviewer biasing should be made.
3. Interviews should be conducted one-on-one, in a mutually agreeable place, and at a mutually agreeable time.
4. Results of interviews, and particularly respondent identities, must be held in the strictest confidence.

### Interview Types

There are three types of interviews used in the needs assessment data-gathering process: structured, semistructured, and unstructured. The depth and extent of feedback being sought should be used to determine which type to use. Due to the dynamic nature of the interview process, considerable latitude must be extended to both the interviewer and the interviewee. Any attempt to limit or otherwise restrict this interchange would defeat the principal contribution that individual interviews are capable of making.

*Structured.* Structured interviews are used when the feedback is confined to a specific area or topic. The interviewer would pose brief but specific questions that can be answered usually by yes or no or by selecting a single answer or response from a predetermined set of choices. Respondents' answers are generally not followed up. Structured interviews work well when the assessment goals are clear. The interview questions should be concise and singularly address the issue at hand. Depending on the desired depth and degree of information, structured interviews do not normally last longer than fifteen to twenty minutes.

*Semistructured.* Many interviews will produce highly specific feedback that also requires some additional probing in order to obtain more in-depth information. This type is referred to as a semistructured interview because it is implemented in a structured manner, but it also mixes quantitatively and qualitatively based questions. Similar to the style of survey questionnaire which uses a combination of both closed-ended and open-ended question formats, semistructured interviews provide a good balance between the sometimes sterile Yes/No structures and the more broadly defined qualitative approach. In essence, this type of interview is mostly applicable in situations where both qualitative and quantitative feedback are required.

*Unstructured.* Similar to the open-ended survey questionnaire format, unstructured interviews are used when the depth of feedback required is broad and nonspecific. They are an excellent choice as a brainstorming tool. Unstructured interviews are good for investigating potentially emotional and/or sensitive personal issues. In order for these interviews to be effective, however, time schedules should be established and adhered to.

### Behavioral Implications

As illustrated in the previous section, interviews, when compared to survey questionnaires, focus groups, and on-site observations, are more individually intrusive because they are conducted in a face-to-face setting that can sometimes be emotionally charged.[12] Questions that are designed to probe our inner feelings are sometimes intimidating and can often create an environment of mistrust and suspicion, particularly where sensitive issues are being discussed. Many people are naturally reluctant to "open-up" and reveal their innermost feelings when confronted with personalized subject matter.[13] Reactions such as a reluctance to participate or to provide candid and truthful answers are symptoms of apprehension and anxiety. For example, individuals may be reluctant to provide a negative yet truthful response to a question because they may feel that doing so could have an equally negative effect on their job or position. This can inhibit both their ability and willingness to respond truthfully. The net result is a failure to produce the desired degree or depth of information interviewers may require. Under such circumstances, interviewers will need to take steps to establish a high degree of trust prior to the interview actually taking place. This can be accomplished in several ways: (1) Before the interview, interviewers could have senior management prepare and distribute a letter informing potential respondents of why the interview is taking place and stressing that all answers will be held in the strictest confidence or (2) interviewers could take steps to personally contact potential respondents to introduce themselves, to set the interview agenda, to provide or otherwise reassert any guarantees of confidentiality, and to set an agreeable time for the interview to take place. To more fully understand the behavioral dynamics and implications associated with interviews, it is important to understand how the communication process between the interviewer and the interviewee works.

### Communication in Interviews

Language, spoken as well as physical, is the major component in interview communications. Any and all questions posed by interviewers must be fully understood by interviewees in order for the communication process to be effective. Figure 4.1 illustrates the basic two-way interview process (sender and receiver) and emphasizes the importance of clarity and conciseness.

Many times respondents will answer a question without fully understanding it because they do not want to appear ignorant. Alternatively, when a question is not concisely phrased, respondents will many times give an eva-

**Figure 4.1**
Interviewer–Interviewee Communication Process

| <sender> | <receiver/sender> | <receiver> |
|---|---|---|
| Interviewer——— | ——> Interviewee——— | ——> Interviewer |
| poses question | receives question, interprets, formulates response, relates response back to interviewer | receives response, interprets, records answer, then determines if answer sufficiently addressed question |

sive or noncommittal answer rather than admit that they do not understand. Therefore, in order to establish clear and effective two-way communication, interviewers should make every effort to explain any technical terms in plain and understandable language.

The communication process is facilitated if the respondents are informed about the purpose of each question. If individuals can see no value in the question they are being asked, it is very probable that they will respond negatively. These kinds of misunderstandings can lead to suspicion, particularly if the interviewees begin to question if the purpose of the interview is something other than what they have been told it is. This can lead to a loss of confidence in the interviewers, which, in turn, can culminate in a refusal to cooperate or, at least, could cause respondents to be less than candid in their responses.

There are a number of techniques interviewers can use to facilitate the two-way communication process. They can engage respondents in small-talk as a means of establishing a basis for rapport, and they can also take steps to assure them that any feedback will be held in the strictest confidence. In effect, interviewers must convey the message that "we're interested in what's said, not in who said what." Once requested and received, however, it is imperative that trust be safeguarded and not violated.

Once under way, interviewers can ask for further information and clarification after respondents have completed an answer. Many times some subtle urging such as "Can you tell me a little more about that?" or "That's interesting. Tell me, what's your view on that issue?" will prompt a respondent to elaborate further. Under no circumstances should interviewers be contradictory or appear to be cross-examining respondents. If respondents are threatened by a particular question (or line of questioning), interviewers should either change the subject or perhaps conclude the session altogether.

Visual communication, or body language, is also an important factor in the interview communication process. Interviewers should be well prepared and appear relaxed. They should maintain eye contact without staring at the respondent. They should speak clearly and succinctly. Physical actions, such as rolling one's eyes, sighing, raising eyebrows, or smiling when asking a question should be avoided, as any of these actions can be misinterpreted by respondents as being indicative of the type of response that they believe interviewers are looking for. Also, interviewers should be seated directly across from respondents at approximately the same level. Interviewers should never be in a position where they are either looking up or down at respondents, as this has the potential to negatively affect the equality balance.

### Interview Planning

It is usually helpful to first develop a plan for using interviews before actually conducting them. This is done so that variables that can (and usually do) impact the outcome(s) of the interview can be identified and addressed.

Factors such as (1) whether the interview will be used independently or in conjunction with one of the other data-gathering methods, (2) identification of the interview population, (3) the preparation of interview scripts or guides, and (4) procedural issues such as note taking and recording all warrant important consideration.

## Using Interviews with Other Data-Gathering Methods

Thoughtfully designed interviews provide one of the best ways to collect needs assessment data. When used as part of a systems approach, interviews are most effective when used for gathering information in the development of survey questionnaire items. They are also very effective when used in tandem with one or more data-gathering methods for obtaining qualitatively based feedback that can be compared and contrasted to quantitative data (such as those obtained through survey questionnaires). There are, however, important factors to consider when using interviews to correlate data that have been obtained via other methods.

First, a key or link must be established between the main purpose or point raised by other data-gathering methods and the composition of the same or similar questions used in the course of an interview. This is done to minimize the chance of respondent misinterpretation. For example, when using interviews to correlate main points that are raised in survey questionnaires, key words, as contained in a survey questionnaire item, should also be mentioned in the interview. To illustrate, consider the following survey question:

Do you believe that managers in our company are effective verbal communicators?
Yes/No (circle your answer)

To correlate the cumulative results of this question through the use of personal interviews, interviewers or analysts would need to first identify key words linking the written survey and interview questions. In this example, the key words are "verbal" and "communicators." The linking word, or rather, the word that identifies association, is "managers." Therefore, when composing an interview script, reference to a survey question like this should contain both the key and the linking words. The results of the interview responses can then be compared to the cumulative results of the survey questionnaire. This helps to ensure continuity. Further, any correlation between written survey responses and cumulative interview responses will indicate that respondents understood the question and did not misinterpret it. This adds validity to the correlation process.

Second, it is extremely important to incorporate links to correlate feedback that has been or will be obtained through one or more of the other methods. To illustrate, assume the following item was included in a survey questionnaire:

Give us your opinion on the degree of team spirit and cooperation present in the organizational structure. Please be specific.

---

---

When framing a question or developing a statement that is designed to be used in an interview to probe respondents' reactions, it is again necessary to identify key links. In the example given, however, there are two of these, namely, "degree of team spirit and cooperation" and "present in the organizational structure." It is very possible to have a significant level of team spirit but not to have similar levels of cooperation because of decentralization, a lack of communication between individuals and departments, and so on. These kinds of issues could be addressed by framing the interview question to first reference the survey item and then probing respondents by using two or more key words contained and embedded within the interview statement (e.g., "team spirit" and "cooperation").

### Background Information on Interviewees

Obtaining background information on potential interviewees is important for a number of reasons. First, it provides insights into how to use the selected interview structure. Second, it enables interviewers to study potential respondents' work habits along with their physical work environments. This combination provides familiarity with the type or types of job-related jargon to either use or to avoid. Third, it provides the means for building an interviewer guide or script containing questions that are related to the areas being investigated. It also presents the opportunity to relate interview questions to other key factors or areas that are being concurrently assessed through another method. Fourth, it provides an opportunity to test the interview prior to actually implementing it. This helps to ensure that it will be done correctly and in a timely manner.

### Scripting

An important part of interview planning lies in the preparation of an interview script or guide. This normally consists of a list of questions that appear in the exact order in which they are to be asked during the interview. This is important for three reasons. First, after the interview process has begun, it may become apparent that some questions may need to be rewritten, particularly for reasons of language, clarity, or relevancy. Second, preparing a list will help to ensure that all interviewees are asked the same questions using the same wording. This lends continuity to the process and contributes to attaining response validity. Third, if interviews are used as a correlational or as a complementary data-gathering method, preparing a script provides an opportunity to compare interview questions with questions in any of the other methods being used. Thus, the process of identifying key words and links between methods is simplified and continuous. An actual sample of an interview script is provided in Appendix D.

### Recording

Taking notes or tape recording an interview is an excellent method to use for archiving or preserving the information collected. Yet, in spite of its potential contribution to clarity and even simplicity, recording interviews also has definite disadvantages.

An obvious disadvantage deals with the issue of anonymity, the guarantee of confidentiality, and the very real possibility of injecting respondent mistrust and untruthfulness into the process. This is particularly applicable where probing questions that deal with sensitive or personal issues are concerned. One way of countering this effect is to alert interviewees of the intention to take notes or tape record the session and then to allow them the option to refuse to participate. This does not, however, contribute to facilitating the process and can actually become a deterrent to other employees' participation. A more appealing way is to inform the respondent of the intention to record or take notes and then to offer to let them review the tape or notes after the interview has been concluded. Experience has shown that this can serve to allay any fears, apprehensions, or anxieties that may have evolved or that have the potential to surface at a later time.

Another disadvantage, particularly to taking notes, is that the physical act of writing responses down can become time consuming and distracting to both interviewers and interviewees. This is especially applicable where qualitative feedback is concerned. Therefore, if significant qualitative information is required, recording the interview on tape is preferable. Taking written notes should be used only when the feedback requires short and focused answers.

One major advantage to tape recording sessions is that it permits a person other than the interviewer to evaluate, clarify, and analyze the responses.[14] This can also reinforce the guarantee of respondent anonymity, providing, of course, that the respondent's identity was not verbally disclosed during the recording.

### Interviewer Training

Regardless of whether the individuals selected to conduct interviews are experienced veterans or inexperienced newcomers, they should be trained so that objective, reliable, and relevant information is obtained. The amount of training required for conducting unstructured interviews is greater than that required for conducting structured ones.

Interviewer training is usually conducted in two parts. In the first part, the interviewer studies the guide or the prepared script and seeks to gain familiarity with respondents' jobs, backgrounds, and working environments. Additionally, they can also familiarize themselves with any key words and links to other needs assessment data-gathering methods that are being (or will be) used. To do this objectively, interviewers must not have any idea about the designer's expectations. This usually requires the use of individuals other than those directly involved in the needs assessment design process.

In the second part, interviewers should undertake practice sessions. This is done to correct timing errors and other irregularities, such as badly worded questions. Also, practice sessions can help to identify scripting deficiencies and, if videotaped, can provide visual feedback useful in evaluating and correcting procedural errors or other concerns.[15]

## FOCUS GROUPS

*Focus groups* (a term coined from the marketing profession) have, over the years, increased in both their importance and use in the HRD profession. In the marketing discipline, focus groups are defined primarily as a group of eight to twelve consumers who are brought together with a moderator to discuss products, promotions, advertising, or other marketing ideas and concepts.[16] However, when used as a needs assessment data-gathering method, focus groups are generally convened to brainstorm problems or situations in which some form of intervention may prove to be needed. When it becomes necessary to include more than twelve individuals in the group, many experts recommend that the group be broken into smaller subgroups with perhaps six individuals per group. These subgroups, led by the same moderator, meet independently of the others. Once each subgroup had completed its particular task they gather in an ending or plenary session to reach common ground or consensus.[17]

Sometimes referred to as problem identification groups, needs assessment focus groups are formed and generally meet in a number of moderator-led sessions. Their principal purpose is to examine a problem or situation and to provide feedback as to its cause(s) and effect(s). This feedback is then recorded by the moderator for subsequent analytical use.

The most applicable use of focus groups is for collectively identifying cause(s) and effect(s) that have been observed and/or measured (see Chapter 2). As such, the feedback obtained through the focus group method will be narrative. Both issues as well as their outcomes are broadly defined. Therefore, focus groups are not commonly used as a means for determining a final solution to a problem but, rather, are used for exploring any cause and effect relationships and for obtaining additional information that will be useful in the data-analysis and recommendation-formulation stages. Like interviews, the principal disadvantages in using assessment focus groups are that they are costly to convene and reconvene (if necessary). Also, there is a very real likelihood that the interpersonal dynamics present in the group can cause it to degenerate into a "gripe session." Over the long term, this can cause greater harm in that it can worsen an already difficult situation.

Although there are no universally accepted standards for determining the composition of a focus group, there are some generally acknowledged principles regarding group size, composition, dynamics, and behavior, which, when appropriately considered, can aid in defining the focus group size and structure.

### Group Structure and Composition

In order to identify the optimal focus group composition, it is first necessary to determine whether to use an objective or a subjective structure.

Objective group structures are usually composed of individuals who are selected at random. Structuring groups in this manner works best when the issue(s) to be discussed are broad and not clearly defined. For example, referring back to Table 3.1, assume that a focus group was to be convened to gather feedback on the cause(s) of poor employee morale—an observed effect. As stated in Table 3.1, the preliminary goal is to identify the reason or cause. The last column in this table shows the organizational level that the assessment should be targeted at. To illustrate, assume again that poor employee morale has been observed across all levels. Since this is an observed effect that has not been quantitatively defined, the feedback obtained from any focus group would be equally broad and contain little in the way of specifics. Thus, an objective approach for defining the group's composition would be the most appropriate path to take. Further, since the observed effect transcends all organizational levels, group participants would need to be enlisted from all organizational areas. This may seem obvious; however, there is an added caveat. If participants from lower organizational levels are placed into groups that also include individuals from senior levels, the degree of open, frank, and candid feedback could be restricted. Known as the *intimidation factor*, it can be (and usually is) disruptive to the focus group process.[18]

One way of overcoming this is to use the subgroup method described earlier, with the exception that each group be composed of individuals selected at random and structured along homogenous lines; that is, each group would consist only of peer levels. In taking this approach, the intimidation factor can be minimalized. Subsequently, when the groups are reconvened in the plenary session, the moderator would be required to present the findings in a balanced and equitable way while also signifying each group's contribution. Then, through a series of controlled discussions, consensus regarding the causes for the observed effects could be rationalized. Of course, if the effect was only observed at one particular level, the group would need to be structured to include only individuals from that level and, again, depending on the number of individuals participating, subgroups may have to be used and reconvened in plenary sessions.

Alternatively, subjective group structures are best used when the effect is predetermined or, in other words, has already taken place and its results are quantifiable. Referring again to Table 3.1, assume that the effect "High cost of goods sold" (#5) has been observed through a review of the company's financial records. In attempting to identify the reasons, an operational audit which included individual interview and focus group data-gathering methods was conducted. Here, the composition of the focus group should include all organizational levels because the cost of goods sold pertains to all of the organization's operational costs. Hierarchical considerations are not necessary in this instance because the organization's task is to collectively determine why costs are as high as they are. Because the emphasis is more on functional and operational issues, sensitive matters dealing with individual behaviors or personalities would not normally arise. Consequently, a more subjective approach can be taken in composing and structuring the focus group because the issues at hand deal with situations that are not of an interpersonal nature. In this example, it would not be necessary to compose the group along hierarchically homogenous lines.

Whichever structure is eventually used, it is important to prepare members for what to expect before the group is actually convened. Three major factors in the group preparation process are (1) determining the group structure and composition, (2) determining its goals and objectives, and (3) holding preliminary meetings with potential group members so that discussions about their individual—as well as the organization's—expectations, can be undertaken.[19] These steps are usually accomplished by the focus group moderator who plays a paramount role in the focus group facilitation process.

### Group Behavior and Communications

In any interaction involving more than one person, there are issues dealing with interpersonal relationships and communications that merit serious consideration. Issues that deal with individual attitudes openly expressed in a group setting have the very real possibility of unleashing emotional responses that, if not controlled, can cause the group to refocus on issues other than those they have been convened to address.[20] This falls under the heading of what has come to be known as *group dynamics*.

Studies of group behavior in the late 1920s and early 1930s by the renowned psychologist Kurt Lewin found that as the size of the group (and hence, the proliferation of different attitudes and beliefs) increases, the social relationships between group members becomes more diluted, while the intensity of the interaction becomes magnified.[21] As a result, the group, as a whole, assumes a behavioral pattern or personality that is unique to itself. This personality, in turn, becomes manifested in the group's approach to addressing situations or problems. Thus, the degrees of varied interaction among the mix of individuals in the group combine to form an aggregate group personality. This phenomenon is known as group dynamics.[22]

Group dynamics are manifested in the group communication process. How smoothly this process is carried out in the group setting will determine how well the group comes together or forms. For example, if the verbal interchange among group members is confined to a select few, the communication process will be hindered because any feedback obtained will be skewed. Thus, it is the responsibility of the moderator to take steps to ensure that all members of the group are given a chance to participate equally in the feedback process.

### The Role of the Moderator

Moderators are the pivotal persons in assessment focus group interaction. They therefore assume responsibility for guiding it toward attainment of the predetermined goals. Because of the behavioral complexities inherent to the group structuring process, the principal role of the moderator is to turn divergent opinions into mutually agreeable outcomes. This provides a sense of direction for identifying areas where potential interventions may be successfully applied.

Moderating an assessment focus group may seem like a relatively easy task, yet the skills required to successfully moderate focus group sessions are not learned from any book. Rather, the art and science of focus group moderation is a learned skill that is acquired through experience.[23] Because of this, many organizations opt to use outside resources or consultants for conducting needs assessment focus groups (although many also have qualified internal expertise as well). The key to deciding which resources to use lies in the word "qualified." Since there are so many variables that can affect focus group moderation, many experts feel this task is best handled by an outside consultant.[24] The following are some general guidelines for those who are considering conducting focus groups sessions:

1. The role of the moderator should be that of facilitator and not that of leader. Group consensus should be reached through mutual agreement and not by directions or parameters set by one individual.
2. It is imperative not to let one or a small number of group participants provide all of the feedback. As mentioned earlier, this can cause subjective biasing.
3. Focus groups should concentrate on present problems and not past ones (unless, of course, unattended past problems have led to the current ones). "The way things used to be" is not an appropriate focus group objective.
4. The moderator must overcome barriers to reaching consensus by motivating the group to think of ways they can move toward agreement. The moderator must be prepared to intervene in any attempt by the majority to bully other participants who hold opposing views. This is done by encouraging healthy debate and resolving interpersonal conflicts by stressing consensus.

5. The moderator must not rush to conclusions. Reaching an early consensus may sometimes appear to be expeditious, but it can also gloss over the real problem in favor of a quick closure.
6. At the point of closure, the moderator should list and have the group reexamine all of the recommendations and/or observations before selecting the best alternative(s) by eliminating those that seem extreme or, for one reason or another, are unfeasible.

Experienced moderators will formulate an approach to facilitate the focus group by first reviewing its goals and objectives. From these they will seek to identify sensitive areas that have the potential to present facilitation problems. Topics related to income, gender, individual performance and evaluation, boss-to-subordinate relationships, and the like are sensitive issues that need to be carefully addressed.[25] The moderator's reaction to sensitive issues provides both visual as well as psychological clues to which the group will quickly respond. Thus, there are a number of facilitation roles moderators can choose from. They are the following: (1) clinical, (2) assertive, or (3) informal.

In the clinical role, moderators pose questions and observe and record respondents' physical reactions and narrative responses. In the assertive role, moderators guide the group through a reasoning process by being not so much facilitators but by being more leaders. Although this is not usually recommended, it is sometimes necessary to intervene, particularly in emotionally charged situations. Through actual examples, moderators use a chronological reconstruction of events leading up to the issue(s) being discussed and pose alternative suggestions that incorporate a variety of observations as well as invoke a variety of responses. In the informal role, moderators assume a more passive position by first presenting the goals and objectives and then urging respondents to provide input in an unstructured and open manner. This role is best used when the issues being discussed are not personally sensitive and the structure of the group is made up of related peer levels.

The way in which moderators ask questions can also introduce error or biasing into the needs assessment focus group process.[26] For example, assume that a moderator presents a question such as "We all know how this problem originated." This is a leading question because it assumes that everyone has the same thoughts or opinions about the origin of a particular problem or issue. Thus, it is likely that the respondents, following the verbal cue of the moderator, will focus on the problem as defined by the moderator as opposed to group consensus. Although unintentional, this kind of biasing will consistently and artificially alter the feedback process.

## ON-SITE OBSERVATIONS

On-site observations are an established and respected method for gathering data. Having long been used in the field of psychological research, it has also found considerable acceptance in the industrial engineering profession.

Used by many manufacturing and service industries in time and motion studies, on-site observations can produce both quantitative as well as qualitative data. The greatest asset to observationally based research is that the results of such studies produce empirical data that can be proved or disproved by continual observation and by statistical sampling methods.[27] However, when used as a needs assessment data-gathering method, on-site observations do not generally provide the level of detail upon which conclusive recommendations can be based. For this reason, it is usually necessary to incorporate them with another type or other types of data-gathering methods.

On-site observations are used to gain firsthand feedback on job and task performance where procedures and work processes can be visually observed and measured. They are generally conducted by individuals (SMEs) who are knowledgeable about the work processes and the behaviors they are observing. Ideally, these individuals will have performed such work themselves in like or similar settings and under like or similar circumstances.[28]

On-site observations are particularly useful for identifying training needs in either a manufacturing- or production-oriented environment. For example, assume a large insurance company wanted to identify the number of claims it processes under its current operational system. It also wants to identify what needs to be done to increase productivity levels. By having an experienced claims processor observe the work-in-progress, direct feedback on what would be needed or otherwise required in both a training and equipment or systems related sense could be obtained. From this, the company could analyze what needs to be done to attain its goal of increasing productive output.

In an administrative or managerial setting, observations can also be used to identify issues related to competency, skill, and morale levels. For example, the reason an organization is experiencing an increase in absenteeism may be due to bad relations between the management and staff. On-site observations could provide a means for observing the work flow along with the interpersonal relations between the groups. The result would be feedback that provides a basis for either a resolution to the problem or, at least, it may indicate other areas where cause and effect relationships should be investigated.

On-site observations are also useful in the retail and customer-service areas. For example, many organizations employ *mystery shoppers* whose job is to engage and interact with sales or customer-service employees to see if they are performing at acceptable levels. Through interaction and careful observation, many needs indicators can surface. To illustrate, consider the case of an automobile dealer who wanted to investigate how well the sales staff was prepared to answer questions from prospective car buyers. The dealer hired three different individuals who were very familiar with the makes and models the dealer was selling. Posing as interested and potential buyers, each observer entered the dealer's showroom about fifteen minutes apart. Each engaged a different sales representative and proceeded to ask technical questions about the vehicles, including financing options, warranties, service, cost of repairs, and so on. The observers made mental notes specifically about how the salesperson reacted and responded to their questions. The results indicated that two out of three of the salespersons were well versed in all of the areas covered. The third sales representative was not familiar with the technical aspects of the vehicle or the cost of repairs or the extent of the warranty. Thus, through the use of skilled and knowledgeable observers, the dealer identified a need in a key employee, which would negatively affect not only the individual's performance but the financial performance of the organization as a whole.

A major disadvantage to using on-site observations is that they are subject to a high degree of biasing by the observer. To illustrate, assume an SME was observing work methods used to produce a particular item. In the observer's opinion, the methods the employees used were satisfactory; however, improvements (and hence, greater efficiency) could be obtained if they would implement other procedures that the observer suggests. The company may come to find that after following the SME's advice, it is actually less productive and efficient than it was before. In this case, the SME perhaps failed to take into consideration the culture and various other environmental elements before making his or her final recommendation to management. In other words, the SME's bias toward a particular approach, although technically sound, did not fit well into this particular organization's operational environment. For this reason, many organizations that use SMEs as part of their needs assessment projects will enlist them from within the company's ranks.

The following is a summary of guidelines for conducting on-site observations:

1. Observations should be carried out as unobtrusively as possible. This is very important, particularly where employees have not been informed beforehand about the observation taking place. In practice, it is usually better to inform employees of what to expect (e.g., the observations), why the observations are being done, and to solicit their input and help in the process.
2. A schedule or plan for conducting observations should be detailed and approved by the company's senior management and the managers of any departments or functions to be included in the observational process.
3. Observations should not interfere with the daily flow of work activities. However, in many instances, this is not possible. Where intrusive observations are required, they should be conducted in a friendly and nonthreatening manner and not cause any more disruption than is absolutely necessary.
4. A detailed summary or log of the observation activities, including the times, dates, and location(s), the outcomes of each observation, and the identities of the observer(s), should be maintained. Any personal notes regarding the observations should be recorded in the summary as well. Where it was necessary for the observer to intrude on an employee during the work process, the reason(s) for the intrusion should be noted along with any results or outcomes.
5. Where managerial activities or behaviors are being observed, attention should be paid to the interpersonal dynamics at play between the various individuals. Any exhibitions of frustration, verbal disagreements, or other nonroutine behavioral actions should be noted, and a follow-up should be conducted between the principals to de-

termine the extent of the situation or problem and, in particular, what can be done to resolve the issue or otherwise to reach consensus. One way in which this can be accomplished is through the use of individual interviews as previously discussed.

## OTHER DATA-GATHERING METHODS

The past decade has seen an extraordinary increase in technological innovation. The advent of the personal computer and quantum leaps forward in other technologies have revolutionized the way in which communications are sent, received, and processed. Paradoxically, as labor costs have spiralled upward, the costs associated with acquiring new technology have actually gone down, thus making the use of new electronic communication mediums more and more attractive. Most notably, this has introduced a variety of optional needs assessment data-gathering methods which are now beginning to find application in HRD.

What follows are three of the most prevalent types of communications technology as applied to the needs assessment data-gathering processes.

### Electronic Mail

With the introduction of electronic mail or *e-mail,* organizations are now able to communicate with greater speed and flexibility. Most larger companies have invested considerable resources in developing their e-mail capabilities. Given this, it is hard to ignore the potential applications and advantages in using e-mail for distributing needs assessment survey questionnaires. As with all other data-gathering methods, there are both advantages and disadvantages to using e-mail to administer survey questionnaires. One obvious advantage is that the costs associated with duplicating and distributing large numbers of paper surveys are virtually eliminated. Another advantage is that studies have shown there is no relative difference in response rates between survey questionnaires administered via a computer system and those that are completed with pencil and paper. Finally, the sophistication and the ease of use of many e-mail programs has increased.[29] This has helped to ease the anxiety levels of users who were originally intimidated by computers.

One obvious disadvantage is that many individuals, even though they have access to sophisticated e-mail systems, still refuse to enter the electronic age and prefer, whether out of anxiety or stubbornness, to use paper and pencil methods. Another disadvantage to administering assessment survey questionnaires through e-mail is the problem it poses regarding respondent confidentiality. Since many electronic responses are accompanied by a signature or other indices of their origin (as is common in e-mail systems), respondents may view this as a breach of any anonymity guarantee(s). This can actually have a negative affect on the overall response rate, although now there are e-mail programs that have built-in safeguards designed to maintain sender anonymity.[30]

### Telephone Interviews

Widely used by polling and marketing research organizations, telephone interviews have become commonplace in our society. As an interviewing method, it offers significant cost savings over face-to-face interviews and can be cost-effectively administered to a broad geographical base. Telephone interviews should be conducted using short answer, closed-ended questions and should not go on for undue lengths of time. As a qualitative feedback method, however, telephone interviews have significant disadvantages. First, respondents' nonverbal actions and reactions to particular questions (e.g., raised eyebrows, smiles, other forms of body language, etc.) cannot be seen by the interviewer. Second, rapport is harder to establish over the telephone, thus making it more difficult for the interviewer to put the respondent at ease. Third, respondents are generally reluctant to truthfully answer sensitive questions over the phone. Last, since many now have electronic answering systems (e.g., "voice mail" and answering machines), it may be more difficult to reach individuals who routinely use these systems to screen their calls.

### Satellite or Long-Distance Conferencing

Significant advances in telecommunications technology has allowed news reporters to broadcast current events from the remotest sections of the world, even as they are happening. An outgrowth of this technological ability, known as satellite or long-distance conferencing, has found its way into business use. Many larger organizations have developed the capacity to interactively conduct meetings or conferences between geographically diverse locations. Video cameras and recorders at each site record the events and discussions at each meeting and instantaneously transmit them to other locations and vice versa. This technological sophistication has greatly reduced both meeting as well as travel time along with their associated costs. In the HRD field, this interactive ability is potentially appealing, especially when it is used to conduct simultaneous focus groups composed of individuals in geographically diverse locations. However, the costs to acquire, operate, and maintain these types of systems are very high, and many organizations question the value they would receive as opposed to the more traditional means of telephone conference calling (where the major difference between the two technologies is one of audio as well as visual communication as opposed to audio only).

From a strictly logistical perspective, conducting focus groups in interactive modes simultaneously at various locations requires multiple on-site focus group moderators—at least one per site. This greatly increases overall facilitation costs. From a behavioral perspective, conducting multiple focus groups over distances from a variety of locations can also have a negative impact on multigroup interactions and feedback, particularly where sensitive issues are concerned. For example, a group in one location may radically oppose the ideas of a group in another location. This could, if not controlled by the moderators (in this case, more like referees), degenerate into a long-distance, video-based shouting match.

Considering the significance of the costs associated with the acquisition and use of this technology—along with the behavioral and logistical problems it poses—it would appear that, at least for the present, its disadvantages outweigh any of its feasible advantages.

## CHOOSING THE APPROPRIATE MIX OF DATA-GATHERING METHODS

Knowing which data-gathering methods (or combination of methods) to use in a needs assessment depends on a number of factors, such as the organization's culture and operational environment, its policies and, in particular, the effects or causality that drove the assessment's goal-setting process. Therefore, it is important to decide which methods are the most appropriate to use with other methods and how each approach will be structured (e.g., which questions in one method will be linked and keyed to which questions in a correlating or complementary method). This is known as an aggregate approach to collecting data. More important, knowing which assessment type and accompanying methods to use in which organizational level or setting are skills largely acquired through experience.

### Criteria

The systems approach to needs assessments is based on input (feedback) and output (analysis of feedback resulting in recommendations).[31] Although there are no hard and fast rules governing which methods to use with a particular assessment type, there are some general guidelines that can be applied to obtain a more appropriate mix. Note that this compilation is not meant to be absolute because the methods listed may or may not be suitable for the type(s) of assessment(s) chosen. For example, survey questionnaires can, and many times will, have applicability in behaviorally based assessments. How these are structured, written, and applied to gather behavioral feedback will determine their particular suitability. Generally, anonymous questionnaires should be used when a high degree of personalized or sensitive information is required. Furthermore, the key to determining the right mix of data-gathering methods lies in knowing which should be used as the principal method and which should be used in a correlationally aggregate role. For example, interviews provide excellent correlational value when used in concert with survey questionnaires (the principal method) in a knowledge/skills assessment. This could also be viewed in reverse order: Survey questionnaires could provide excellent correlational value when used primarily in tandem with interviews. In this example, the interviews would provide qualitative value while the questionnaires would provide quantitative correlational value.

For these methods to produce consistency, however, key words, common to both methods, should be used as a linking element.

Using key words to link salient portions of aggregate data-collection methods is important in a systematic needs assessment because they provide a common basis from which causal correlational value between responses to questions that originated with different data-gathering methods can be obtained.[32] However, regardless of which methods are used, care must be taken to ensure that these words (and, in some instances, phrases) are stated so they will produce consistent results. For example, if an individual responded to a survey questionnaire item in a certain way, he or she should also respond in a like or similar manner when queried with the same or similar question in an interview. Similarly, if two methods employing closed-ended questions were used, the results should be consistent and identifiable.

Alternatively, if a question was constructed in an open-ended format (e.g., as an option in a multiple-choice closed-ended questionnaire) and was also posed in the same format in an interview, the key words in the survey item should be linked to the key words contained in the interview question. Thus, when analyzing the data, narrative answers obtained from the interviews should closely resemble the cumulative results obtained from the survey questionnaires. Where two different assessment populations are involved (e.g., one group undergoing only interviews and another participating only in the survey questionnaire process) there will always be slight variations in the cumulative responses received. This is because two similar yet separate methods are being applied to a nonstratified sample. Comprehensive data analysis should, however, reveal the emergence of repetitive patterns while also indicating causality (see Chapter 3). Thus, in a systematic needs assessment, it is vital that consistency be established and maintained between the data-gathering methods used.

As illustrated in Table 4.2, the survey questionnaire is one of the most widely used needs assessment data-gathering methods. Of the ten different types of assessments listed, the survey questionnaire is included as a primary method in each category. The reason for its widespread popularity lies in its flexibility. It can be either quantitatively or qualitatively based, or it can include a combination of both data types. This flexibility, however, also requires that a high degree of consideration be used in questionnaire design so that (1) the risk of misinterpretation by potential respondents is minimalized, and (2) they provide the kinds of feedback necessary for determining the cause(s) of the observed effect.

## Aggregation and Weighting of Data-Gathering Methods

Although there are no hard and fast rules governing the selection of correlational data-gathering methods, there are some generalities that can be applied. In using aggregate data-collection methods (where the sums of both data

**Table 4.2**
Needs Assessment Type, Data, Method, and Application Suitability

| Assessment Type | Method* | Types of Data Produced | Application |
|---|---|---|---|
| 1. Competency/ Skills | Questionnaire | Quantitative/ Qualitative | Suitable for assessing needs in all jobs and positions. |
| | Interviews | Quantitative/ Qualitative | Applicable across entire organizational spectrum for all job positions. Excellent for generating qualitative data when used in conjunction with survey questionnaires. |
| | Focus Groups | Qualitative | Applicable across organizational spectrum, but care should be taken to keep groups homogenous, particularly if issues involving boss-to-employee relationships are to be discussed. Excellent tool when used to correlate quantitative data obtained through survey questionnaires. |
| | Observations | Qualitative | Applicable across organizational spectrum, with emphasis on job and task relationships. Good for correlating quantitative data obtained using survey questionnaires. |
| 2. Knowledge/ Experience | Questionnaire | Quantitative/ Qualitative | Applicable from the first through the middle management levels and, in particular, for screening job applicant potential when used in conjunction with interview method. |
| | Interviews | Qualitative | Appropriate for obtaining narrative feedback from all organizational levels but are most suitable for use at senior and/or executive management levels. Excellent correlation use with survey questionnaires. |
| | Observations | Qualitative | Appropriate from the first through the middle management levels. Good correlational use with questionnaires and interviews. |
| 3. Behavioral | Interviews | Qualitative | Appropriate throughout all organizational levels, but care must be taken so that they are not presented in a confrontational or emotionally charged manner. |
| | Questionnaires | Quantitative | Appropriate for anonymously gathering sensitive information (e.g.,personalized demographic data). |
| | Observations | Qualitative | Suitable particularly for all levels. |

| | | | |
|---|---|---|---|
| 4.Attitudinal/ Morale | Questionnaire | Quantitative/ Qualitative | Suitable for assessing needs across all organizational levels. |
| | Interviews | Quantitative/ Qualitative | Suitable for all levels, particularly when used in a narrative approach and in conjunction with quantitatively based questionnaires. Care should be taken when addressing demographic information. |
| | Observations | Qualitative | Suitable throughout first and middle levels for providing feedback that can be used in conjunction with survey questionnaires. |
| 5.Organizational Climate | Questionnaire | Quantitative/ Qualitative | Suitable for use across all organizational levels for providing mainly quantitatively based data. |
| | Interviews | Qualitative | Suitable for use across all organizational levels for obtaining feedback in correlation with either quantitative or qualitatively based survey questionnaires |
| | Focus Groups | Qualitative | Appropriate mainly for lower to middle levels, although attention should be paid to maintaining homogenous groups to avoid intimidation factors. |
| | Observations | Qualitative | Applicable throughout lower to middle levels for providing narrative feedback in conjunction with any of the other types of data gathering methods listed. |
| 6.Cultural | Focus Groups | Qualitative | Used to broadly define issues related to organizational culture. |
| | Questionnaire | Qualitative/ Quantitative | Applicable across all organizational levels, although would generally have a qualitatively based format. |
| | Interview | Qualitative | Excellent for use at all organizational levels and especially as a method to correlate narratively based feedback obtained through the use of the survey questionnaire. |
| 7.Leadership | Questionnaire | Qualitative/ Quantitative | Suitable for use at mainly middle to senior or executive levels for obtaining qualitative and some quantitatively based feedback. |
| | Interviews | Qualitative | Very appropriate for use at all levels, particularly for correlating quantitative feedback obtained through survey questionnaires. |

**Table 4.2** *(continued)*

| Assessment Type | Method* | Types of Data Produced | Application |
|---|---|---|---|
| 8.Benchmarking | Questionnaire | Quantitative/ Qualitative | Applicable to use to gather internal (throughout all levels) as well as external feedback (e.g., from customers, suppliers, etc.). |
| | Interviews | Qualitative/ Quantitative | Suitable as a correlational method to survey questionnaires or can be used as a stand-alone method to gather mostly qualitative feedback. |
| | Focus Groups | Qualitative | Suitable as a means for "brainstorming" across all organizational levels. |
| | Observations | Qualitative/ Quantitative | Particularly applicable in manufacturing or production-based environments. |
| 9.Operational | Questionnaire | Quantitative/ Qualitative | Applicable to use across all organizational levels for generating mainly quantitatively based data. |
| | Interviews | Qualitative/ Quantitative | Excellent use as a survey questionnaire correlational method. |
| | Focus Groups | Qualitative | Particularly suitable for "brainstorming" operational environment. Not restricted to any particular level(s). |
| | Observations | Quantitative/ Qualitative | Excellent for correlating quantitative data obtained from survey questionnaires. Should be conducted by knowledgeable SME. |
| 10.Job/Task Analysis | Questionnaire | Quantitative/ Qualitative | Excellent for obtaining both quantitative and qualitative data in order to better define jobs through incremental task(s). |
| | Interviews | Qualitative | Suitable at lower to middle levels as a survey questionnaire correlational method. |
| | Focus Groups | Qualitative | Suitable at lower to middle levels as both a survey questionnaire and observation correlational method. |
| | Observations | Quantitative/ Qualitative | Suitable for observing work in progress. Should be conducted by knowledgeable SME. |

*Data-gathering methods are listed in the order they are most used with the type(s) of needs assessment(s) specified.

sets will be combined and analyzed to produce a single set), some consideration must be given to the significance levels of individual questions, regardless of whether they originated in survey questionnaires, interviews, focus groups, or on-site observations. Invariably, common questions posed through different methods will produce different outcomes or results. These differences can be addressed by *weighting*, or rather, the assigning of numerical values to the feedback or outcomes obtained from the aggregate data sets.[33] Weighting is also used to account for the difference in opinions that can arise in observations conducted by two different SMEs. For example, in studying work processes, two SMEs base their observations and recommendations on both their personal work experiences and on their intuition. The results from survey questionnaires that were administered to individuals who were performing the observed work produced different outcomes. By weighting the results of the SMEs' observations against the results obtained from the survey group, decisions regarding the validity of the data and the aggregate responses from the three different sources can be obtained, measured, and analyzed.

When deciding which data-gathering methods will provide the most valuable aggregate feedback, HRD analysts often choose the survey questionnaire because they are inexpensive, convenient, and their data yield can be considerable. Therefore, they are generally chosen as the principal method. The exceptions to this are the following: (1) the behavioral assessment, which, because of its interpersonal and somewhat sensitive nature, uses the interview as the principal method; and (2) the organizational culture assessment, which, because culture is defined through group interaction on an organizational level, uses both the focus group and interview as its principal methods.

Due to costs and logistical requirements, interviews are most often used with survey questionnaires as an aggregate correlational method. They are well-suited for providing high degrees of narrative feedback that is useful for correlating closed-ended quantitative data obtained through survey questionnaires.

Focus groups also provide excellent aggregate correlational data when used in conjunction with survey questionnaires, providing that either of the following applies: (1) that they be used to address issues that are broadly related to the assessment goals, or (2) that they be used as a means for introducing peripheral issues associated with the goals that would otherwise not be apparent through the use of a more structured approach. For example, to broadly define issues affecting an organization's culture, one could first employ focus groups and then correlate the feedback through a more rigorous method, such as survey questionnaires or interviews. In this example, narrative data is first obtained through the focus groups (the principal method) and further investigated in detail through one or more of the other methods.

For the most part, on-site observations, because of their highly subjective nature, are best applied aggregately as a means for producing both narrative and qualitative feedback. This is then used to correlate any quantitative data obtained through another method. To illustrate, assume that interviews were conducted as part of an operational audit. The results indicated that certain work methods were outdated and should be redesigned or otherwise revised. On-site observations conducted by SMEs could either confirm or dispute the findings and would also provide narrative as well as quantitative feedback on the work methods observed, the equipment used, and the time it took to produce a given number of units.

One of the major criticisms of using aggregate data obtained from two or more methods is that many times a cumulative analysis may illustrate a sharing of procedural characteristics between the methods used but differ in the findings or outcomes.[34] In those instances where aggregate correlational methods provide feedback that conflicts with the findings provided through another method, the degrees of compatibility between the methods used should be examined by focusing first on how and at what stages in the needs assessment process they were used and second, on what correlational values, if any, actually do exist between the data sets. The key to establishing reliability is to make each data-gathering method as compatible as possible with the other methods particularly when there is more than one individual involved in the data-gathering process.[35] More detailed information on analyzing data that originated from multiple sources using aggregate methods will be presented in Chapters 7 and 8.

### Data-Gathering Decision Options

The type of assessment used (e.g., operational, leadership, knowledge/experience, etc.) will to a great extent dictate which data-gathering method (or combinations of methods) to use. There are, however, a number of other factors which must be considered as part of the decision process:

1. Which methods are the most complementary and will, through integrated application, aggregately yield the desired amount(s) of data?
2. Which methods will work best in an aggregate correlational manner, given the differences in organizational levels and in the degrees of sensitivity?
3. Given that there will undoubtedly be cost constraints involved, which mix of methods is the most cost-effective but able to provide the desired levels of quality data?

Once the type of assessment and accompanying data-gathering methods have been chosen, attention should then be directed at exploring how well the assessment will work under real-world conditions.

## SUMMARY

Needs assessment data consist of two types: quantitative and qualitative (or narrative). Quantitative data are produced from methods that involve and rely on numerical answers, while qualitative data are based on summary statements and narrative feedback. Analyzing quantitative data is easier because they lend themselves to numerical tabulation and ranking. Narrative data, on the other hand, are based primarily on statements and other conversational-type input and require one to read and then interpret the response. Because of this, qualitative data are subject to higher degrees of interpretative biasing than are quantitative data. However, the depth of qualitative information is significantly greater. Many survey professionals recommend a combination of both data types because, while quantitative data can be used to investigate and quantify a specific point, qualitative data can be used to investigate peripheral yet related issues.

There are four major methods for gathering needs assessment data. They are (1) survey questionnaires, (2) individual interviews, (3) focus groups, and (4) on-site observations. Survey questionnaires are the most widely used type of data-gathering methods. They require composing and writing questions that are designed to obtain feedback on the areas or issues under consideration. Questions should be written clearly and concisely and should, where appropriate, contain key words and jargon germane to potential respondents' jobs. If questions are of a highly demographic or sensitive nature, respondent anonymity should be guaranteed in an effort to obtain as high a response rate as possible.

One way of addressing respondent truthfulness is to use special codes on survey questionnaires. These codes contain the identities of the potential survey respondents and are kept in confidence. They can be used to identify who has completed and returned the questionnaire and who has not. Before coding anonymous questionnaires, potential respondents should be informed of why the coding is being used.

There are a variety of question types used in survey questionnaires. These are closed-ended questions (e.g., Yes/No, True/False, multiple choice, ranked order or ranked choice, and rating scales), open-ended questions (e.g., questions requiring the respondent to write a statement), and a combination of the two (e.g., those seeking both quantitative as well as qualitative feedback). Because of its comprehensiveness, many survey professionals prefer to use the combined question type.

The readability level of a questionnaire is also very important. It should be kept relatively low because keeping the questions simple and straightforward will generally produce higher response rates. Research has shown that including positively and negatively worded questions should be avoided, as they may serve only to confuse potential respondents. Also, in the interest of maintaining high response rates, questionnaire length should be kept to within reasonable levels (usually not more than two to three pages).

Interviews are also a commonly used needs assessment data-gathering method. They involve the collection of feedback through direct and verbal interaction between two individuals. The depth and quality of the information obtained is significantly greater than that obtained through survey questionnaires because the interviewer has access to verbal as well as visual and physical cues. These can indicate how a respondent reacts (or will react) to certain questions. The interview method is very adaptable and can provide a more realistic picture of opinions and true feelings.

Three types of interviews most commonly used are the following: structured, semistructured, and unstructured. Structured interviews usually contain the highest number of quantitatively based questions. Respondents' answers are generally not followed-up. Semistructured interviews are designed to produce highly specific feedback but also allow for additional probing. These consist of both qualitatively as well as quantitatively based questions and are similar in content to the combination format used in survey questionnaires. Unstructured interviews are very much like open-ended survey questions and are used primarily for brainstorming an issue or a problem. All interview types have behavioral implications, particularly where sensitive and demographic issues are discussed. The respondent should be informed about the purpose of the interview and should be guaranteed that their identity will remain confidential.

Assessment interviews must be planned well in advance, especially if they are to be used in conjunction with other data-gathering methods. This is necessary if links between the interview and any other methods (e.g., certain questions in a survey questionnaire) are to be established. Also, the interviewer should prepare background information on prospective interviewees to familiarize themselves with the individuals' job responsibilities.

Scripting of interviews is also an important factor to consider in the needs assessment planning stages. Preparing scripts in advance has definite advantages: (1) Writing questions in the exact order that they are to be asked adds continuity to the data-collection process; (2) questions can be changed if they need to be; and (3) writing interview scripts allows more than one person to conduct the interviews. This is critical if the interview population is large or geographically diverse.

Recording of interviews allows the actual give and take of the interchange to be recalled or played back later so that any discrepancies can be addressed and clarified.

Prior to actually conducting interviews, potential interviewers should undergo training. This is necessary to make certain that the way in which they conduct the interview is acceptable. Videotaping and playback critique of simulated interviews is an excellent way to build on the interviewer's strengths and also to identify any weaknesses.

Focus groups are used to brainstorm a particular subject. Made up of anywhere from six to perhaps twelve individuals and sometimes referred to as problem identification groups, they are generally convened under the guidance of a skilled and experienced moderator. Focus groups are useful for identifying causes and effects that have either been measured or observed. Focus group moderators should be skilled in group facilitation processes and have a keen understanding of group dynamics and communications.

On-site observations have long been used as data-gathering methods and have found considerable acceptance in various professions. As a needs assessment data-gathering method, however, on-site observations by themselves usually do not provide the levels of detailed feedback upon which conclusions or recommendations can be based. They are useful, however, when they are incorporated with other data-gathering methods. On-site observations are used primarily to gain firsthand feedback on job and task performance where work processes and procedures can be measured. They can also be used in managerial or white-collar settings to identify KSA deficiencies. Observations should be carried out unobtrusively. They should not interfere with the normal conduct of the organization's business and should be carried out in a nonthreatening and cordial manner. A detailed summary or log should include all observed activities along with any personalized notes or opinions of the observer(s). Where at times it is necessary for the observer to intrude or otherwise interrupt an employee in an attempt to further clarify a point or to gain some additional feedback, the observer or SME should record the reasons for the interruption along with the information received.

Other data-gathering methods include electronically administering survey questionnaires over computerized mail systems (e-mail), telephone interviews, and satellite or long-distance video-based conferencing. Using e-mail as a means for distributing surveys eliminates the costs associated with printing and distributing large numbers of paper questionnaires and also provides, in certain instances, acceptable return rates. Telephone interviews are widely used by the polling and marketing professions. They offer considerable cost savings over face-to-face or individualized interviews because they can be administered to a large number of people situated in geographically diverse locations. They should be designed using concise, brief, short-answer, closed-ended questions.

Satellite or long-distance video-based conferencing has met with mixed degrees of acceptance. It provides simultaneous levels of interaction, immediacy, and feedback to and from a number of remote sites. This can reduce travel costs normally associated with convening groups of individuals from a variety of different locations. Its major disadvantage lies in the cost to obtain, operate, and maintain the required technology and expertise. Also, from a logistical standpoint, this method would require individual on-site moderators when convening multiple focus groups from different locations. This would significantly increase the costs.

The survey questionnaire is the most common and widely used type of needs assessment data-gathering method. Because of its flexibility, it can be used to gather both quantitative as well as qualitative data. It is particularly useful in the systems approach to needs assessment design and implementation.

When using aggregate data methods to produce a singular data set, the HRD analyst or consultant must give serious consideration to the issue of question significance levels. This applies regardless of whether the questions are used in survey questionnaires, individual interviews, focus groups, or on-site observations.

Questions posed through different data-gathering methods will always produce different outcomes. One way of compensating for these differences is to assign significance levels to similar questions in the aggregate data sets. Known also as weighting, this technique can be used to account for opinions that are expressed in observations (and focus groups) as well.

Interviews are often chosen to be used in tandem with survey questionnaires because they yield substantial amounts of high-quality data. Focus groups are also commonly used in concert with survey questionnaires when the issues to be addressed are broadly defined or the organization has a need to introduce other goal-related issues. Because they are highly subjective, on-site observations are generally used to produce feedback that is aggregately correlated to quantitatively based data that has been obtained through other methods (e.g., through survey questionnaires).

A major criticism of using aggregate data-collection methods is that while a cumulative analysis may show commonality between procedures, there may be differences in the findings or outcomes. Standardizing question content between aggregate data-gathering methods is often necessary to attain reliability. The type of assessment being initiated will often indicate or otherwise determine which combination of data-gathering methods to use.

Organizations conduct surveys for a variety of purposes—from obtaining feedback on their operations to determining employee training and development needs. The types of methods used have considerable impact on the content and value of the data produced because they can introduce biasing or otherwise influence (either positively or negatively) the outcome of the needs assessment project. One way to reduce biasing is to strive to maintain a high degree of objectivity.

## NOTES

1. R. Dunnington, "New Methods and Technologies," in *Improving Organizational Surveys: New Directions and Methods*, P. Rosenfeld, J. Edwards, and M. Thomas, eds., *American Behavioral Scientist*, Vol. 36, No. 4, pp. 512–530.

2. J. Geer, "Do Open-Ended Questions Measure 'Salient' Issues?" *Public Opinion Quarterly*, Vol. 55, No. 3, pp. 360–370.

3. S. McClelland, "Training Needs Assessment Data Gathering Methods—Part I: Survey Questionnaires," *Journal of European Industrial Training*, Vol. 18, No. 1, pp. 22–26.

4. J. Edwards and M. Thomas, "The Organizational Survey Process," in *Improving Organizational Surveys: New Directions and Methods*, P. Rosenfeld, J. Edwards, and M. Thomas, eds., *American Behavioral Scientist*, Vol. 36, No. 4, pp. 419–442.

5. F. Fowler, "How Unclear Terms Affect Survey Data," *Public Opinion Quarterly*, Vol. 56, No. 2, pp. 360–370.

6. T. Rotondi, "The Annonymity Factor in Questionnaire Surveys," *Personnel Journal*, Vol. 68, No. 2, pp. 92–101.

7. Ibid.

8. Lori Long, "Surveys from Start to Finish," in *Info-Line*, G. Spruell, ed. (Alexandria, Va.: American Society for Training and Development, 1986).

9. Fowler, pp. 360–370.

10. Edwards and Thomas, pp. 419–442.

11. S. McClelland, "Training Needs Assessment Data Gathering Methods—Part II: Individual Interviews," *Journal of European Industrial Training*, Vol. 18, No. 2, pp. 27–31.

12. L. Stoneall, "Inquiring Trainers Want to Know: What Kinds of Questions Should Trainers Ask?" *Training and Development Journal*, Vol. 45, No. 11, pp. 31–39.

13. W. Wymer and J. Carsten, "Alternative Ways to Gather Opinion," *HR Magazine*, Vol. 37, No. 4, pp. 66–71.

14. R. Croft, "How to Minimize the Problem of Untruthful Response," *Business Marketing Digest*, Vol. 17, No. 3, pp. 17–23.

15. K. Karl and J. Kopf, "Guidelines for Using Videotaped Feedback Effectively," *Human Resource Development Quarterly*, Vol. 4, No. 3, pp. 303–310.

16. R. Tedlow, "Glossary of Marketing Terms," in J. Quelch, R. Dolan, and T. Kosnik, eds., *Marketing Management: Texts and Cases* (Homewood, Ill.: Richard D. Irwin, 1993).

17. H. Brightman, *Group Problem Solving: An Improved Managerial Approach* (Atlanta: Business Press, Georgia State University, 1988).

18. S. McClelland, N. Harbaugh, and S. Hammond, "Improving Individual and Group Effectiveness," *Journal of Management Development*, Vol. 12, No. 3, 1993, pp. 48–58.

19. R. Martell and R. Guzzo, "The Dynamics of Implicit Group Performance: When and How Do They Operate?" *Organizational Behavior and Human Decision Processes*, Vol. 50, No. 1, pp. 51–74.

20. G. Coleman and E. Van Aken, "Applying Small Group Behavior Dynamics to Improve Action-Team Performance," *Employment Relations Today*, Vol. 18, No. 3, pp. 343–353.

21. K. Lewin, *Field Theory in Social Sciences* (New York: Harper & Row, 1951).

22. Ibid., pp. 35–62.

23. T. Greenbaum, "Do You Have the Right Moderator for Your Focus Groups?" *Bank Marketing*, Vol. 23, No. 1, p. 43.

24. T. Greenbaum, "Outside Moderators Maximize Focus Group Results," *Public Relations Journal*, Vol. 47, No. 9, pp. 31–32.

25. H. Miriampolski, "Focus Groups on Sensitive Topics: How to Get Subjects to Open Up and Feel Good about Telling the Truth," *Applied Marketing Research*, Vol. 29, No. 1, pp. 6–11.

26. D. Potts, "Bias Lurks in All Phases of Qualitative Research," *Marketing News*, Vol. 24, No. 18, pp. 12–13.

27. D. Nich, "Inquiry and Observation—Effective Internal Auditing Techniques," *Internal Auditing*, Vol. 3, No. 2, pp. 11–17.

28. D. Gayeski, L. Wood, and J. Ford, "Getting Inside an Expert's Brain," *Training and Development*, Vol. 48, No. 8, pp. 55–62.

29. P. Rosenfeld, S. Booth-Kewley, and J. Edwards, "Computer Administered Surveys in Organizations," in *Improving Organizational Surveys: New Directions and Methods*, P. Rosenfeld, J. Edwards, and M. Thomas, eds., *American Behavioral Scientist*, Vol. 36, No. 4, pp. 485–511.

30. Dunnington, pp. 512–530.

31. G. Rummler, "Determining Needs," in *Training and Development Handbook: A Guide to Human Resource Development*, 3rd ed., R. Craig, ed. (New York: McGraw-Hill, 1987), pp. 218–219.

32. C. Ostroff and J. Ford, "Assessing Training Needs: Critical Levels of Analysis," in *Training and Development in Organizations*, I. Goldstein, ed. (San Francisco: Jossey-Bass, 1989), p. 55.

33. W. Hannum and C. Hansen, *Instructional Systems Development in Large Organizations* (Englewood Cliffs, N.J.: Educational Technology Publications, 1989).

34. H. Cooper, "The Integrative Research Review/A Systematic Approach," *Applied Social Research Methods Series* (Beverly Hills, Calif.: Sage Publications, 1984), pp. 80–81.

35. Hannum and Hansen, p. 61.

PART III

# Facilitation, Administration, and Control

CHAPTER 5

# Assessment Project Preparation

## PRETESTING THE ASSESSMENT

Pollsters, researchers, and other professionals who regularly conduct surveys and assessments will always prefer to perform tests on their projects before formally implementing them. Known as pretesting, this serves a variety of purposes:

1. It provides a means for identifying and correcting errors and ambiguities that were unforeseen during the design stage.
2. It increases the probability that any survey questionnaire used in the assessment will yield the quality of data required, thereby saving time, expense, and the embarrassment of possibly having to recall and correct them.
3. It will indicate how well the selected data-gathering methods will work in an aggregate and correlational manner.
4. It provides a means for preliminarily validating the selected needs assessment data-gathering instruments.
5. It provides a means for conducting the assessment on a representative sample of individuals in order to obtain realistic feedback.

Pretesting is a way of simulating the mechanics of the assessment under quasi-real-world conditions before actually implementing it. It involves collecting data from a sample population comprised of individuals who may or may not be part of the actual target assessment population. Any of the data-collection methods discussed in Chapter 4, with perhaps the exception of the on-site observation methods, can be used in an assessment pretest. The main advantage to pretesting is that it gives the analyst a means for implementing the assessment system under low-risk conditions while also providing a way to make changes (if necessary).[1]

The decision of whom to include in the assessment pretest is another important question. Whether to conduct pretests that include only individuals from outside of the target assessment population or whether to conduct them using individuals to be included in the actual assessment population basically can be determined best by the type of assessment being conducted. If it is more generalized (e.g., skills, competencies, knowledge, etc.), then a pretest involving individuals from outside of the target group would be acceptable. On the other hand, if it is to be directed at obtaining very job-specific feedback or is behaviorally related, it is preferable to direct pretests at individuals from within the targeted assessment population. This provides better insight as to the appropriateness and validity of the assessment methods being used. However, conducting pretests on individuals who are also part of the actual assessment population presents another problem, namely, exposing them to the actual survey, interview, or focus group questions may send inappropriate signals of what potential respondents can expect in the actual needs assessment. This can influence or otherwise bias their responses once the formal data-gathering process has begun.

Regardless of who is included in the pretest group, it is highly unlikely that everyone—either directly or indirectly connected with the assessment—will be able to participate. Therefore, in order to get a realistic idea of how the actual assessment design will perform, a pretest is conducted on a representative sample of respondents.

## Sampling

Selecting an appropriate sample of respondents is a very important step in the pretest process. There are two critical issues the HRD analyst should be concerned with. They are (1) the composition or make-up of the sample and (2) the sample's size.

There are a variety of sampling techniques that can be used. Some of these are *simple random sampling, stratified sampling, cluster sampling,* and *systematic sampling.*

*Simple Random Sampling.* This is the most basic of all sampling procedures and will in most circumstances provide an acceptable degree of feedback. Simple random sampling means that all members of a group or population have an equal and independent chance of being included in the sample.[2] There are two principal stages in simple random sampling: (1) define and list the total assessment sample population or assessment group; and then (2) devise the actual sample by employing a procedure whereby sheer chance determines which members are drawn and included in the sample.

The first step is to generate a table of random numbers (see Table 5.1). This can be done using a computer and statistical software. Using a computer ensures that a random order of the numbers will also be generated. Next, each member of the assessment sample population is assigned a distinct or unique number that is also drawn at random from the computer-generated table. Finally, the computer is used to select the assigned identification numbers of the individuals to be included. Table 5.1 illustrates a computer-generated table of random numbers for a total assessment population of forty-eight individuals. Table 5.2 contains an example of a computer-generated selection of 25 percent (twelve individuals) that were randomly drawn from the total population of forty-eight qualified individuals.

**Table 5.1**
Computer-Generated Table of Random Numbers for an Assessment Group of Forty-Eight Individuals

| | | | |
|---|---|---|---|
| 10284 | 10164 | 04839 | 21928 |
| 22429 | 54193 | 19274 | 21954 |
| 32228 | 01823 | 10854 | 19285 |
| 33285 | 29377 | 00283 | 20044 |
| 15664 | 21999 | 81652 | 67917 |
| 53916 | 27001 | 81647 | 14441 |
| 97735 | 46883 | 00555 | 95012 |
| 09763 | 32427 | 55657 | 61680 |
| 05998 | 14778 | 09118 | 19070 |
| 25669 | 33371 | 01074 | 04146 |
| 27163 | 39921 | 20069 | 50407 |
| 88813 | 26267 | 81772 | 01067 |

**Table 5.2**
Computer-Generated Selection of Twelve Random Numbers (nonordered sequence)

| | | | |
|---|---|---|---|
| 39921 | 53916 | 01823 | 22429 |
| 09118 | 05998 | 27163 | 46883 |
| 15664 | 95012 | 01067 | 00283 |

*Stratified Sampling.* If the assessment population is composed of subgroups (also known as strata) that differ in certain characteristics (such as organizational level, technical expertise, span of authority and responsibility, etc.), it would be desirable to use a sampling procedure known as stratified sampling. Here, job-related criteria are first identified along with any similarities that exist between members of each strata. Then, using a computer, numbers are assigned to each member of each strata. The computer is then used to select either equal or odd numbers from each, or it is used to make a selection that is proportional to the size of each stratum contained in the sample population. The latter of these two approaches is known as proportional stratified sampling, meaning that the stratum is represented in the sample according to its exact proportion to the total population.

Stratified sampling often provides a truer representation of the actual assessment population as compared to that obtained through simple random sampling. Its major advantage is that it guarantees representation throughout the defined assessment population.

*Cluster Sampling.* Because it is sometimes impossible to include all members from a target assessment population, it is more convenient and cost-effective to identify and include only certain subjects from within defined areas or clusters. For example, in conducting a needs assessment for a multinational corporation with 10,000 employees, the analyst would choose individuals from a list of departments whose personnel have the same or similar job titles and responsibilities. The determinants for being included in the sample population are not based on individual criteria but rather on criteria reflecting groups of individuals who share similar characteristics (e.g., peer levels where an effect has been observed, measured, predetermined, etc.). The clusters included in this type of sampling method must be chosen at random because if only one cluster were used, then the analyst could not draw generalizations that would be representative of the entire assessment population. A principal procedural requirement to cluster sampling is that once a cluster is selected, then all members from within that cluster must be included in the sample.[3]

*Systematic Sampling.* This involves sampling by including every $k$th person from a list of all possible candidates in the population. The first step is to decide how many subjects to include in the sample ($n$). Once that is done, the analyst would then divide the number of the total population ($N$) by the number to be included in the sample ($n$). The result provides the sampling interval ($k$). Then, the first person is randomly selected from at or near the top of the list and then every $k$th member of the entire population is subsequently included. To illustrate, assume a population of 1,000 and a desired sample size of 100:

$$k = N/n = 1{,}000/100 = 10.$$

Thus, every tenth person on the list would be included in the sample. The various choices associated with systematic sampling are not independent because once the first person is selected, then all subsequent selections to be included in the sample are predetermined by the sample interval (*k*).[4] Alphabetically compiled lists should not be used in systematic sampling because they do not normally give a good representative sample. This is because last names can and often do fall into clusters (e.g., more last names begin with the letters s or m as compared to the number that begin with an x, an e, or a z).

Note that the sampling methods presented here are not mutually exclusive and various combinations may be used. The key to selecting an appropriate combination of sampling methods lies in first identifying the parameters of the sample (e.g., size, whom to include, etc.) and then determining how much representation throughout and across various levels is necessary in order to produce the desired amounts of quality data.

### Determining Sample Size

Since there are no universal rules that apply to determining sample sizes, one way is to simply estimate what will be needed to ensure confidence that the data obtained from the sample will be valid and that it is representative of all groups who are to be included in the assessment population. One general rule regarding sample size is that survey professionals will always strive to use as large a sample as possible because its mean and standard deviation are more likely to be representative of the survey population's mean and standard deviation.[5] (Mean and standard deviation are discussed in detail in Chapter 7.) Increasing the sample size will also control and reduce sampling error (margin of error) that occurs when all units in a given population are not included and measured. Most professionals specify a sampling error of ±5 percent or less, meaning that responses in the survey accurately represent the entire population within plus (+) or minus (–) 5 percentage points.

One caveat to estimating sample size is that larger samples alone do not guarantee precision nor accuracy. Comprehensive representation across all organizational levels to be included in the assessment is mandatory to ensuring accuracy and confidence. For example, assume that an assessment was conducted in an organization employing 210 people. The organization consisted of three departments: sales/marketing, accounting/finance, and operations. The goal of the assessment was to identify ways of lowering overhead costs. Of the 210 employees, 20 were managers, 25 were clerical/administrative, 10 were professionals (e.g., engineers, computer specialists, etc.), and the rest (155 persons) were nonexempt hourly workers. Clearly, if one were to draw a random sample from across the organizational spectrum, it is very possible that the results could be biased in favor of the operations department, the one with the largest number of workers. In order to compensate for this and to obtain a balanced yet comprehensive sample that more accurately represents the organization as a whole, one could draw an averaged sample from each of the three departments. To simplify, assume that a 25-percent sample (53) of the total number of employees (210) was considered acceptable. Fifty-three individuals divided by three departments would produce a subsample of seventeen individuals from two of the departments and nineteen individuals from the other. The addition of two individuals from one department would not be significant enough to statistically bias or offset the results. Therefore, a balanced average sample drawn from across the organization would have been obtained.

## PRETEST RESULTS

Pretest results should give a good indication of how the system design will actually perform once it is formally implemented. Some concerns related to this are the following:

1. How well do the aggregate data-gathering methods perform?
2. How accurately were the data-gathering instruments interpreted by respondents in the sample or samples selected?
3. Do the methods chosen have the ability to generate the degree(s) of quality data desired?
4. Is the type and quality of feedback useful for determining causality? In short, do the data directly relate to and address the goals of the assessment?

If the answer to any of these concerns is negative, then a detailed review of the system design should be conducted. Some important factors to consider here would be the following:

1. The appropriateness of the data-gathering methods relative to the assessment type and sample population (groups)
2. Individual team member attributes (e.g., are they the right or best persons for their assigned roles?)
3. A detailed review of the goal-setting process to determine whether the assessment goals are realistic and attainable

Once it is shown that the system design is appropriate and once there is a high degree of confidence that it will produce sufficient levels of quality feedback, all steps, processes, procedures, and instruments that were developed throughout the design phase should be documented for future reference and use.

## PREASSESSMENT LOGISTICAL CONSIDERATIONS

Part of a formal preproject review should include in-depth examination of the project's logistics, particularly as they relate to the implementation and use of the aggregate data-gathering methods.

### Questionnaire Completion and Return Times

Adequate time should be allowed for respondents to receive, complete, and return written survey questionnaires. In order to estimate how much time to allow, the following items should be considered:

1. *Questionnaire length and clarity*: As was previously discussed, the length and complexity of the questionnaire will significantly impact not only the amount of time it will take respondents to complete it, but will also affect the overall return rate. Questionnaires comprised of closed-ended, concisely worded questions take less time to complete than ones that are many pages long and contain a number of open-ended questions.
2. *Respondent absences*: Vacations, sick leave, court or jury duty, distractions due to other projects, business trips, military service, and a variety of other reasons will also negatively impact completion and return times. Deadlines for returning completed survey questionnaires should never fall in line with recognized holidays.

Generally speaking, the larger the group, the more time should be allowed for questionnaire completion and return. However, this time period should not be extended beyond normal reason. Research has shown that where completion and return times are concerned, respondents who have received coded questionnaires are more prone to return them within the specified time frame(s).[6] Anonymous questionnaires should be sent out with a cover letter or should contain a paragraph stating (1) the time the completed survey is due to be returned, (2) where it should be sent, (3) to whose attention, and (4) by what means (e.g., interoffice mail, regular postage, special deliveries, etc.). Where e-mail is used, instructions on how to electronically route the return should be included.[7] An explanation from senior management as to why the survey is being conducted, what the organization hopes to gain, what will be done with the information once it is received, and guarantees of anonymity in those cases where respondents are asked to identify themselves should also be included.

### Scheduling Individual Interviews

Individual interviews should be scheduled around respondents' available work time. They should be conducted in a nonthreatening manner, be nonintrusive (e.g., they should not interfere with the respondents' work schedule), and should be conducted in private. Interview times should be agreed to well in advance, and a follow-up letter or note from the interviewer should be sent to the respondents reminding them about the interview time and place. Interviewees should be advised as to how long the interview will take, why it is being conducted, and what will be done with the information once it has been received. Finally, the note should contain a guarantee of anonymity from senior management.

Scheduling interviews is similar to scheduling regular types of meetings. Since they are subject to a number of variables, it will undoubtedly be necessary to reschedule many of them, sometimes more than once. The interviewer should be prepared to make allowances for this by being flexible yet persistent.

Many needs analysts struggle with the question of whether to schedule interviews with respondents who are also participating in another data-gathering method (e.g., survey questionnaires, focus groups, etc.). Participation in multiple methods is largely influenced by a number of factors, such as the amount of time that has been allocated to complete the data-gathering phase of the assessment, the number of individuals selected from the overall population to participate in both methods (e.g., survey questionnaires and individual interviews), and whether the interview is being used as the principal data-gathering method or whether it is being aggregately used to provide correlational feedback. Generally, when respondents are designated to participate in multiple data-gathering methods, it is more convenient to schedule interviews within the same time frame (unless the content of the survey or other method[s] and that of the interview[s] are mutually exclusive).

A log of scheduled interviews should be maintained by the team leader. It should contain information such as the participant's name, the date and time the interview was conducted, the interviewer's name, and the length of time it took to complete the interview.

## Scheduling Focus Groups

Scheduling focus groups can be frustrating, particularly where multiple groups are concerned. Since each group will normally contain between six and twelve individuals, analysts (or focus group moderators) are faced with the task of trying to manage a number of individual schedules. Multiply that by two or three groups and the challenge of scheduling multiple focus groups can become daunting indeed.

Out of sheer necessity, focus groups will need to be planned well in advance. Each employee selected to participate should be contacted and time frames agreed to. Due to individuals' work as well as personal schedules, changes and rescheduling of focus groups will without doubt occur. Given this, it is a good idea to designate alternate participants who can make themselves available when first-choice members cannot attend. One way of doing this is to elect one, or sometimes two, alternate participants for every primary one. This makes the scheduling process more manageable.

Each participant should receive a letter highlighting the time and place where the sessions will be held. Information about why the group is being convened and what will be done with the information once it is collected should also be included. Many professional moderators also include a broadly stated topic agenda. Some even elect to include the names of other participants. Doing so has both advantages and disadvantages. The advantages are that a framework becomes established and the agenda can serve to prompt participants into thinking about the subject(s) to be discussed. This can aid in the group facilitation process. The principle disadvantage is that upon receiving this information, participants may contact other members and form internal group coalitions that can be distracting once the formal group is convened.

The focus group moderator should keep accurate notes of the dialogue and interchange including the time (and date) the session(s) started, when they ended, and, in particular, what significant information was produced as an outcome.

### Scheduling On-Site Observations

Since their very nature is to obtain feedback as unobtrusively as possible, scheduling on-site observations is more easily accomplished. For example, in a manufacturing or production-oriented environment where work processes, methods, systems, and so on, are the targets of the observation(s), scheduling can be done by first alerting the appropriate personnel (e.g., the department manager, supervisor, foreman, and, in some instances, the workers who will be observed) about the observation, what types of work or processes are to be observed, and what will be done with the data once they are collected. Once this has been done, it is simply a matter of scheduling the SMEs and placing them where they need to be.

Placing SMEs in an environment where interpersonal relations and behaviors are to be observed (which usually involves a number of employees who are simultaneously undergoing the observation) will require tact and finesse. With the objective to obtain realistic and unbiased feedback, it may be necessary to announce to the employees at the outset that an observation is going to take place but refrain from divulging when it will begin or who will be conducting it. It may even be desirable to begin the observations before making this announcement in order to obtain a before- and after-announcement comparison base.

In both circumstances, the SME or observer must keep accurate records detailing the dates, times, locations, and what outcomes were observed.

## PROJECT REVIEW

Once the design stage is complete, there are a number of other factors to consider prior to the assessment's formal implementation. Among these are (1) the development and review of a project chronology (time line), (2) a comprehensive budgetary review, (3) finalization of the project team, (4) presenting the project plan and budget to senior management for their review and approval, and (5) formally announcing the assessment to the organization's employees.

## Project Chronology

Time line models are a favorite tool with project managers because they provide a visual representation of the various tasks and events, critical time frames (also known in project management terminology as Critical Path Method or CPM), the interrelationships between various tasks and events and, most important, the interdependencies between tasks which have precedent relationship(s).[8] The time line model is especially useful in planning needs assessment activities for the following reasons:

1. It provides a means for viewing the project in a macro sense.
2. It forces reconsideration of the choice(s) of data-gathering methods to be used.
3. It places each of the tasks in sequential order and illustrates the impacts and consequences of time on the project overall.
4. It places significant emphasis on task and event interrelationships, interdependencies, and precedent relationships.

Time line models are constructed by including each and every task, event, and activity that the project could conceivably encompass. The steps to constructing a time line model are as follows:

1. List all tasks or events in the project from start to finish.
2. Arrange this list in the order in which tasks and events are supposed to occur (or are most likely to occur), paying particular attention to any event/task precedent relationships (e.g., Task B must occur before Task C, Task C and Task D can occur simultaneously but both must occur before Task E, and so on).
3. Assign a starting time to each task or event.
4. Note which tasks/events can be accomplished simultaneously.
5. Assign an estimated duration time to each task/event.
6. Determine the time durations between task accomplishment or event occurrence (e.g., time between Tasks/Events A and B is one week, between B and C is one week, C and D are accomplished together within one week, and so on).
7. List all tasks/events on a line noting which events occur simultaneously within the estimated time durations.
8. Take note of which tasks/events occur simultaneously and which will require the least amount of time to accomplish. Note free time, or rather, time in which an event will more than likely conclude with an amount of spare or slack time remaining.
9. Total all task/event times from first to last. This figure is the estimated assessment project duration.

An example of a time line is provided in Figure 5.1. This is a hypothetical time line indicating the accomplishment of overlapping multiple tasks within a given period as relates to the systems model illustrated in Figure 2.1.

**Figure 5.1**
Needs Assessment Time Line Model

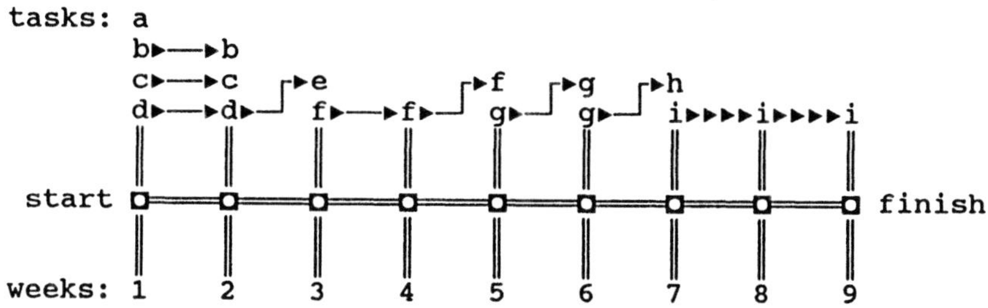


Tasks:

a. Define Preliminary Assessment Goals
b. Conduct Preliminary Planning
c. Review/Select Assessment Methods and Instruments
d. Finalize Project Preparations
e. Schedule and Implement
f. Gather Feedback
g. Analyze Feedback
h. Draw Conclusions
i. Present Findings and Recommendations and Formulate Corrective Actions

**Estimated assessment duration: 9 weeks**

The time line model illustrated shows the interrelationships between multiple tasks and activities over a given period of time. For example, Tasks A through D can be theoretically accomplished during *week 1*, while Tasks B and C may be completed sometime during *week 2*. Likewise, Task E may conclude along with Task F during *week 3*, and so on. The purpose for constructing a time line model like this is that it forces attention to the accomplishment of tasks within a given time frame. Thus, it can serve as a useful project planning tool when dozens of tasks are involved. It also serves to illustrate task precedent relationships along with each task or event's degree of independence as well as any interdependence.

## Budgetary Review

After a project time line has been prepared, a review of the project budget is usually undertaken. This is done to update any estimated costs which may have changed since the budget was proposed. A budgetary review also provides the opportunity to record and review any changes that may have occurred with the organization's personnel (e.g., promotions or demotions, new hires). The review allows finalizing of the budget so that it reflects realistic and not hypothetical costs.

A budgetary review begins by comparing the details and results of past assessment projects to the current one. This is done so that reliable information on the project's actual costs can be obtained. Where previous information is not available (e.g., if this is the first time an assessment has been undertaken), the budgetary review will serve to highlight those areas where the amounts of time or funds allocated are perhaps not sufficient. Alternatively, it can highlight areas where too much time (and expense) is allocated.

When forecasting costs where no previous information, data, or experience exists, costs are usually estimated at higher rates. For example, assume that 400 hours of an HRD analyst's time, totaling $4,500, was originally estimated. After the project time line was developed, this estimate was revised upward to reflect a 450-hour involvement. The additional costs associated with this increase would have to be calculated and adjusted with the revised figure(s) included in the budgetary update.

All costs associated with the project should be listed with particular emphasis placed on their itemization. A justification for each cost should also be included. It is important to note that during the original budget development stage, costs related to time allocations would normally have been averaged. Notes to this effect should be included on the final budget to be presented to senior management.

### Finalizing the Project Team

After the budgetary review process has concluded, a meeting of all project team members should be convened. This is done for a variety of reasons:

1. To discuss last-minute issues relating to scheduling and logistics
2. To discuss issues relating to administration and project support
3. To clarify team member roles (e.g., who is responsible for what)
4. To resolve any problems or questions still outstanding

Perhaps the most important reasons are the ones relating to personnel roles and responsibilities. It is imperative that the members of the team be familiar with their assigned task(s). Any disagreements, disputes, differences of opinion, or other ambiguities should, at this point, be brought forward, discussed, and decided upon. Finally, a complete set of notes containing the results of the meeting should be shared with each team member. The project team should be organized so that once schedules and time frames have been set, there is adequate support and back-up to handle scheduling conflicts that are certain to arise.

In order to harmonize the team, it is necessary to establish open and clear channels of communication between all members. It is critical to making the project—which could involve literally hundreds, even thousands, of people—run smoothly and efficiently. A paramount responsibility of the project team leader is to ensure that all members are current in the information and status of the project at any and all times. This can be accomplished through formalized ongoing status meetings, an example of which is included in Figure 5.2. The team leader should also serve as the liaison between the team members, senior management, and the organization's employees. This provides those outside of the project team with a focal point where questions or concerns can be addressed.

## PRESENTING THE PROJECT PLAN TO MANAGEMENT

The final steps in the project preimplementation phase involve presenting the plan to management for their approval and then formally announcing it to the organization's employees.

**Figure 5.2**
Time Line Model Indicating Team Status Meetings

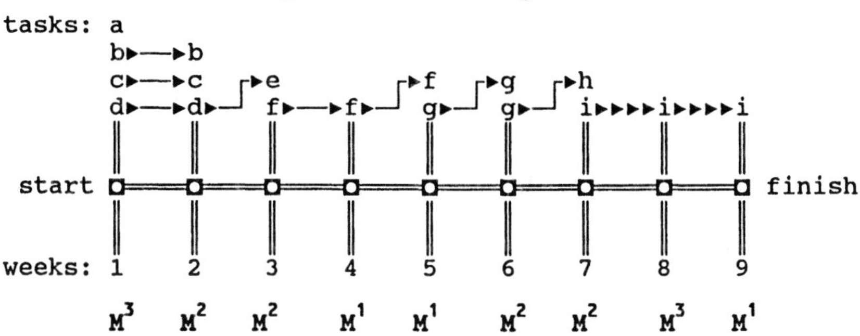


Tasks:

a. Define Preliminary Assessment Goals
b. Conduct Preliminary Planning
c. Review/Select Assessment Methods and Instruments
d. Finalize Project Preparations
e. Schedule and Implement
f. Gather Feedback
g. Analyze Feedback
h. Draw Conclusions
i. Present Findings and Recommendations and Formulate Corrective Actions

**$M^X$ Team Status Update Meetings (number of meetings Within Given Time Frame Indicated)**

The plan presented to management should contain all information that is relevant to the assessment. This normally includes an explanation of what led to the project's inception (observed or measured effect), how the assessment system design was accomplished, all budgetary information, the results of the assessment pretest, and the project chronology or time line. The plan should contain an executive summary that focuses attention on attaining the assessment goals. It should emphasize the necessity for action once the feedback has been analyzed, the conclusions drawn, and all recommendations have been made. It should also state that any recommended interventions drawn from the assessment's outcome will be accompanied with a similar type of plan, including costs, goals, logistics, and means for evaluating and measuring the intervention's short- as well as long-term effectiveness.

### Gaining Management's Commitment and Support

Perhaps one of the most prevalent reasons why so many assessment projects fail to deliver what was desired or expected lies in a failure to secure senior management's commitment and support. The worst thing that can happen to any assessment project is for management to give only tertiary support or implied approval.[9] Since a needs assessment relies mainly on employee participation, their (the employees') enthusiasm and acceptance can be obtained only through the equal enthusiasm, support, and active participation of management. Likewise, commitment by management to act on the recommendations resulting from the assessment sends a clear signal that this is not only a worthwhile endeavor, but is necessary to maintain a competitive and productive advantage.

In order to emphasize this importance, the following case taken from an actual incident is provided.

### Case: A Lack of Support

An HRD manager was directed by the vice president for human resources to conduct an assessment to identify employee training needs. The manager, not being skilled in assessment methods, received permission to hire an external consultant who had expertise in the area. The project included survey questionnaires, individual interviews, and on-site observation data-collection methods and involved over 250 employees. It required approximately 420 hours (or 52.5 eight-hour working days) to implement, gather the data, analyze it, and present the conclusions to management. Employee enthusiasm and acceptance for the project, once they learned why it was being done and what results they could expect to see from it, was high. The assessment was implemented and a survey completion and return rate of better than 90 percent was obtained. Additionally, the overall interview and observation completion rates were better than 70 and 80 percent, respectively. The results highlighted various needs that were substantiated by a quantitative analysis of productivity and performance records. A list of recommendations was included in the final report which was then presented to the vice president.

After some time had passed with no comments or feedback on the assessment report and recommendations, the HRD manager asked the vice president about the status of the project. The reply was that the organization had pressing problems of more immediate concern. Consequently, the results and recommendations had been filed and a decision regarding any subsequent actions had been postponed. News of management's decision to shelve the report and recommendations spread among the employees.

Some months later, management expressed concern that productivity appeared to be in decline. They also noted that employee morale was low, as evidenced by an increase in absenteeism. In an effort to get at the root of the problem, management had the HRD manager initiate another assessment project. This time employee participation was only slightly better than 40 percent. Moreover, during the interview and observation stages, many employees rescheduled their interview times and were absent during the scheduled observation periods. Of those that did meet their times, it was readily apparent that many lacked the enthusiasm they had previously exhibited during the first assessment. Input was slow in coming and there seemed to be an overall lack of desire to participate.

What had happened? Even an elementary review can provide the answer. The original assessment was initiated by senior management (the vice president of human resources) and involved considerable resources. Additionally, a consultant was retained which pushed the costs and perhaps employee expectations even higher. The results and recommendations were given to management who then ignored them. Management's seeming lack of concern had been interpreted by the company's employees to mean that the assessment was seen by them (management) to be unimportant and that there never were any real intentions of addressing employee training needs. As a result, it was inevitable that management's apparent lack of concern and failure to act on the recommendations proved to be a demoralizing factor. The net result was a decrease in performance and productivity, lower employee morale, and increased absenteeism.

The message here is simple: Any type of organizational assessment is in itself an intervention and will draw attention. In this instance, the attention drawn was in the form of heightened employee expectations. Therefore, management's approval for any assessment project must not only be sincere, but they should take measures to act on the recommendations made, even if this involves only an acknowledgment that the recommendations presented are under active consideration. If, for whatever reason, this does not happen, the employees need to be told why.

## MAKING THE FORMAL ANNOUNCEMENT

Once all of the design and preimplementation phases of the project are complete, an announcement, usually done via a formal letter or memo from senior management, should be made. This should emphasize why the assessment is being done, what types of information are being sought, what will be done with the information once it has been collected, and, in those instances where employee anonymity is an issue, contain specific guarantees that identities will be protected. This is particularly important where coded survey questionnaires are being used. Many such announcements will call specific attention to the fact that the survey questionnaires are coded and will provide detailed information on why coding was considered necessary (e.g., for contacting nonrespondents so that a greater response rate can be obtained, etc.).

## SUMMARY

Pretesting provides a means for simulating the needs assessment in a quasi-real-world environment. It is performed on a sample of individuals drawn from either or both the actual assessment population or from those employees who are not scheduled to participate. The major advantage to pretesting is to obtain feedback indicating how well the selected data-gathering methods will perform.

There are essentially four types of sampling techniques. Simple random sampling is where all members of a particular group have an equal and independent chance of being included in the sample. Stratified sampling, although similar to simple random sampling, differs in that individuals with certain job-related criteria are chosen to be included, and from this, a sample is chosen for inclusion in the pretest. Its major advantage is that it guarantees representation of each strata across the entire assessment population. Cluster sampling is used because it is sometimes more efficient and cost-effective to select individuals for inclusion in the assessment based on group characteristics (e.g., job-related activities and peer levels). Clusters must be selected at random and must include all members from within that particular cluster. Systematic sampling sequentially selects individuals from across the entire population in an orderly manner. In systematic sampling, the various choices are not independent because once the first person is selected, all subsequent selections are predetermined.

Once the sampling method has been chosen, the next decision involves estimating the size of the sample. This is usually done by first estimating the number of individuals to be included in the formal assessment. Professional researchers usually prefer to have as large a sample size as possible because a larger sample tends to be more representative of the actual assessment group. However, size alone does not guarantee precision. Comprehensive representation across all organizational levels should be the final determinant in any attempt to ensure accuracy.

The results of the pretest should indicate the appropriateness of the data-gathering methods chosen. It should also provide a good indication of how the assessment project team will function and how well the assessment design addresses the goals established in the goal determination process. From a logistical standpoint, there are issues which need to be addressed before formally implementing the assessment. They are questionnaire completion and return times and the scheduling of individual interviews, focus groups, and on-site observations.

Once the design stage is completed, a comprehensive review of the project should be conducted. This includes a review of the project time line, budgetary revisions, finalization of the project team, presentation of the assessment project plan to management for their approval, and formally announcing the assessment to the organization's employees. This serves to focus attention on the details of the project and also establishes time frames for its completion.

Once the project has been reviewed and approved by management, it is important to formally announce it to the organization's employees. This can be done through a memorandum or some other type of written correspondence. The announcement should include information on why the assessment is being done and what kind of information is being sought. It should also contain guarantees of anonymity (if applicable), stress the importance of employee participation, and highlight information on what actions might result. In taking this approach, management will send a signal to the employees that they not only approve of but actively support the assessment. This, in turn, helps to solidify employee support and participation.

## NOTES

1. K. Ludeman, "Measuring Skills and Behavior," *Training and Development*, Vol. 45, No. 11, pp. 61–66.

2. G. Henry, *Practical Sampling* (Newbury Park, Calif.: Sage Publications, 1990).

3. W. Hines and D. Montgomery, *Probability and Statistics in Engineering and Management Science* (New York: Wiley & Sons, 1980).

4. F. Fowler, *Survey Research Methods* (Newbury Park, Calif.: Sage Publications, 1988).

5. C. O'Muircheartaigh, "Simple Response: Estimation and Determinants," in P. Biemar et al., eds., *Measurement Errors in Surveys* (New York: Wiley & Sons, 1991), pp. 551–574.

6. P. Sheatsley, "Questionnaire Construction and Item Writing," in P. Rossi, J. Wright, and A. Anderson, eds., *Handbook of Survey Research* (Orlando, Fla.: Academic Press, 1983), pp. 195–230.

7. R. Dunnington, "New Methods and Technologies in the Organizational Survey Process," in *Improving Organizational Surveys: New Directions and Methods*, P. Rosen-

feld, J. Edwards, and M. Thomas, eds., *American Behavioral Scientist,* Vol. 36, No. 4, pp. 512–530.

8. S. McClelland, "Performance and Productivity Improvement: Applying a Time-to-Progress Model," *Industrial Management*, Vol. 29, No. 4, pp. 10–14.

9. D. Bowers and L. Stambaugh, "Making Organizational Surveys Pay Off," in *Organizational Development: Targeting Change*, C. Jackson, ed. (Alexandria, Va.: American Society for Training and Development, 1986), pp. 41–54.

CHAPTER 6

# Assessment Organization and Control

## RESOLVING SCHEDULING CONFLICTS

No matter how well an assessment is planned, scheduling problems will inevitably arise. The frequency with which they surface increases with the size and complexity of the project. Understanding why scheduling conflicts occur and what measures can be taken to effectively manage them is an important part of needs assessment organization and control.

Scheduling conflicts affect all data-collection activities. While they are sometimes unavoidable, they should not be allowed to go on unresolved because they have the very real potential to derail the overall project. There are a number of ways in which scheduling conflicts can be managed while still keeping within the established time line(s).

### Resolving Interview Scheduling Conflicts

When interview scheduling conflicts occur, it will sometimes be necessary to attempt to reschedule all subsequent activities. In a systematic needs assessment, rescheduling can often require a comprehensive adjustment of the entire project due to the existence of interrelationships between different activities.

Where interpersonal or sensitive issues are to be discussed in the interview, interviewees may become apprehensive, particularly as the actual interview time draws near. This can raise anxiety levels, which can lead them to reschedule or, in many instances, attempt to postpone or cancel the interview altogether. Situations like this present formidable challenges to both the interviewer and the assessment project team leader. The reasons as to why the potential interviewees chose to reschedule, postpone, or otherwise avoid the session should be thoroughly investigated. Many times, in spite of formal notification from senior management, the postponement results from inaccurate information obtained through informal communication channels (e.g., miscommunication through an informal grapevine). Situations like this are indicative of employee suspicion and must be dealt with in a tactful manner. One way of effectively managing this is for the interviewer to contact the individuals and attempt to allay any fears or anxieties that may have built up by stressing the importance of their (the respondents') input. Another way is to contact the persons through a letter or memorandum. Under no circumstances, however, should threats or any other type of coercion be used. This would only make an already bad situation worse.

Scheduling conflicts are more common at the senior management levels. Because of various time constraints, executives are more likely to have to reschedule than are lower-level personnel. When this occurs, the interviewer should contact the individuals and request alternate dates and times when they will be available. When interviews are formally rescheduled, a confirmation letter should be sent from the interviewer and a copy provided to the team leader (assuming, of course, that they are different persons) who in turn notes and records it on the project time line.

A major consideration in the rescheduling of face-to-face interviews relates to logistics and their associated costs. Where individual interviews are scheduled to be conducted in a variety of locations (which requires the interviewer or perhaps some of the interviewees to travel to different sites), the costs related to travel and per diem must be weighed against the predicted value and quality of the data to be obtained. Depending on the interview population sample size and the project budget, rescheduling face-to-face interviews may actually be cost prohibitive. However, because a high response rate is obviously desirable, it may be a good idea to attempt to reschedule but to actually conduct them over the telephone. Another way is to disqualify the interviewee from the list of potentially eligible candidates in favor of another person who is considered equally suitable but is logistically or more geographically accessible. This is known as substitution.

### Resolving Focus Group Scheduling Conflicts

As stated earlier, scheduling focus groups can be frustrating because one is dealing with multiple individual schedules. Because of this, it is very probable that last-minute scheduling conflicts will arise. One way to manage focus group scheduling conflicts is to designate alternate personnel who can substitute for those who are unable to participate. In order to do this effectively, however, any alternates must be kept informed as to the status of the focus group composition and schedule. Where no suitable alternates are available, two other options should be explored:

1. Attempt to reschedule *all* members. All group members should be contacted and presented with a variety of optional dates and times.
2. Do nothing. Simply consider the individual(s) who are not able to participate as ineligible and proceed with the focus group anyway.

The problem with the first option is, given that focus groups are normally comprised of between six to twelve persons, the probability of reaching consensus on alternate yet mutually agreeable dates and times is low. The problem with the second option is that the depth and amount of feedback becomes diminished by going ahead and conducting the focus group without the desired number of participants. This can degenerate the quality of data that the focus group was intended to produce. These problems are further compounded where multiple groups are concerned and increase exponentially with subgroups who are scheduled to meet at varying times and then again in plenary sessions (see Chapter 4). Also, as with individual interviews, cost factors relating to travel and so on must also be considered. Many times the costs involved prohibit rescheduling entire focus group sessions altogether.

### Rescheduling On-Site Observations

As with individual interviews and focus groups, there are a number of factors affecting the rescheduling of on-site observations. Personnel who are the subjects of observations may harbor the same fears and apprehensions as those designated to undergo individual interviews and may, therefore, be absent during periods when the observations are to take place. Of course, if the observations are unannounced, the subjects have no knowledge of when they are to occur and, therefore, cannot plan to be absent.

When subjects are going to be absent during scheduled on-site observations, the observer or SME should first attempt to contact the individuals and, in certain cases, their supervisors, in an effort to reschedule the observation times. Every attempt to determine why the subjects will not be available should be made. In those cases where anxieties or fears about the intent and purpose of the observation are discovered, the observer or SME should use approaches similar to the ones used to reschedule interviews, namely, to calm employee anxieties by stressing why the observation is being conducted, why certain individuals were chosen as observation subjects, and what will be done with the observation data once they have been collected. Moreover, the observer should stress the importance of the individual's role in the observation process and should make every effort to motivate them to participate. Again, cost factors must be taken into consideration, especially if they require the observer or SME to travel to different locations. A cost–benefit analysis may show that rescheduling the observation would be cost prohibitive when weighed against the quality and value the data are expected to produce.

## DETERMINING RESPONSE RATES

Of special concern to needs analysts are response rates or, rather, the number of survey questionnaires projected to be completed and returned. Some estimates place this at fewer than half of all the questionnaires mailed. A low response rate can be detrimental because it not only reduces the size of the population sample but it can also skew the results. Moreover, valid generalizations regarding the assessment's outcome cannot be confidently made.

Ideally, one would like to obtain a questionnaire return rate of 100 percent; however, due to variables beyond anyone's control, this is highly improbable. Although there are no concrete rules governing the estimation of response rates, a realistic goal is to try to obtain a minimal rate of between 70 to 80 percent.[1] This is based on the assumption that if there are more than 30 percent nonreturns, the results of the assessment would be questionable. However, response rate estimates are generally not expressed in such concrete terms because they are tied to a number of factors, such as the scope and tone of the questionnaire topics, the composition of the assessment sample population, the time frame in which it is conducted (e.g., an assessment conducted over the summer months may have a lower response rate due to vacations, etc.), and the type of plan devised to compensate for nonresponse.[2]

A simple formula for determining an acceptable questionnaire response rate is this:

$$(N \times E) = R$$

where

N = number of eligible population members

E = minimum level of response acceptability expressed as a percentage

R = the desired response rate

To illustrate, assume a survey questionnaire was distributed to a sample population of 2,000 individuals. Given a minimum acceptability level of 70 percent, the estimated response rate (R) would be 1,400 or, using the formula, $(2{,}000 \times 0.70) = 1{,}400$.

Alternatively, response rates for individual interviews, focus groups, and on-site observations are generally estimated to be higher because of the absence of most of the variables that are associated with survey questionnaires.

These are usually set at a 90 percent threshold or better. For example, assuming an eligible interview population of thirty individuals, the minimum number that would need to be conducted in order to establish validity would be 27 (i.e., $[30 \times 0.90] = 27$).

### Handling Nonresponses

*Contacting Questionnaire Nonrespondents.* Although this is not a scheduling problem per se, individuals who have not completed and returned the questionnaire (nonrespondents) present obstacles to the successful management and completion of the assessment project. Nonresponses adversely affect not only the quantity of data collected but also their quality. Although a large response rate alone does not guarantee quality (see Chapter 4), one would want as high a rate as possible in order to produce broader representation across the assessment population. This lends validity to the results and subsequent recommendations. As stated earlier, a 100-percent response rate is desirable, albeit improbable, even with a small population of fifty or so individuals. Where respondents are situated in varied geographic locations, an even smaller response rate would be predictable. In an effort to increase the rate, it is imperative that, where possible, nonrespondents be contacted and urged to complete and return the questionnaire.[3]

Where coded questionnaires are used, the assessment team leader should identify nonrespondents by accessing the key list and then contacting them. This can be done by calling the individuals or by sending an informal memorandum reminding them that the questionnaire completion and return date is approaching (or has already passed) and urging them to complete and return it. As an added incentive, the notification could also include a statement stressing the importance of their input. An example is included in Figure 6.1.

Where noncoded questionnaires are used, there is no way to identify individual nonrespondents. In these instances, it is best to use some type of generalized announcement. This can take the form of interoffice memorandums, posters or notices on company bulletin boards, e-mail notices on the organization's computer network, and announcements in any of the company's internal publications (e.g., newsletters and so on). The reminder should originate from senior management and include a restatement of why the assessment is being conducted and the importance of getting each person's candid and frank feedback. It should also highlight where and to whom the completed questionnaires should be sent and by what means. An example of a generalized announcement is included in Figure 6.2. Overall, the tone for any such announcement should be motivational.

Another way for managing questionnaire nonresponse is known as the *proxy method.* A proxy respondent is essentially an individual who is considered to be a suitable substitute when an individual who was originally selected cannot or should not, for one reason or another, participate.[4]

**Figure 6.1**
Informal Nonrespondent Reminder Memorandum

MEMORANDUM TO: TRAINING NEEDS ASSESSMENT RESPONDENT CODE #: 26449

FROM: JOHN SMITH, PRESIDENT

In looking through our records we have noticed that we have not yet received the training needs assessment survey questionnaire sent to you. Because the information and feedback obtained from this survey is important to each of us individually as well as collectively, I urge you to please take a few minutes and complete all sections and return it by September 30 via the interoffice mail to:

Brenda Garrett
Administrative Assistant
Human Resources
5th Floor
Phone (interoffice) 3418
E-mail address: BGHR3418

If you have misplaced the original survey questionnaire sent to you, please contact Ms. Garrett who will send you another copy. Your input is vital to the continued growth and success of our organization. Please be assured that your responses will be held in the strictest confidence. We're interested in "*what's* said, not in *who said what*!" Thank you for your cooperation.

## DATA-PROCESSING DECISIONS

The advent of the personal computer and the ever-increasing sophistication of software has had a profound impact on needs assessment administration, data input, manipulation, and analysis. Technology now provides the ways and means for electronically tabulating and analyzing data and adds to the variety of reporting options.[5]

### Computer Systems and Software Considerations

With the technologies now available, organizations have access to both the hardware and software needed to design and administer organizationally specific needs assessments. Since the costs of the equipment (hardware) and software continue to decline, investing in them is wise, even if they would be infrequently used. When compared to the amount of time required to hand record, compile, and perform statistical tests on the assessment data, the initial costs involved in purchasing equipment and software become minimal.

All software requires time to learn its use (the *learning curve*). A major factor associated with this learning curve is deciding which software package best fits the organization's needs. Depending on the extent of available resources, many organizations have chosen not to purchase commercially available packages but have opted instead to have them custom developed

**Figure 6.2**
General Needs Assessment Questionnaire Return Announcement

| | |
|---|---|
| MEMORANDUM TO: | ALL EMPLOYEES |
| FROM: | JOHN SMITH, PRESIDENT |
| RE: | TRAINING NEEDS ASSESSMENT SURVEY QUESTIONNAIRE'S |

As you know, the Human Resource Development department has been conducting an organization-wide training needs assessment project. The goal is to develop information that leads to a planned approach to meeting organizational and individual training and development needs. Each of you will benefit by participating in two distinct ways: (1) you will have the opportunity to have your individually perceived needs considered, and (2) you have the opportunity to influence the organization's priorities in meeting strategic training and development goals.

Participation in this survey is with a guarantee of complete anonymity and security of your response. No identification with individuals is associated with survey responses nor is it assumed. Only selected staff within the HRD department will see the completed survey questionnaires.

Please complete all questions in each part of the survey and return it by September 30 to:

Brenda Garrett
Administrative Assistant
Human Resources
5th Floor
Phone (interoffice) 3418
E-mail address: BGHR3418

for their own internal use (IBM Corporation's *On-Line Opinion Survey* is such an example). For those who decide to purchase a commercially available software package, there are a number of programs available. Most modern relational data bases that are designed to run on a personal computer can provide considerable value. Most are user friendly and many have their own language which can be used to custom design specific software solutions. Also, many of the popular spreadsheets such as *Lotus 1-2-3, Quattro Pro,* and *Excel* can be very useful. Each can be set up to facilitate the data-entry process. Many such programs also have a variety of mathematical tabulating and statistical processing capabilities that are useful in the data organization, analysis, and reporting stages. Additionally, other types of software programs such as *SPSS/PC+*, *SPSS-X*, *Stat-Pac*, and *SAS/STAT* all have tabulation, organization, statistical analysis, and reporting capabilities.

There are also a number of specialized software programs now available. Although most were written for designing and administering survey questionnaires, many are also useful for entering and processing narrative data obtained from individual interviews, focus groups, and on-site observations. Known as groupware, programs such as these can be used simultaneously by groups of people over computer networks. They are designed to facilitate the qualitative and narrative data-gathering process. They can be very useful in brainstorming and decision-making sessions. They are also useful in sessions where prioritizing issues is required.[6]

A number of specialized software programs originally developed for use in marketing research have also found a place in the organizational needs assessment field. The *Survey Software System* from Insync, the *Organizational Universe Survey System* from Organization Universe Systems, and *ASTD ASSESS* from the American Society for Training and Development are three such examples. An example of a program that is used for surveys that are to be administered electronically (e.g., distributed, completed, and returned through a computer network) is *VisionQuest* from Collaborative Technologies Corporation.

Another software technology known as multi-rater assessment systems (MRAs) has also emerged. Designed primarily as a feedback instrument for appraising an individual's job performance, much of the data produced by an MRA are also useful for identifying organizational needs. *20/20 Insight—Team Leader & Team Player* from Performance Support Systems, Inc., *Synchrony* from Development Dimensions International, and *Team Member Performance Assessment* from Feedback Plus are all examples of MRAs which produce performance-appraisal data that are also useful for identifying individual as well as organizational needs.

Whatever the requirement, the use of computers and software for designing, collecting, organizing, tabulating, analyzing, and reporting needs assessment data is highly recommended.

### Establishing a Central Location for Receiving Incoming Data

Another factor in needs assessment project organization and control is the importance of establishing a central location where all incoming data is received and recorded. Although this is not imperative where feedback from individual interviews, focus groups, or on-site observations is concerned, it is critical for handling survey questionnaire data. This aspect of assessment organization and control is often overlooked until such a time when incoming data are not entered and recorded properly. Then it becomes a crisis situation.

Questionnaires are often received en masse, generally shortly after their initial distribution, later again as the deadline for their return draws near. As large numbers of surveys are received, the risk of data becoming misplaced increases. In the rush to get data entered or recorded, other handling, entry, or recording errors are prone to occur. For example, in one project 5,000 surveys were sent out. Within two weeks, 2,000 of them were returned. Since there are ten working days in a two-week period, the returns averaged 200 per day. Even with two or perhaps three receivers (i.e., data entry or recording persons), it is not difficult to see how mishaps can easily occur.

The probability for data handling or entry errors increases when more than one receiving point is involved. This is particularly true for organizations whose employees are situated in geographically diverse locations. For example, assume an organization administered a needs assessment survey to 8,000 of its employees. If each of these individuals were instructed to return the surveys to one central location, the potential for mishaps could be tremendous.

Alternative approaches to managing this problem could be to administer the survey to groups at staggered times or establish return points at each location and then transfer them from the remote to the central location one location at a time. The major disadvantage to the latter approach is that the probability for potential mishaps (e.g., missing or misplaced questionnaires) that exist with just one location is multiplied by the number of alternate or remote locations. One way to compensate for this suggests that where multiple locations are concerned, personal computers connected or networked to a central computer or bulletin board system could be used.[7] This assumes, of course, that appropriate measures to safeguard respondent anonymity (if applicable) have been taken.

Given that considerable potential for errors and other mishaps exists, the importance for sound administrative support within the assessment project team cannot be overstated. One way of controlling the handling of incoming data suggests that the team should be structured so that only specific individuals be designated as data receivers and handlers. This task usually befalls the project or team administrative support staff, which may also include any data-processing or computer systems personnel. Procedures for receiving and processing survey questionnaires should include setting up a log where codes (given that questionnaire codes are used) can be recorded. This will greatly enhance future prospects for contacting nonrespondents.

### Consistency in Data Entry and Recording

Another factor is the importance of establishing and maintaining consistency in the way that data is entered or recorded. Because the data ultimately will be subjected to statistical manipulation and testing, it is important that steps be taken to ensure consistency and conciseness in the data entry process.[8] This is applicable for all of the data gathered, regardless of the methods used (e.g., survey questionnaires, individual interviews, focus groups, on-site observations, etc.).

*Survey Questionnaire Data.* No matter how rigorous the pretest, it is not uncommon for respondents to write in their own individualized response. Because there is a significant likelihood of this occurring, some ground rules for handling questionable or incomplete answers should be established. For example, it is very possible that in attempting to answer a closed-ended True/False or Yes/No question, respondents would write in an answer like "maybe" or "possibly" rather than make a selection from the options provided. Strictly speaking, this is not an incomplete answer; however, the respondents' intentions become questionable. Therefore, at the onset of the assessment, it is necessary to decide how to treat such responses.[9] In an effort to make the task of interpreting a question as well as the response less ambiguous, many survey professionals use a format which contains options labeled "No Opinion" or "Undecided."

Two other ways in which write-ins can be effectively managed are the following: (1) Where coded questionnaires are used, one should first refer to the key list to obtain the respondents' identity and then contact them for clarification; or (2) completely dismiss or otherwise disqualify the answer (and the question).

The latter approach presents problems that can surface in the analysis stage, namely, in the form of diminished response rates.[10] Alternatively, respondents will sometimes write in an answer in an attempt to clarify why they chose their own response as opposed to selecting one from the options provided. Treating questionable responses like these can be done by including special categories in the tabulation process. If a computer is used to record the data, a commercially available software package that has this capability will be required. Where the organization is using its own internally developed custom program, the persons responsible for developing it must also include alternate response categories.

*Data from Individual Interviews.* Since the data obtained from interviews are mostly narrative, they should be carefully reviewed prior to recording them. Where tape recordings were used, they should be reviewed by both the interviewer and the project team leader in order to qualify response appropriateness and applicability. The interviewer's observations should be carefully weighed, especially those linked to keyed questions used in either (or both) the primary and any correlational data-gathering methods (e.g., survey questionnaires). This helps to establish correlational value between any aggregate methods used.

Some experts advocate a word-for-word transcription of the interview.[11] This requires considerable input which is neither central or even peripheral to the goals of the assessment. Under such circumstances, the team leader or HRD analyst with the help of the interviewer must first determine the extent to which an entire transcript is helpful for determining causality.

The interviewer should provide feedback on observed respondent behavioral patterns, keeping in mind that such feedback be kept as neutral and as unbiased as possible. This should be submitted with the interview scripts and notes. This information should also include the dates and times the interviews were conducted as well as any additional commentary provided by the interviewer that is not contained in the script or in any taped recordings.

*Data from Focus Groups.* All notes and comments from focus group sessions should first be reviewed by the moderator and the HRD analyst or team leader prior to formally recording them. This requires that a format agreed to by both the analyst and the focus group moderator be developed.[12] Since most of the data provided by the focus group moderator will be in commentary format and, therefore, is subject to personal biasing, debriefing sessions between the moderator and the analyst should be conducted after each group has concluded. The results of this debriefing should then be compared to the moderator's comments as a way of identifying correlational values.

When entering or recording this type of data, they should be arranged to complement the structure and conduct of the focus group session(s). Feedback directly related to the goals of the assessment should be highlighted or otherwise emphasized along with feedback that is linked to key questions obtained through an aggregate data-gathering method.

*Data from On-Site Observations.* Debriefing sessions should be conducted between the team leader/analyst and the observer (SME) after each scheduled observation has concluded. The notes taken from the observations can then be used to compare and correlate any feedback that was obtained from other methods. Because this type of information can be both qualitative as well as quantitative, a concerted effort must be made to minimize personal biasing. Where observations have been conducted in a production or manufacturing environment that has centered on work processes, systems, and procedures, the data will usually contain significant quantitative information. Provisions should be made in the data entry system to allow for input of quantitatively based feedback, the results of which can provide useful information for monitoring productivity improvement efforts.

*Data from Other Sources.* Feedback can also come from sources outside of the target assessment population. For example, informal comments and observations from senior management and other employees as well as from customers and suppliers are all potentially valuable sources that should be included in the data-collection process (see Chapter 3). Additional information can also be obtained through reviews of the organization's personnel records and from any training evaluations or other interventions previously implemented. This type of data should be kept separate from that obtained from the target assessment population. It should be treated as peripheral information because its primary use will be to add additional breadth and depth to the data analysis phase.

## PRELIMINARY BIASING OF INCOMING DATA

Once the assessment is formally underway and incoming data is being entered or recorded, patterns relating to *how* individuals responded to certain questions will inevitably begin to emerge. While this may at first appear to be of little significance, the simple act of reading incoming data can and many times does introduce bias into the subsequent data analysis phases. Known as *preliminary biasing*, the potential of this happening is not very important where quantitative data are concerned, however, it is critical when dealing with qualitative or narrative feedback. Thus, it is important to discuss how to avoid or, at least, to minimize, preliminary biasing. Taking steps to prevent this from occurring early on is crucial in preventing one from forming any preconceived notions about the assessment's outcome before all the data have been received, recorded, and analyzed.

Preliminary biasing occurs when individuals are exposed to information they will eventually use as a basis for analysis and formulating recommendations. Previously, emphasis was placed on formulating needs assessment objectives through a variety of goal determination processes that were driven by (1) cause-and-effect relationships (e.g., predetermined, measured, observable, or desired), (2) intuitive or deductive reasoning, and (3) various types of forecasting methods. These were used as the foundation for developing questionnaire items, interview scripts, and focus group and observation agendas, all of which may contain key questions directly related to the type of effect that was observed or measured. These are important because they drive the entire needs assessment process. Therefore, as incoming data are received and reviewed for completeness, analysts' attention can be easily yet unintentionally drawn to key questions and responses.

Depending on how closely analysts review the incoming data, patterns will begin to emerge, particularly where closed-ended quantitative data are concerned. Patterns in qualitative and narrative feedback, usually caused by repetition of key words or phrases, will also begin to appear. Since all of this information has to be compiled and put into some semblance of order, analysts are continuously exposed to it prior to initiating any formal type of analysis. This exposure, even though many times only randomized, can easily bias or otherwise influence the analysts and cause them to subconsciously form a preconception about the assessment's final results before all the data have been collected and analyzed. This impairs objectivity and can have negative consequences on the conclusions and recommendations that eventually will be made.

Although it is virtually impossible to completely eliminate preliminary biasing, there are steps that can be taken to offset its effects. Some of these are the following:

1. When randomly spot-checking for data entry consistency, analysts should focus only on how the data were recorded rather than on their content. This applies to both quantitative as well as qualitative data.
2. Feedback, comments, and so on from interviewers, focus group moderators, and observers should be received in a structured, written format which can then be briefly scanned for completeness as opposed to content. During the formal analysis stage, questions regarding content can be addressed through debriefings in an effort to clear up any vague or ambiguous points or discrepancies.
3. Because it is often necessary to hold debriefings before beginning the formal data analysis phase, every attempt should be made to focus on the conduct and the mechanics of the data-gathering methods as opposed, again, to their content.

Overall, uniformity and consistency are keys to entering, recording, and verifying incoming data.

## SUMMARY

Since scheduling conflicts will invariably arise, it is useful to predict and plan for them. Scheduling adjustments are frustrating and can disrupt the entire assessment project. The reasons or causes for scheduling conflicts should be investigated by the project team leader. In the interest of obtaining as large a response from the sample population as possible, every effort should be made to resolve conflicts. It is often necessary to examine the costs associated with rescheduling interviews, focus groups, and so on because rescheduling may be cost prohibitive when compared against the predicted quality and value of the data.

A critical part of the needs assessment process lies in accurately predicting response rates, especially where survey questionnaires are concerned. Most professional pollsters advocate a minimum response rate of 70 to 80 percent, while others feel that a rate of 50 percent is sufficient to attain a minimal degree of accuracy and relevancy. However, with the ideal being 100 percent (i.e., everyone who is included in the sample population participates), it appears that the 70 to 80 percent range represents a threshold below which the validity of the survey results may be called into question. In an effort to obtain as high a response rate as possible, careful examination of alternative approaches to handling nonrespondents should be made. These usually take the form of personal contacts (where nonrespondents are identifiable, as in the case where anonymously coded questionnaires are used) or follow-up letters. Follow-ups should be designed to motivate individuals to participate by stressing the importance of their input. Where individual interviews are concerned, personal contacts supported by follow-up or confirmation letters will generally yield satisfactory results.

Rescheduling focus groups presents a unique challenge. This problem is further compounded when subgroups are involved. To resolve focus group scheduling problems, the analyst must first weigh the necessity for conducting them against the expected level of quality information to be gained. Many times, rescheduling focus groups does not make good financial sense, particularly where individuals that are designated to participate originate from geographically diverse locations. Where on-site observations are used, the same considerations apply.

The advent of the personal computer and the ever-increasing sophistication of software programs have opened up new and broad opportunities for organizations wishing to custom design their own needs assessments. With the software readily available and reasonably priced, organizations would find it wise to invest in the technology, even if it were to be infrequently used. When compared to the costs of hand tabulating assessment data, the investment in computer software becomes minimal.

When using computers to enter and tabulate assessment data, a central receiving and processing point must be established. This is important because survey data are often received in clusters and the potential for misplacing or improperly recording them is relatively high. To offset this, only certain individuals in a centralized location should be designated to handle and process incoming data.

Consistency in data entry is critical. In particular, the data entry persons should be given clear instructions on how to record questionable responses. These usually take the form of write-ins where respondents provide their own answer as opposed to selecting one from the choices provided. Proactively anticipating this and developing plans on how to compensate for it will greatly facilitate the data-handling process. Likewise, procedures for recording data received from individual interviews, focus groups, and on-site observations should also be devised and put into place. Of particular importance is the necessity to make a conscious effort not to allow emerging data patterns to influence or to otherwise cause the formulation of preconceived notions about the outcome until all of the data have been received, recorded, and analyzed. Uniformity and consistency in data handling is mandatory if the subsequent analysis is to be done objectively.

## NOTES

1. N. Bradburn and S. Sudman, *Polls and Surveys: Understanding What They Tell Us* (San Francisco: Jossey-Bass, 1988).

2. J. Lessler and W. Kalsbeek, *Nonsampling Error in Surveys* (New York: Wiley & Sons, 1992).

3. D. Miller, *Handbook of Research Design and Social Measurement*, 5th ed. (Newbury Park, Calif.: Sage Publications, 1991).

4. Lessler and Kalsbeek, p. 169.

5. R. Dunnington, "New Methods and Technologies," in *Improving Organizational Surveys: New Directions and Methods*, P. Rosenfeld, J. Edwards, and M. Thomas, eds., *American Behavioral Scientist*, Vol. 36, No. 4, pp. 512–530.

6. P. Rosenfeld, S. Booth-Kewley, and J. Edwards, "Computer Assisted Surveys," in *Improving Organizational Surveys: New Directions and Methods*, P. Rosenfeld, J. Edwards, and M. Thomas, eds., *American Behavioral Scientist*, Vol. 36, No. 4, pp. 485–511.

7. Ibid., p. 495.

8. R. Miller, "The Design and Implementation of Employee Opinion Surveys," *Employment Relations Today*, Vol. 16, No. 4, pp. 315–319.

9. H. Schuman and S. Presser, *Questions and Answers in Attitude Surveys: Experiments on Question Form, Wording, and Context* (New York: Academic Press, 1981).

10. S. McClelland, "Training Needs Assessment Data Gathering Methods—Part I: Survey Questionnaires," *Journal of European Industrial Training*, Vol. 18, No. 1, pp. 22–26.

11. R. Little and D. Rubin, *Statistical Analysis with Missing Data* (New York: Wiley & Sons, 1983).

12. D. Sink, "Focus Groups as an Approach to Outcomes Assessment," *American Review of Public Administration*, Vol. 21, No. 3, pp. 197–204.

PART IV

# Data Analysis and Evaluation

CHAPTER 7

# Statistical Analysis Methods

In Chapter 6, a significant amount of emphasis was placed on the use of computers for processing incoming needs assessment data. The speed with which it can be entered and statistically analyzed gives the organization an efficient and cost-effective means for designing custom needs assessments. However, to more fully understand what the computer-generated statistics mean, it is necessary to develop an understanding of statistical terminologies, techniques, and procedures.

Statistics are a fundamental tool used in virtually all types of research. They are indispensible to analysts because they provide a way to arrange, rearrange, and manipulate data. Statistics can be used to describe the various relationships between different sets of data. They also can be used to infer general relationships that are observed in a small population to a much larger one. They also can uncover hidden relationships that are not readily observable. Thus, they serve a variety of purposes, from identifying hidden relationships to solving routine as well as nonroutine problems.

One major problem associated with the use of statistics is that most people lack a fundamental understanding of what statisics are, what they are supposed to do, and how they should be used. This lack of understanding has created a fear of statistics. Many individuals consider statistics to be too complicated and to involve too much time. To others, statistically produced outcomes mean very little unless there is some sort of factual evidence to support what the statistics represent.

To become a good needs analyst does not require an in-depth knowledge of statistics. That is not to say that one should not acquire a fundamental understanding of what statistics are and, more appropriately, how they are used. Indeed, one should have at least a cursory understanding of what statistical methods should be used under certain circumstances. However, the variety of excellent statistical software programs now available takes the mystery out of statistics and places the ability to perform complex analyses at everyone's fingertips.

This chapter is designed to provide an overview and summary of some of the statistical methods commonly used in analyzing needs assessment data. It is not intended to be an in-depth review. Many of the examples used are provided for illustrative purposes only. For more detailed information of the various methods presented, the reader is advised to consult any reputable text on research and statistical methods.

## STATISTICS AS A FUNDAMENTAL RESEARCH TOOL

*Descriptive* and *inferential* statistics are used to translate quantitative and qualitative data into meaningful information. Descriptive statistics are used to summarize information while inferential statistics are used to predict if what has been observed in a sample can—and probably will—be observed in the whole. Descriptive statistics are useful for summarizing, logically arranging, and presenting needs assessment data. Alternatively, inferential statistics are useful for drawing inferences from a sample of employees and then applying the results across organizational levels.

Even though many of the software programs mentioned in the previous chapter have descriptive and inferential capabilities, one must develop a working knowledge and understanding of statistical terms and methods so that assessment research data can be accurately interpreted and communicated to others.

### Types of Scores

Measurements are fundamental to statistical needs assessment research. They consist of scores that are usually referred to in one of five ways: as the *continuous score*, the *rank*, the *artificial dichotomy*, the *true dichotomy*, and as a *category*.

Continuous scores are scores that theoretically occur at any point along a continuum. Examples are scores that are drawn from intelligence and other types of standardized tests. Rank scores are scores that express the position of a person or item as a variable that is relative to the positions held by other persons or items. An example of ranked scores is a test that shows the number of units produced by individuals from two separate groups with those having the highest output being ranked first and those producing less ranked second, third, and so on. Artificial dichotomy is a variable that has only two values. An example of an artificial dichotomy would be a pass or fail test. True dichotomy exists when members of two groups have some type of characteristic that makes it possible to differentiate them from other groups. For example, a study that is designed to investigate the impact that gender has on survey responses would examine the differences between male and female values and/or perceptions. Categories contain values of a variable that can yield more than two discrete noncontinuous scores. For example, a group of employees participating in an on-site observation could be divided into categories such as (1) their willingness to participate, (2) their unwillingness to participate, (3) their correct performance of designated tasks, and (4) their incorrect performance of designated tasks.

## DESCRIPTIVE STATISTICS

Descriptive statistics are used to draw generalizations from data that have been logically organized. This is useful when large amounts of data are too cumbersome to present as part of a final report and when including large amounts of statistical information in a report is inappropriate.

The organization of research data is fundamental in descriptive statistics. Frequency distributions and the presentation of data in a graphical format are methods that are most frequently used.

### Scales of Measurement

In research, measurement is a process for translating observations into numbers. Basically, there are four types of measurement scales: *nominal*, *ordinal*, *interval*, and *ratio*.

The nominal scale involves placing numbers into categories that are qualitatively different. The only relationship between these categories is that each is different from the others. For example, classifying a needs assessment sample population according to gender is a form of nominal measurement. The principal purpose of the nominal scale is to identify the members or objects of a given category.

Ordinal scales are used to identify the relationship between individuals or objects with respect to a particular attribute. It does not, however, indicate the distance or how much difference there is between them. For example, ordinal measurement can be used when managers are ranked on certain leadership characteristics, such as vision, risk taking, decision making, and so on, rather than on a more subjective measurement, such as their contribution to profitability.

Interval scales are used to rank or to provide order to a given number of items and then to measure the distance between them. Interval scales are used, for example, in IQ tests, where the difference in one set of scores may approximate the differences between another.

Ratio scales are used to establish equal intervals between two or more points. This provides an "absolute zero" reference. From this, the ratios between any two given values can be found. For example, one can say that a three-foot yardstick is three times the length of a twelve-inch ruler, but one cannot say that an employee with a 0-percent manufacturing defect rate is twice as smart or as skilled as an employee who has a 50-percent defect rate.

One can, however, say that the rate (a tangible reference point) of one employee is twice as good as that of the other. Ratio scales can, for example, provide a way of identifying gaps between the performance levels of two different individuals because it is quantitatively measurable. Once a discrepancy like this is uncovered, an assessment could be initiated to determine why such gaps exist.

### Frequency Distributions

Frequency distributions arrange individual data into a logical and systematic order from the lowest value to the highest. They involve developing a list of individual measures in a column format starting with the highest measure at the top and then continuing downward and ending with the lowest score at the bottom. Since several identical scores will customarily occur in any distribution, it is common practice to not list each score separately but rather to indicate in a separate column the number of times a particular score occurred. Table 7.1 shows the frequency distribution of responses to an Agree/Disagree, closed-ended question.

Frequency distributions are useful for examining the general shapes of a given distribution of scores. Organizing scores in this manner permits observation of their *spread* (i.e., whether they are distributed evenly or whether the scores appear in clusters and where these clusters occur). From this, some immediate generalizations about how each question was answered and how groups (or clusters) of respondents answered certain questions can be drawn. One can then see what questions provoked what types of responses and at what level(s) these occurred.

## MEASURES OF CENTRAL TENDENCY

A convenient way of summarizing data is to find a single score or number that can reliably represent a set or group of measures. This can be done

**Table 7.1**
Frequency Distribution for Agree/Disagree Question

| Question No. | "AGREE" | Frequency ($f$) | "DISAGREE" | Frequency ($f$) |
|---|---|---|---|---|
| 1. | ///// // | 7 | ///// | 5 |
| 2. | ///// / | 6 | ///// / | 6 |
| 3. | /// | 3 | ///// //// | 9 |
| 4. | ///// /// | 8 | //// | 4 |
| 5. | ///// //// | 9 | /// | 3 |

through *measures of central tendency* consisting of the *mode*, the *median*, and the *mean*.

The mode is that value which occurs with the greatest frequency in a given distribution. For example, the following represents data that were taken from a production schedule and reflects the number of units produced per worker:

| | | | | | | | | |
|---|---|---|---|---|---|---|---|---|
| Employee: | 2 | 6 | 7 | 1 | 8 | 3 | 5 | 4 |
| Units produced: | 10 | 11 | 11 | 12 | 13 | 13 | 13 | 11 |

From this, one can calculate the mode to be 13 (the number of units produced which appears with the greatest frequency). The mode, however, is generally not reliable as an indicator of central tendency because it is unstable. For example, observations drawn more than once from the same sample group may produce very different modes due to factors that cannot be controlled (e.g., employees' psychological state, their attitudes, fears, or uncertainties, the condition of the company's equipment, etc.). Because of their simplicity, modes are the only measure that may be legitimately used with nominal scales.

The median is essentially that point in a distribution below which 50 percent of the scores fall. For example, using the numbers from the previous example, the median (12.5) falls halfway between 12.0 and 13.0. To find this value, the scores of the distribution are first placed in ranked order. Next, the point below which 50 percent of the given scores lie is found.

The mean is the most widely used measure of central tendency. It is the sum of all numbers in a distribution divided by the number of cases in the same distribution. For example, the following represents the numbers of units produced per worker:

| Employee | Group A | Group B |
|---|---|---|
| 1 | 20 | 23 |
| 2 | 24 | 23 |
| 3 | 21 | 25 |
| 4 | 23 | 21 |
| 5 | 19 | 20 |
| 6 | 22 | 19 |
| 7 | 25 | 26 |
| 8 | 27 | 26 |

The mean for Group A is 22.63 while the mean for Group B is 22.88. Thus, the mean or standard number of units produced between the two groups would be 22.75 [(22.63 + 22.88) ÷ 2]. This figure could be interpreted to represent the average number of units each worker is expected to produce within a given period of time. Information like this can be valuable for establishing production standards or expected output levels.

When comparing the three measures, the mean is generally regarded as being most precise because it takes every score into account. It is considered to be most stable because if a number of samples are randomly drawn, the mean will vary less from one sample to another than the median or the mode.

### Distribution Shapes

Distribution shapes are used to visually display relationships between the measures of central tendency. When a distribution is symmetrical and consists of only one mode, the three measures of central tendency will coincide. If it is not symmetrical, the distribution is said to be skewed, either positively, where the mean will appear to the right of the mode, or negatively, where it will appear to the left. Skewed distributions occur when the measures of central tendency differ. Figure 7.1 illustrates a symmetrical distribution, while Figures 7.2 and 7.3 show negatively and positively skewed distributions, respectively.

### Measures of Variability

While useful, measures of central tendency only describe data in terms of averages. They do not provide information on the variations between a set of scores and the mean. The most commonly used measure to accomplish this is known as the *range*. The range is calculated by subtracting the smallest value in the distribution from the highest. For example, given the data listed previously for production groups A and B, the range for Group A is 8 (27 – 19) and the range for Group B is 7 (26 – 19). When applied with the means, these data could be used to establish minimal or required performance levels or standards.

The *variance* represents the average value of the squares of deviations from the mean and is mathematically expressed as

$$\sigma^2 = \frac{(\Sigma x^2)}{N}$$

where

$\sigma^2$ = the variance

$\Sigma$ = the sum of . . .

x = the deviation of each score from the mean

N = the number of cases in the distribution

Although variances show the degree to which a set of numbers vary from the mean, they are not particularly useful because they represent squared values.

**Figure 7.1**
A Symmetrical Distribution

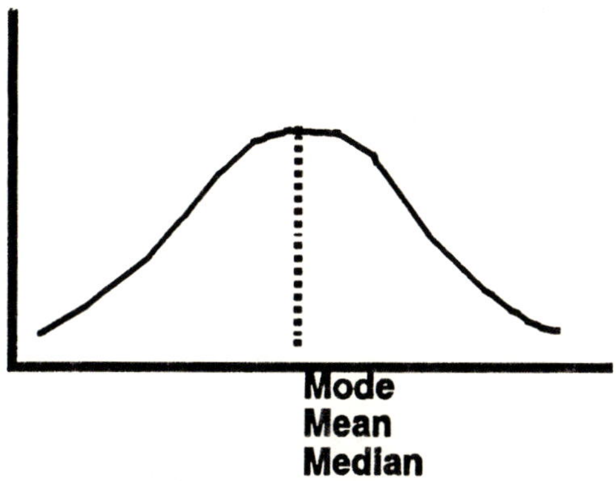


**Figure 7.2**
A Negatively Skewed Distribution

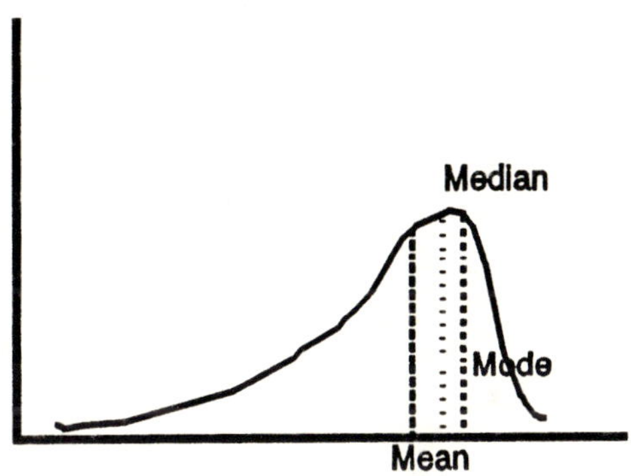


**Figure 7.3**
A Positively Skewed Distribution

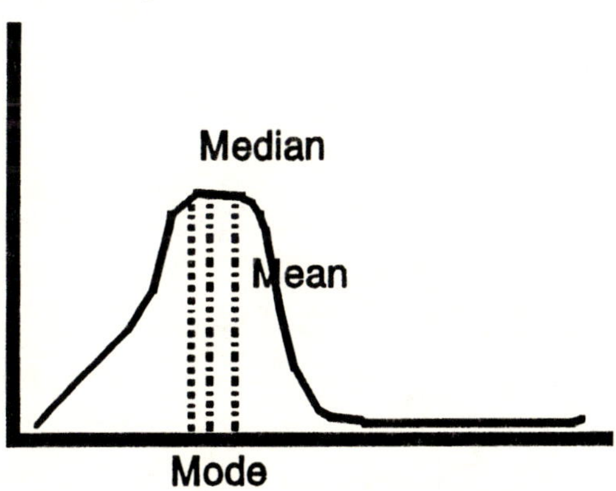

Alternatively, the measure of *standard deviation* (SD) is more useful because it represents the degree to which a set of scores deviates from the mean value. To illustrate, consider the data in Table 7.2. Column B contains production data (number of units produced) for seven employees. The mean is calculated to be 22.00. Column C shows the deviation for each of these scores, and Column D shows the squares of each of the deviation scores, whose sum equals 50.00. By placing this value into the formula and then dividing by the number of employees, the value received is 7.14. The square root of 7.14 = 2.68. Using the formula provided, the calculation would appear as

$$\sigma = \sqrt{(50 \div 7)} = \sqrt{7.14} = 2.68$$

The standard deviation is useful because it is stable, meaning that in a normal distribution repeated samples taken from the same population are likely to produce similar results. It provides a way for describing the scores of a group based on a single measure. The standard deviation is also used to form the basis for various types of scores. One example is known as *z-scores*. The z-score is a type of standard used frequently in needs assessment research to express one person's performance in relation to the performance of the group. Z-scores are calculated by first subtracting the mean score of the total group from a person's raw score. The result is then divided by the standard deviation of the group. What makes z-scores useful is that they enable one to view over time an individual's performance in relation to the performance of an entire group.

**Table 7.2**
Computation of Standard Deviation

| (A) Employee number: | (B) X | (C) $x = X - Y$ | (D) $x^2 = (X - Y)^2$ |
|---|---|---|---|
| 1 | 22 | 0 | 0 |
| 2 | 24 | -2 | +4 |
| 3 | 24 | -2 | +4 |
| 4 | 20 | 0 | 0 |
| 5 | 26 | -4 | +16 |
| 6 | 21 | +1 | +1 |
| 7 | 17 | -5 | +25 |
| $\Sigma X = 154 \div 7 = 22$ | | | $50 = \Sigma x^2$ |

## CORRELATIONAL STATISTICS

Correlational statistics are used to identify relationships between two or more groups of data known as variables. One approach to identifying whether a relationship exists between two variables is to plot them on a *scatter diagram* (which is actually a two-dimensional table). Here, one set of scores on one variable is plotted on a horizontal axis (the x-axis) with the lowest value on the left and the highest value on the right. The other set of scores is plotted on the vertical axis (the y-axis) from the lowest on the bottom to the highest on the top. The position of each score on the diagram is then indicated by a single point. Figure 7.4 illustrates a positive correlation scatter diagram.

The relationship between two variables is not, however, always positive. For example, two variables, such as productivity and absenteeism, may be found to have a negative relationship; that is, as absenteeism increases, productivity decreases. Figure 7.5 is an example of a negative correlation.

### Correlation Coefficients

Correlation coefficients show the linear strength between two variables which result in a value between -1.00 and +1.00. A -1.00 indicates a perfect negative relationship between the two variables, while a +1.00 indicates a perfect positive relationship. The midpoint, 0.00, indicates that there is no relationship between the variables at all. Figure 7.6 provides an approximate interpretation of correlation coefficient ranges, while Figure 7.7 shows scat-

**Figure 7.4**
Positive Scatter Diagram

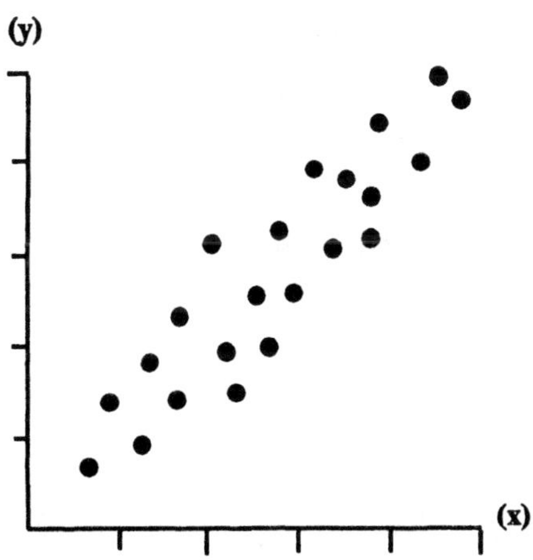


**Figure 7.5**
Negative Scatter Diagram

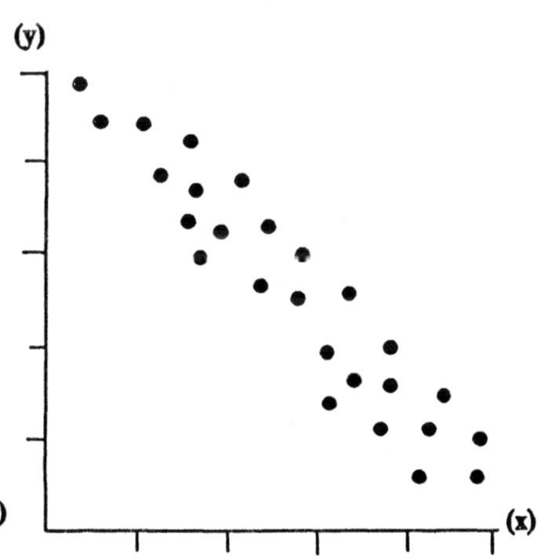

ter diagrams reflecting perfect positive, perfect negative, and zero (0.00) correlation coefficient relationships.

Another way of displaying and revealing the amount of variations between variables is called a *histogram*. A histogram takes measurement data and displays their distribution. It provides a quick pictorial representation of any surprises or irregularities in data distributions that should otherwise be normal or symmetrical. Figure 7.8 is an example of a histogram showing variations between response rates (variable #1) and survey questionnaire length (variable #2).

An English statistician by the name of Karl Pearson developed the most commonly used correlation index. Known as *Pearson's product–moment correlation coefficient*, it states that each person's z-score on one variable ($x$) is multiplied by their z-score on the other variable ($y$). The results are then added and the sum is divided by the number of pairs. *Pearson r*, as it is also known,

**Figure 7.6**
Approximate Interpretation of Correlation Coefficient Ranges

| VALUE | APPROXIMATE INTERPRETATION |
|---|---|
| -1.0 | Perfect (Negative Correlation) |
| -.8 | High Degree (Negative Correlation) |
| -.6 | Medium Degree (Negative Correlation) |
| -.4 | Low Degree (Negative Correlation) |
| -.2 | Little to No Degree (Negative) |
| 0.0 | No Degree |
| .2 | Little to No Degree (Positive) |
| .4 | Low Degree (Positive Correlation) |
| .6 | Medium Degree (Positive Correlation) |
| .8 | High Degree (Positive Correlation) |
| 1.0 | Perfect (Positive Correlation) |

**Figure 7.7**
Perfect Positive, Perfect Negative, and Zero (0.00) Correlation Coefficients

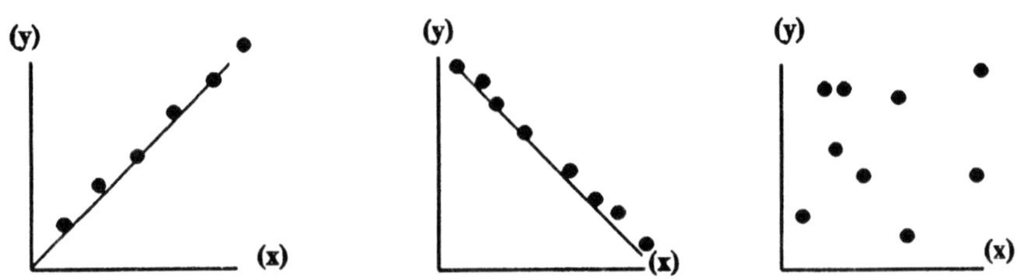

**Figure 7.8**
Histogram Showing Effect of Survey Length on Response Rate(s)

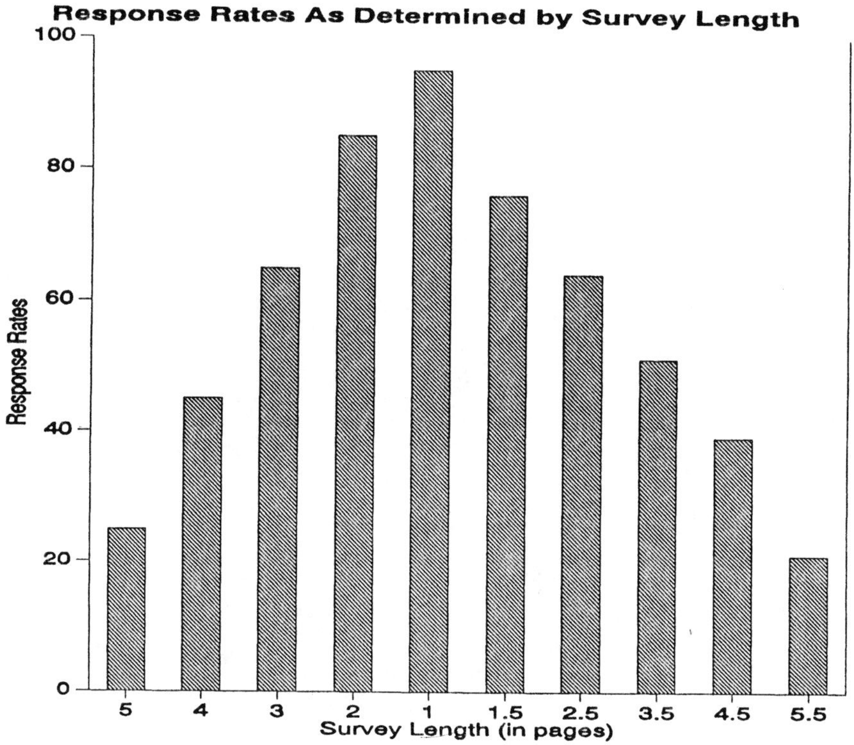


is used for calculating the mean of the z-score products. The mathematical formula for Pearson r is

$$r = \frac{\sum z_x z_y}{N}$$

where

r = the product–moment correlation coefficient (Pearson r)

$\sum z_x z_y$ = the sum of the z-scores

N = the number of paired scores

Where a large number of cases is concerned (as in a large assessment sample population), converting individual z-scores becomes tedious. Therefore, the following formula can be used:

$$r = \frac{\sum xy - \frac{(\sum x)(\sum y)}{N}}{\sqrt{[\sum x^2 - \frac{(\sum x)^2}{N}][\sum y^2 - \frac{(\sum y)^2}{N}]}}$$

This formula will be used to compute Pearson r from the information contained in Table 7.3.

$$r = \{3279 - [(143)(159)] \div 7\} \div \sqrt{\{2945 - [(143)^2 \div 7]\}\{3653 - [(159)^2 \div 7]\}} = 0.98$$

Looking back at Figure 7.6, we see that the correlation for these two values is very high. To illustrate further, Table 7.4 shows the Pearson r correlation between financial incentives and improved productivity. One can readily see there is a high degree of correlation between them.

$$r = \{9292 - [(417)(443)] \div 20\} \div \sqrt{\{8751 - [(417)^2 \div 20]\}\{9871 - [(443)^2 \div 20]\}} = 0.96$$

## Interpreting Coefficient Correlation

Statistical correlation between two variables provides a mathematical indication of their relationship. However, it is also useful to keep the following points in mind when interpreting the results of coefficient correlations: (1) Causation (cause of the measured or observed effect) is not necessarily indi-

**Table 7.3**
Values for Computing Pearson Product–Moment Correlation Coefficient

| (1) Respondent | (2) $x$ | (3) $y$ | (4) $x^2$ | (5) $y^2$ | (6) $xy$ |
|---|---|---|---|---|---|
| 1 | 23 | 26 | 529 | 676 | 598 |
| 2 | 23 | 26 | 529 | 676 | 598 |
| 3 | 21 | 24 | 441 | 576 | 504 |
| 4 | 20 | 22 | 400 | 484 | 440 |
| 5 | 19 | 21 | 361 | 441 | 399 |
| 6 | 19 | 20 | 361 | 400 | 380 |
| 7 | 18 | 20 | 324 | 400 | 360 |
| **N = 7** | **Σ = 143** | **Σ = 159** | **$\Sigma x^2$ = 2945** | **$\Sigma y^2$ = 3653** | **Σxy = 3279** |

**Table 7.4**
Pearson r Computations for Correlation between Financial Incentives and Improved Productivity

| (A) Employee | (B) (X) | (C) (Y) | (D) ($X^2$) | (E) ($Y^2$) | (F) (XY) |
|---|---|---|---|---|---|
| 1 | 24 | 25 | 576 | 625 | 600 |
| 2 | 23 | 24 | 529 | 576 | 552 |
| 3 | 23 | 24 | 529 | 576 | 552 |
| 4 | 23 | 24 | 529 | 576 | 552 |
| 5 | 23 | 24 | 529 | 576 | 552 |
| 6 | 22 | 24 | 484 | 576 | 528 |
| 7 | 22 | 23 | 484 | 529 | 506 |
| 8 | 21 | 23 | 441 | 529 | 483 |
| 9 | 21 | 23 | 441 | 529 | 483 |
| 10 | 21 | 22 | 441 | 484 | 462 |
| 11 | 20 | 22 | 400 | 484 | 440 |
| 12 | 20 | 22 | 400 | 484 | 440 |
| 13 | 20 | 22 | 400 | 484 | 440 |
| 14 | 20 | 21 | 400 | 441 | 420 |
| 15 | 20 | 21 | 400 | 441 | 420 |
| 16 | 19 | 20 | 361 | 400 | 380 |
| 17 | 19 | 20 | 361 | 400 | 380 |
| 18 | 19 | 20 | 361 | 400 | 380 |
| 19 | 19 | 20 | 361 | 400 | 380 |
| 20 | 18 | 19 | 324 | 361 | 342 |
| N=20 | $\Sigma x=417$ | $\Sigma y=443$ | $\Sigma x^2=8751$ | $\Sigma y^2=9871$ | $\Sigma xy=9292$ |

cated by correlation. Correlation between two variables shows that positions in one variable are associated with positions in the other. It does not necessarily mean that changes in one variable are or can be caused by changes in the other. (2) The interpretation of correlation coefficients should be tempered with sound judgment, intuition, and experience.

For example, financial incentives were shown to have a statistically positive effect on productivity; however, the amounts of such incentives may outweigh the values or benefits actually received. In essence, a higher production volume may actually increase the cost per unit as the number of units produced likewise increases.

### Rank Coefficient Correlation

While Pearson r is used to determine the relationship between two variables, it is often useful to explore how sample populations rank certain types of criteria. This can be done by computing the correlation coefficient between rank-ordered measures or scores. This ranking of objects is highly subjective because it is based on interpretation of respondents' criteria. For example, when presented with a set of possible training topics, respondents could be required to rank them in the order of priority which they believe to be the most to the least important.

Because two or more rankings may differ in their order does not mean that there is no relationship between them. One way of identifying whether correlation between two or more ranked orders exists is to use a technique known as the *Spearman rho correlation coefficient*, which is expressed mathematically as

$$\rho = 1 - \frac{6\sum D^2}{N(n^2 - 1)}$$

where

$\rho$ = the Spearman rho correlation coefficient

$\sum D^2$ = the sum of the squares of the difference between rankings

N = the number of cases being ranked

For example, Table 7.5 contains two separate rankings of training needs.

$$\rho = 1 - [6(34) \div 8(64 - 1)] = 1 - (204 \div 504) = 0.60$$

Interpretation of the Spearman rho is the same as with Pearson r. Using the interpretation scale previously presented in Figure 7.6, one can see there is collectively a degree of positive correlation between the rankings. However, note that the individual relationship between both rankings for Item 5, Decision-Making Skills, is the same for both groups. Similar ranking approximations also exist between Items 1, 2, 3, 4, 6, and 7. Only Item 8, Accounting Skills, shows a significant difference between the two ranked scores. When taken on an individual, case-by-case basis, however, one cannot say that there is a symmetrical, a positive, or a negative correlation between the rankings.

**Table 7.5**
Ranking of Perceived Training Needs and Computation Using the Spearman rho

| Item | Training Needs | $R^1$ | $R^2$ | Difference (D) | $D^2$ |
|---|---|---|---|---|---|
| 1 | Communication Skills | 3 | 5 | -2 | 4 |
| 2 | Motivational Skills | 4 | 2 | 2 | 4 |
| 3 | Coaching Skills | 1 | 3 | -2 | 4 |
| 4 | Time Management Skills | 5 | 7 | -2 | 4 |
| 5 | Decision-Making Skills | 6 | 6 | 0 | 0 |
| 6 | Computer Skills | 2 | 1 | 1 | 1 |
| 7 | Leadership Skills | 7 | 8 | -1 | 1 |
| 8 | Accounting Skills | 8 | 4 | 4 | 16 |
| | | | | 0 | 34 |

One can only say that there are definite relationships between several items when viewed on a singular, item-by-item basis. In the example given, there appears to be agreement between respondents on the ranking of Item 5 and close agreement on the others. Yet, if one item were chosen as being more significant than the others, it would be Item 6.

The Spearman rho correlation coefficient index is useful for ranking needs that have been defined through the assessment process and also for understanding their cumulative significance.

## Multivariate Correlational Methods

In needs assessment research, it is often necessary to explore the relationship between three or more variables (e.g., how performance at work is affected by a person's social environment, behavioral characteristics, and so on). This can be done through the use of *multivariate correlational methods*. These include *multiple linear regression*, *canonical correlation*, *partial correlation*, and *factor analysis*.

Multiple linear regression is used to describe the strength of a relationship between several independent variables and one dependent variable. For example, multiple linear regression could be used for exploring the strength of the relationship between job satisfaction, performance, and morale (independent variables) and productivity gains (dependent variable).

Canonical correlation is used to describe the relationship between several independent and several dependent variables. Canonical correlation could be used for exploring the strength of the relationship between factors such as work environment, organizational politics, and incentives (independent variables) and productivity, profitability, and compensation (dependent variables).

Partial correlation is used to describe the strength of relationships between two variables after the influence of a third variable has been controlled. An example of this could be in exploring the strength of the relationship between absenteeism and productivity (independent variables) and company work rules (controlled variable).

Factor analysis is used to explore whether a set of variables can be reduced to a smaller number of factors. For example, if a survey questionnaire was designed to measure ten different variables relating to employee attitudes, factor analysis could be used to explore whether each variable measures a different type of attitude or whether two or more variables contribute to measuring the same or similar attitudes.

## INFERENTIAL STATISTICS

Inferential statistics are used when research is conducted on a group or a sample that is drawn from a larger group or population. The results of the research on the sample are then generalized or inferred to the larger population from which the sample was drawn. Initially presented and discussed in Chapter 5, sampling is a fundamental technique of inferential statistics. In this section, some selected techniques used in conducting research on samples that are drawn from larger populations will be presented and discussed.

### The Null Hypothesis

The *null hypothesis* is a basic tool in inferential statistics. It is essentially a statement that says there is no actual relationship between variables and that any observed relationship is only a product of chance. For example, assume that the results of a survey questionnaire that had been administered to two different and mutually exclusive groups of employees in a large auto assembly plant was designed to measure the skill and knowledge levels associated with auto frame assembly. The results of the questionnaires administered to both groups were very similar. Yet, how does one know that any similarities (or, in some cases, the dissimilarities) observed between the groups was a function of experience, technical acumen, training, and the like? Moreover, were the results obtained purely a matter of chance? Since there is no way of being absolutely certain that the results contain any correlation, one would need to estimate the likelihood of chance being responsible for what has been observed. Further, they would need to explore how the obtained results actually occurred. To reject the null hypothesis, or rather, to state that the results observed occurred only by chance is, in effect, the strategy of inferential statistics.

### Statistical Significance

Tests of statistical significance are performed before rejecting a null hypothesis. This is done because rejecting a null hypothesis when, in fact, it is correct, results in what is known as a *Type I error*. In needs assessment research, a Type I error results from implementing unwarranted interventions that were developed as a result of rejecting an otherwise correct null hypothesis.

Type I errors have the potential to produce undesirable consequences (e.g., initiating policy changes when no such changes are necessary). Errors such as this can have long-term damaging effects. Alternatively, *Type II errors* result from a maintenance of the status quo; that is, nothing is done even though the situation warrants some form of intervention. Testing for statistical significance permits the analyst to measure the differences between samples drawn from the general population and, further, to make inferences from the samples to the population as a whole.

A variety of tests are commonly used to test for statistical significance. These can be broken down into two major groups: *parametric* and *nonparametric.*

Parametric tests assume that the scores in a population are normally distributed about the mean and that the population variances of comparison groups are approximately equal. Some commonly used parametric tests are the *t test*, *analysis of variance (ANOVA)*, *analysis of covariance*, *trend analysis*, and *confidence limits*.

The t test is used to determine whether two means differ significantly from each other and whether a single mean differs significantly from a specified population value. An example where the t test can be applied is in exploring mean differences between employee anxiety levels and performance evaluations. ANOVA is used to explore whether mean scores on one or more factors differ significantly from each other, whether these factors interact significantly with each other, and whether (and by how much) sample variances differ. ANOVA can be used, for example, for exploring intergroup and intragroup variations in the levels of compensation between two work groups or teams and, further, what effects these variations have on output as well as quality. Analysis of covariance is similar to ANOVA except that the influence of one or more independent variables on the dependent variable is controlled. Analysis of covariance could be used, for example, to explore what effects incentives (controlled variable) and employee attitudes (uncontrolled variable) have on productivity (dependent variable). Trend analysis is used to test the significance of a hypothesized trend, such as exploring what effects a TQM program has on employee morale. Confidence limits are used for estimating a population value based on what is known about a sample value. An example of an estimation of confidence limits would be when a comparison of the results of an assessment conducted on a sample group indicated a need that is common throughout all organizational levels.

Nonparametric tests are used when large deviations are present. Commonly used nonparametric tests include the *Mann-Whitney U test*, the *Wilcoxon signed-rank test*, and the *chi-square test*.

The Mann-Whitney U test is used to investigate whether two uncorrelated means differ significantly from each other. For example, it can be used to investigate whether and by how much the results of a survey involving two groups from two different locations differ. The Wilcoxon signed-rank test is used to determine whether two correlated means differ significantly from each other. The chi-square test is used to identify whether two frequency distributions differ significantly from each other.

The following are examples of how the Wilcoxon signed-rank and the chi-square nonparametric tests can be applied.

### The Wilcoxon Signed-Rank Test

The Wilcoxon signed-rank test is a nonparametric method that is useful for investigating whether two distributions of scores differ from each other when the scores of the samples are correlated. The following example illustrates the usefulness of the Wilcoxon signed-rank test.

After considerable financial losses, an organization's board of directors replaced the president with another individual who subsequently ordered a complete restructuring of the company. Sensing there was considerable doubt as to the new president's ability to turn the organization around and return it to a level of profitability (hence, the null hypothesis states that there is a lack of confidence in the new president's leadership abilities), the company's HRD manager, with the support of the new president, undertook an assessment to explore the levels of confidence employees had in the new president's ability. A series of thirty Yes/No, closed-ended questions designed to probe employees' perceptions about the new president's leadership abilities were devised in a script format and administered through personal interviews to a sample of ten employees drawn at random from throughout the organization. The results of the interviews are shown in Table 7.6.

The first step involves ranking the scores based on their levels of difference (see Table 7.7). Next, one must locate a table of critical values for the Wilcoxon signed-rank test. Assuming that a probability level of 0.05 was desired, the first step would be to locate the sample size (*n*) and then the critical value corresponding to the value calculated (in the example, 5 was the minimum value). In the table consulted, the 0.05 value is given as 8.[1] Therefore, since $R_{0.05}$ (8) is greater than $R_{min}$ (5), the null hypothesis which states that there was a lack of confidence regarding employees' perceptions of the new president's leadership abilities could be rejected. Note, however, that caution should be used when attempting to literally interpret these results. In the example given, there would be a number of other factors that could actually inhibit the new president's effectiveness (e.g., poor employee morale, lack

**Table 7.6**
Responses to Closed-Ended Questions Relating to Leadership Ability

| Respondent | YES Responses | NO Responses | Difference | Sign |
|---|---|---|---|---|
| 1 | 14 | 16 | −2 | − |
| 2 | 13 | 17 | −4 | − |
| 3 | 20 | 10 | 10 | + |
| 4 | 24 | 6 | 18 | + |
| 5 | 18 | 12 | 6 | + |
| 6 | 25 | 5 | 20 | + |
| 7 | 9 | 21 | −12 | − |
| 8 | 10 | 20 | −10 | − |
| 9 | 7 | 23 | −16 | − |
| 10 | 19 | 11 | 8 | + |

**Table 7.7**
Ranking of Scores Based on Levels of Difference

| Respondent | Difference | Signed Rank |
|---|---|---|
| 1 | -2 | - |
| 2 | -4 | - |
| 6 | 5 | + |
| 5 | 6 | + |
| 10 | 8 | + |
| 3 | 10 | + |
| 8 | -10 | - |
| 7 | -12 | - |
| 9 | -16 | - |
| 4 | 18 | + |

$R^+$ (positive rating) = 5 and $R^-$ (negative rating) = 5. $R_{min}$ = 5.

of motivation or incentives, poor market or economic conditions, etc.). Although these variables were not isolated and tested for in this example, it is realistic to assume that under the circumstances as presented they have the potential to exist in one form or another.

### The Chi-Square Test

A nonparametric technique that is used for measuring and comparing what is with what ought to be is known as the chi-square test.[2] This compares two frequencies: the observed with the expected.

To illustrate, suppose an HRD analyst in an insurance company sent out twenty survey questionnaires to each of the company's six field offices. The survey was anonymous and had a return date of September 30. In a previous yet similar experience, the analyst received a return rate of 60 percent from each office. In an effort to increase the overall response rate, she arranged for a letter from senior management to go out on September 15 urging employees to complete and return the questionnaire. As part of her research, she wanted to explore how effective the reminder letters would be in increasing the response rate. Column 1 in Table 7.8 shows the number of surveys received from each of the six field offices by September 10. Column 2 shows the additional number of surveys received by the due date of September 30 after the reminder letters were distributed.

Looking only at the information contained in Table 7.8 can be misleading. The data are only descriptive and do not show any relative importance. In order to find out if, indeed, the reminder letters contributed to increasing the response rate, the analyst would use the chi-square test.

First, what is expected based on what had previously been received must be determined. This can be done by computing the mean for the expected, which is 11 (i.e., 55 ÷ [6 – 1] = 11). Next, a table containing the following columns is constructed: Expected (E), Observed (O), Expected minus observed (E – O), Expected minus observed squared $(E - O)^2$, and finally, Expected minus observed squared divided by the expected $[(E - O)^2 \div E]$[3].

At this point, the data from Table 7.8 would be inserted and the calculations performed. An example of this in provided in Table 7.9.

The analyst would now need to consult a table of chi-square values. First, he or she would need to locate the *df* line containing the value that is one less than the sample size (which, in this case, would be 5). The next step would be to locate the value on this line that most closely approximates the chi-square value calculated (18.06). In the reference consulted, the chi-square value at a *df* level of 5 is above both the probability of significance levels of 15.09 (at the 0.01 level) and 20.52 (at the 0.001 level).[4] This means that the result obtained has a probability of less than 1 in 100 but greater than 1 in 10 of having occurred by chance. Given these results, it would be relatively safe to say that the use of the reminder letters did contribute to increasing the questionnaire return rate.

**Table 7.8**
Number of Surveys Received by Date from Each Field Office

| Field Offices | 9/10 | 9/30 |
|---|---|---|
| 1 | 10 | 7 |
| 2 | 9 | 6 |
| 3 | 10 | 3 |
| 4 | 11 | 4 |
| 5 | 7 | 5 |
| 6 | 8 | 8 |

**Table 7.9**
Chi-Square Computations

| Office | Expected (E) | Observed (O) | Expected Minus Observed | $(E - O)^2$ | $(E - O)^2 \div E$ |
|---|---|---|---|---|---|
| 1 | 11 | 7 | 4 | 16 | 1.45 |
| 2 | 11 | 6 | 5 | 25 | 2.27 |
| 3 | 11 | 3 | 8 | 64 | 5.81 |
| 4 | 11 | 4 | 7 | 49 | 4.45 |
| 4 | 11 | 5 | 6 | 36 | 3.27 |
| 6 | 11 | 8 | 3 | 9 | 0.81 |
| | | | | | Chi-Square: 18.06 |

## DEALING WITH MISSING DATA

Problems with data analysis will always result when respondents leave items unanswered. Individuals will leave questions unanswered for a number of reasons, some of which are the following:

1. They did not consider the question as it was written to be relevant to them;
2. The question was threatening or was of a highly personalized nature; or,
3. In the case of forced-choice questions, the answers that were provided were not acceptable or applicable.

Exactly why an item has been left blank is, in reality, rarely discovered.[5] Although there is no prescribed best way to handle missing data, one approach suggests that a code—one that is used consistently by the data entry person—be assigned to unanswered questions. Questions that have higher degrees of missing answer codes are easily identifiable and signify a need to reexamine their composition, structure, clarity, and appropriateness.

## CAUTIONS ABOUT STATISTICAL ANALYSES

Using statistical methods poses as many problems as solutions. The problems are manifested in a misunderstanding of what statistics are supposed to do versus how they are used. Choosing the correct statistical technique or test is paramount to conducting reliable and meaningful research. For this reason, it is important to emphasize how statistics can mislead, thus resulting in unintentionally erroneous conclusions.

### The "Rush to Conclusions" Syndrome

As mentioned in Chapter 6, recognizable patterns in incoming data often result in the formulation of preconceived notions and opinions. As such, it is easy to become temporarily blinded by what appears to be foregone conclusions. In these instances, preliminary conclusions are easily drawn from data that only has been through an elementary analysis. These conclusions can be reinforced by analyses that focus only on a singular issue, particularly if that issue just happens to coincide with and support a stated hypothesis.

As the analysis phase draws to a close, there is a natural tendency to want to bring the project to closure. In the rush to complete the data analysis, attention is sometimes directed at what are believed to be relevant issues, while less attention is given to factors which upon further analysis have significant influence upon the major goals of the needs assessment project. Likewise, if a project's completion time is behind schedule, the chance of making arithmetic or computer keying errors increases.

Conclusions and recommendations should only be made after a thorough and systematic analysis has been carried out. Data summaries, particularly those drawn from statistical inferences, should be reevaluated to ensure they have been correctly interpreted.

### Graphical Misrepresentations

Any graphs, charts, tables, or illustrations that provide a pictorial view of the data should be accurate. They should be checked and rechecked prior to being formally incorporated into the final report. Also, recalculations and checks for errors in processes that were used to condense data into graphs should be performed in order to identify errors or other discrepancies.

## Choosing the Appropriate Statistical Analysis Methods

Choosing the appropriate statistical methods for analyzing and interpreting data is critical. Since the final results and recommendations will be based on the results these methods have produced, every effort should be made to ensure that all of the statistical tests that were performed were correct. One way of ensuring this is to look at similar types of projects and then to seek to replicate the procedure(s) used. Assuming that there is similarity in the null hypotheses, the results of the original study and the replication should to some degree coincide. Where no precedent exists (or cannot be found), the analyst should consult a professional statistician or researcher to determine which methods and techniques are appropriate to use.

## Avoiding Analysis/Paralysis

Analysis/paralysis is jargon for going to extremes in the data analysis phase. It is easy (and sometimes fun) to be able to apply a variety of statistical techniques just to see what kinds of results are obtained. Doing so, however, can often result in delays in conducting evaluations and making recommendations because the data can become contaminated and the results obscured. Overanalysis often causes undue attention to be focused on vague or distant ambiguities that have little or no significance on the eventual outcomes.

It is easy to become confused and frustrated with assessment analysis. This frustration can lead to mistakes and oversights which can ultimately result in erroneous conclusions.[6] Since future assessments may be based on the results of past projects, it is crucial that steps be taken to avoid data contamination. Record keeping should be stringent, and any and all tests that were performed on the data should be able to be replicated with consistent results. Even though the type and quality of data collected will be influenced by the type of systematic assessment approach adopted, extreme care should be taken to be as thorough and exacting as possible without letting the analysis phase of the assessment go on indefinitely.

## Ethical Considerations

Because needs assessment research involves participation and objective as well as subjective observation, analysis, and evaluation, it becomes susceptible to deception. There are some who subscribe to the view that purposeful deception helps to minimize biasing. Others support the view that purposeful deception is unethical and discredits not only the researchers but, indeed, the project itself.[7] Researchers continually wrestle with this question, but, since there are no clearly defined parameters, it appears that the adage "let your conscience be your guide" seems to be the best advice to follow.

One form of purposeful deception that clearly violates both the intent and purpose of needs assessment research is the willful manipulation of data to either support or refute a hypothesis, belief or position, or particular point of view.[8] Under certain circumstances the pressures to commit such acts can be significant. Consider, for example, a situation where analysts are directed by their manager to alter the findings of an assessment so that it conforms to the manager's point of view. By failing to comply with this directive, the analysts risk the possibility of some form of recrimination (e.g., job loss, etc.). Yet, by carrying out the deception, they risk losing something of much greater value: their integrity and credibility.

The analysis of organizational needs assessments is composed of research methodologies that must be subjected to the same rigors and safeguards as any other type of research effort. The findings should be presented intact, and recommendations should be based on actual and not manipulated results. In order to maintain credibility, absolute integrity must be maintained throughout the analysis, evaluation, and reporting stage(s). Opting for or accepting anything less runs a high risk of producing undesirable long-term results.

## SUMMARY

Statistics are useful for translating quantitative and qualitative data into understandable information. Descriptive statistics are used to summarize data and then present it in a graphical or visually oriented format. Inferential statistics are used to analyze data that were obtained from a sample group drawn from a larger population. The results of the data analysis are then inferred from the sample to the larger population. Scores are measurements consisting of five primary types: continuous, rank, artificial dichotomy, true dichotomy, and categories.

Descriptive statistics involve organizing data into frequency distributions and then summarizing and presenting the findings. They use scales of measurement for translating observations into hard data. Four types of measurement scales commonly used are the following: (1) nominal scales, which place data into categories that are quantitatively different; (2) ordinal scales, which are used to explore the relationship(s) between individuals or items; (3) interval scales, which are used to order or to rank criteria so that the extent of any difference between them can be measured; and (4) ratio scales, which are used to establish an absolute zero reference between two or more points.

Frequency distributions are useful for visually organizing, displaying, and examining the general shapes of data. They permit quick observation of the relationship(s) between data sets. This allows some immediate generalizations to be made. Distribution shapes can appear symmetrical where all measures of central tendency appear equal, or, when the measures differ, the shapes can appear to be either positively or negatively skewed.

Measures of central tendency are used for organizing and arranging data. They include (1) the mode, which is the value that appears with the greatest frequency, (2) the median, which is a point in a distribution below which 50 percent of its scores fall, and (3) the mean, which is the sum of all numbers in a distribution divided by the number of cases in the same distribution. Of these, the mean is regarded as being the most precise because it accounts for every score in a distribution.

Measures of variability are used to describe distributions in terms of variations in scores. This is accomplished through the use of (1) the range, which provides information on scores from lowest to highest, (2) the variance, which calculates the average value of the squares of deviations from the mean, and (3) the standard deviation, which measures the amount or distance that a set of scores deviates from the mean.

Correlation is used to explore relationships between two or more groups of means, while correlation coefficients show the linear strength of the relationship between the variables. There are a variety of techniques used to calculate correlation coefficients. Some of them are Pearson's product–moment correlation coefficient, which measures the relationship between two sets of scores relating to two different variables, the rank correlation coefficient, which computes the correlation coefficient between scores or measures that have been rank ordered, and the Spearman rho, which determines the correlation between two or more ranked orders.

Multivariate correlational methods are used to explore and to describe the existence of any relationships between three or more variables. Such methods include multiple linear regression, canonical correlation, partial correlation, and factor analysis.

A basic technique in inferential statistics is the null hypothesis, which states that any observed relationship between variables occurred by chance. Accepting or rejecting the null hypothesis is done by determining its level of significance, which calculates the risk of incurring a Type I error. In needs assessment research, Type I errors represent the effects of changes or interventions that were implemented but were actually unwarranted and unnecessary. Type II errors result in a maintenance of the status quo, meaning that nothing was done even though there were indications that some sort of intervention was warranted. In organizational needs assessments, Type I errors are considered the more serious of the two.

Inferential statistics use parametric and nonparametric tests. Parametric tests include the t test, ANOVA, analysis of covariance, trend analysis, and tests of confidence levels. Nonparametric tests include the Mann-Whitney U test, the Wilcoxon signed-rank test, and the chi-square test.

Missing data pose many problems. Although there is no universally accepted means to manage or to otherwise compensate for it, one way that has met with some success is to consistently use specially devised codes. Coding permits easy identification of missing data and may indicate problems with certain questions or observation criteria, particularly with those where the missing data code frequently appears.

Statistical analysis must be used with caution. Conclusions must not be drawn until a comprehensive analysis has been completed. Data should not be summarized until they have been checked and rechecked for accuracy. Analyses should not be allowed to continue indefinitely because recommendations and decisions about their outcomes must be made.

Finally, data should be summarized and presented based on the results of the analysis. They must not be subjected to willful manipulation, deception, or distortion just to support a hypothesis, theory, position, or belief.

## NOTES

1. E. Pearson and H. Hartley, *Biometrika Tables for Statisticians*, Vol. 1, 3rd ed. (Cambridge: Cambridge University Press, 1966).
2. O. Westgaard, "Measuring Performance," *Performance and Instruction Journal*, June/July, 1986, pp. 10–11.
3. R. Iman and W. Conover, *Modern Business Statistics* (New York: Wiley & Sons, 1983).
4. Ibid., pp. 686–687.
5. J. Edwards and M. Thomas, "The Organizational Survey Process," in *Improving Organizational Surveys: New Directions and Methods*, P. Rosenfeld, J. Edwards, and M. Thomas, eds., *American Behavioral Scientist*, Vol. 36, No. 4, pp. 419–442.
6. J. Phillips, *Handbook of Training Evaluation and Measurement Methods*, 2nd ed. (Houston: Gulf Publishing, 1991).
7. W. Borg and M. Gall, *Educational Research: An Introduction*, 4th ed. (New York: Longman, 1983).
8. S. McClelland, "Training Needs Assessment Data-Gathering Methods—Part I: Survey Questionnaires," *Journal of European Industrial Training*, Vol. 18, No. 1, pp. 27–30.

CHAPTER 8

# Formulating and Presenting Recommendations

Once the statistical computations on the data have been completed, many people are often left with the following question: How does one actually go about interpreting or otherwise evaluating the results of the analysis? In other words, what do the numbers really mean? Since statistics will provide only a mathematically based interpretation, one must look beyond the numbers in order to develop a more in-depth understanding of the real story they tell.

An important distinction in needs assessment data evaluation lies in understanding the function it serves. There are two principal methods that can be applied to the evaluation of needs assessment data: *formative* and *summative* evaluation. Formative evaluation is used in-process to form or to modify a project as it is being implemented. It is useful for determining how well the assessment project is proceeding. Alternatively, summative evaluation is used to make decisions and to formulate recommendations based on an analysis of the data.[1] In needs assessment research, summative evaluation has greater application because it takes a more macro view of the assessment and allows one to concentrate on formulating recommendations that are based on a comprehensive review of the data.

When formulating decisions and making recommendations, there are no absolute rules that can be applied universally. Rather, the analyst must rely on good judgment, intuition, common sense, and experience. There are, however, some general guidelines and techniques that can aid in the data-evaluation process.

## SUMMARIZING QUANTITATIVE DATA

Because quantitative data are easier to organize, tabulate, and analyze, they are the type most commonly used in needs assessment research. By using the various statistical methods outlined in Chapter 7, the task of evaluating quantitative data is made much easier. After an analysis of the data has been completed, one must then interpret what relationships exist between the data sets. This can be accomplished through exploring the data's *programmatic significance*.[2]

Programmatic significance is analogous to reliability and validity. It is a way of evaluating what effects the statistical analysis has produced. This is important in a systematic needs assessment because

1. It provides the analyst with a means for assembling the assessment data in a logical format.
2. It can indicate deficiencies in the assessment process, particularly in the data-gathering methods used.
3. It allows the analyst to reject the null hypothesis based on sound analysis, validity, and verification.

For example, if the results produced by two or more aggregate data-gathering methods did not provide correlation or consistency between them, it would become necessary to review the design elements associated with each data-gathering method used. This could uncover inconsistencies in the design and preparation of the data-gathering instruments and also identify errors in the sampling procedures used. Furthermore, it could highlight any areas where interviewer, focus group leader, or SME biasing exists. Last, an exploration of the assessment's programmatic significance could help to detect any mathematically based errors that resulted from an inappropriate use of the statistical analysis methods.

One way to summarize quantitative data is to first organize them into clusters and then rank the responses based on the frequency of their appearance. Clusters, in this sense, would be items that are related (e.g., communications, making verbal presentations, writing skills, etc.). Scores that are drawn from any of the quantitative scales used (e.g., Likert scales) are calculated by first totaling the responses in each category and then dividing the outcome by the number of items contained within each cluster. At some point, a threshold based on the averaged scores must be established. Any individual or cluster scores that fall below the threshold would indicate a need or highlight an area for some form of intervention.

## SUMMARIZING QUALITATIVE (NARRATIVE) DATA

The very nature of qualitative feedback makes it much more difficult to summarize. Because of this, qualitative data should be evaluated on their content and on the conditions or circumstances under which they were obtained. For example, assume an assessment designed to explore employee confidence levels in management's decision-making abilities was conducted. Further, assume that while the survey questionnaire was being administered, the company had simultaneously announced a downsizing program. It is almost certain this would surface in the data retrieved even though confidence levels in management's abilities may have been very high prior to the announcement. Factors such as this can and will significantly influence the relationship(s) between identified cause(s) and measured or observed effects.

Other factors that must be taken into consideration when summarizing qualitative data are the following:

1. In the case of interviews, the interviewer's demeanor and manner
2. The composition and structure of any open-ended questions used in survey questionnaires
3. The degree of influence, if any, that the structure, composition, and conduct of focus groups had on feedback that was obtained from them
4. How unobtrusively any on-site observations were carried out and whether the observer's report is objective and unbiased

Since qualitative data are prone to individual interpretation, summarizing them, as compared to summarizing quantitative data, is less exacting.[3] Because of its open-ended nature, it is more susceptible to biasing and misinterpretation. Since qualitative data also have a definite behavioral aspect to them, the true meanings behind narrative or open-ended responses often lie hidden within what was actually recorded and/or reported. To uncover these hidden meanings requires considerable time and rigorous objectivity.

### Pattern Analysis

One of the most useful ways of organizing and summarizing qualitative data is to use a modified form of a statistical technique known as *pattern analysis*.[4] Pattern analysis involves computing the statistical significance between responses and then comparing the results for similarities as well as differences. Pattern analysis is used to analyze and summarize response patterns between individuals as well as groups (or clusters) of individuals. Patterns can be traced to things like gender, age, socioeconomic status, levels of authority and responsibility, ethnic origin, and so on. For the purposes of analyzing qualitative needs assessment data, pattern analysis can best be described in terms of repetition, or rather, those patterns that surface consistently over time. For example, during a pattern analysis, one first looks for repetitive responses, particularly where keyed or weighted questions are concerned. These are examined with respect to their content by noting the frequency of similar statements made by a numerically significant number of individuals. As this process continues, a clearer picture of what the qualitative data are actually saying begins to emerge.

### Peripheral Information

In the course of writing responses to open-ended survey questions or in verbally expressing an opinion during an interview, individuals' thoughts may wander from the main point of the question to issues that they (the respondents) feel are related and are important enough to be included in their response. Some may feel so strongly about these issues that they may elaborate on them more than responding to the questions asked. This presents a dilemma when summarizing responses: whether to treat such elaboration or commentary as miscellaneous rambling and consequently disregard it, or to carefully scrutinize its content and its validity.

Peripheral information can be just as valuable as the mainstream feedback. It can contain significant information on issues that are (or can be) of great importance to the organization. Therefore, it should not be discarded or overlooked. However, the needs analyst must make certain to place emphasis on the issues that are relevant and contribute to attaining the goals of the assessment, albeit sometimes indirectly. Specifically, caution should be used when any of the following are encountered:

1. Assumptive statements that begin with phrases like "Well, it's common knowledge that . . ." and "Everyone here knows that . . . "
2. Broad and sweeping generalizations
3. Answers that appear to be planned or indicate preconceived notions or hidden beliefs
4. Answers that appear to be more cosmetic than descriptive and informative

### Scheduling Follow-Up Activities

Misinterpretation of qualitative data can be minimized by scheduling follow-up interviews with individuals whose responses are thought to be questionable. Where anonymous survey questionnaires containing open-ended questions are concerned, follow-up interviews are impossible to conduct. However, respondents whose identities are known should be contacted with a list of questions that was derived from their initial responses. Follow-up interviews should be tightly structured and focus only on those items that are questionable. They should be conducted in a nonthreatening manner, and any additional questions asked should be able to be understood clearly by the respondent as being necessary to clear up ambiguities or to seek further input on unclear issues. Questions should be very specific, direct, and to the point but never posed in a threatening or an intimidating manner.

## SUMMARIZING AGGREGATE DATA

A central theme of this book has been the utility and value in combining two or more data-gathering methods for the purposes of identifying organizational needs (see Chapter 4). Summarizing data that have been obtained through aggregate methods can be complex and tedious, particularly where open-ended qualitative feedback is concerned. Therefore, the following recommendations are provided: (1) As was previously stated, the use of computers and statistical software is highly recommended. The speed and flexibility they provide for summarizing diverse sources of information make them invaluable. Computers are also very useful for drawing conclusions using "what if" scenarios and in preparing final reports. (2) Where statistical software is not available, the use of relational data bases or spreadsheets are suitable substitutes, particularly those that have cross-tabulation and statistical manipulation capabilities. Although the depth and breadth of analysis is not as great as it is with statistical programs, data bases and spreadsheets can quickly organize and present data. This greatly facilitates the process of reaching conclusions and formulating recommendations. (3) Paper, pen, and calculator methods may also be used to analyze aggregate data. However, because of the complexities involved, this approach is not recommended. It is particularly unsuitable for large assessment samples. To illustrate the complexities associated with the paper, pen, and calculator methods, the following procedure is provided. It assumes the use of survey questionnaires and that these contain keyed questions which are common to another type of data-gathering method. It also assumes that numerical significance or weighting factors have been applied to these questions. This procedure is based on the use of survey questionnaires as the principal method and on the use of individual interviews as the secondary method.

Step 1. Organization: identify and isolate all responses to key questions.

Step 2. Tabulate and record the weights assigned to regular as well as keyed quantitative questions contained in the survey questionnaire.

Step 3. Read each narrative response obtained from the individual interviews and assign a weighted value (assuming this has not already been done during the data entry or recording process).

Step 4. Tabulate and record the weighted values from the responses of each regular and each keyed qualitative question.

Step 5. Calculate an ideal value for each question by combining absolute maximum values for each data type (i.e., the maximum value if everybody had responded in the positive to any positively worded questions used or the maximum value if everybody had responded in the negative to any negatively worded questions used).

Step 6. Determine an upper-limit threshold. This is normally done at the 75-percent level, indicating that correlation between responses for each question received from both methods should total at or above 75 percent (0.75).

Step 7. Calculate and record for all questions the absolute maximum value for both methods.

Step 8. Calculate the difference between the two.

Step 9. If the difference is equal to or greater than the 0.75 threshold, then correlation between the two methods with respect to the question(s) for which it is being applied will have been attained. If the difference is less than the 0.75 threshold, then correlation between the two methods for that particular question has not been attained.

Step 10. Questions where correlation has not been received should be reevaluated in regards to their appropriateness, their readability, and so on. This applies to the written item in the survey questionnaire as well as to how the question was posed and the response interpreted during the interview process. An example containing each of these steps is shown in Table 8.1.

The reader should note that this approach is highly subjective when compared to using a computer and statistical or data base software and is considerably less precise on an order of magnitude. One of its major faults is that it greatly oversimplifies the analysis and evaluation process and is prone to leading one to make broad and sometimes sweeping generalizations. Also, since each question from each method has to be manually accounted for, the process is unrealistically tedious and time consuming. For example, assume that the survey questionnaire contained one hundred questions and that twenty-five of these were closed-ended keyed items. Also assume that twenty-five interviews were conducted and each interview contained fifty open-ended questions, twenty-five of which were keyed items that were linked to and corresponded with the twenty-five keyed, closed-ended survey questionnaire items. This means that one would first have to read 625 open-ended responses and assign weighted values to each of them prior to even setting up the calculation and summary table, and then perform the calculations for each question. One can easily see why this approach is not recommended for large or even medium-sized population samples.

This method is not, however, without any value. It can be used, for example, when there is a need to assess a relatively small group (e.g., ten individuals) in a relatively short period of time. The information it provides, while by no means precise, can provide valuable insights about the validity of the aggregate data-gathering methods used and can give at least a cursory indication of whether the keyed questions yielded any correlational value.

## FORMULATING RECOMMENDATIONS

This is the final phase of the summary and evaluation stage. It is where the evaluation and data summaries are analyzed. Technically speaking, it is also one of the most important stages of the entire needs assessment process because any interventions or activities that are developed and implemented are based on the recommendations drawn from the evaluation and summary.

Recommendations can be made in an operative context, in an environmental context, or in a combination of the two. Furthermore, recommendations

**Table 8.1**
Sample of Aggregate Data Correlation Calculations Using Pencil, Paper, and Calculator Method

| Primary Method (PM) Question # | Weighting Factor (PWF) | Primary Method Response Totals (PTR) | Weighting Factor (SWF) | Secondary Method Response Totals (STR) | Ideal Value(IV) (PWF x PM) +(SWF x SM) | Threshold (IV/.75) (T) | Value Received (PTR+STR) (VR) | Correlation? Y=VR≥T N=VR<T |
|---|---|---|---|---|---|---|---|---|
| 2 | 4 | 300 | 3 | 50 | 475 | 356 | 350 | N |
| 12 | 4 | 300 | 3 | 60 | 475 | 356 | 360 | Y |
| 19 | 2 | 200 | 1 | 24 | 225 | 169 | 224 | Y |
| 26 | 4 | 260 | 2 | 36 | 450 | 338 | 296 | N |
| 27 | 4 | 320 | 3 | 63 | 475 | 356 | 383 | Y |
| 40 | 3 | 210 | 2 | 32 | 350 | 263 | 233 | N |

Primary Method (PM) = 100 Survey Questionnaires; Secondary Method (SM) = 25 interviews.

may be immediate (i.e., tactical), intermediate (i.e., tactical to medium-range), or ultimate (i.e., long-range).[5] For example, recommendations to change a routine operational process or procedure is immediate in its effect. On the other hand, a fundamental change in a company's culture represents an ultimate effort, one that in most cases will take longer to implement and measure.

How the recommended action(s) or intervention(s) will address causality is a principal concern. In essence, will the recommendations solve a problem by addressing the goals of the needs assessment, and, if so, what results can be realistically expected, observed, and/or ultimately measured? Another important factor to consider is the extent to which the goals of the assessment or the needs as they have been defined can be met by the recommended intervention. One must always try to predict and identify the value or worth of any recommended activities. Therefore, any recommendations should be based on facts that are grounded in both theory and intuition. This is where experience becomes an invaluable and indispensable asset.

### Levels of Risk

Any recommendation resulting from an analysis of needs assessment data bears an element of risk. For example, a recommendation to fundamentally alter an organization's culture would be operationally as well as environmentally based. Given that it is also likely to have significant behavioral implications, some thoughtful forecasting and planning should precede its implementation. Under these circumstances, it may be advisable to institute such a change over a longer term because doing so could allow the organization time to monitor the intervention's progress on an incremental basis. Doing so permits the analyst to implement in-process changes or alterations should problematic areas be encountered. In short, the risk of incurring a Type I error (see Chapter 7) under such circumstances is reduced. Alternatively, implementing such changes on an immediate basis increases the potential (and probability) of producing Type I errors. This could have potentially disastrous implications. For these reasons, a careful study of any recommendations and their possible outcomes and effects should be made.

Many times the results of a needs assessment are paradoxical because even though some form of intervention is called for, none of the possibilities presents a scenario of minimal risk. This means that the probability of incurring negative results or outcomes is significant, no matter what is done. Under these conditions, one can easily become risk averse and, subsequently, recommend that nothing be done. As a result, ongoing monitoring and evaluation may be undertaken so that any incremental in-process adjustments may be made at a time where more fundamental or comprehensive changes are warranted.[6]

### Consensus Recommendations

One of the best ways to gather input, opinions, and ideas for formulating recommendations is to conduct a series of debriefing meetings with members of the assessment project team. This is done so that important feedback from team members involved in the project can be obtained. The meetings should focus on arriving at a consensus about the kinds of interventions being considered and, in particular, on brainstorming the possible effects or outcomes. Other individuals who can provide equally valuable input are company managers, other employees, and customers. Ultimately, however, it is the analyst or the person in charge of the assessment project who must make the final determinations and recommendations. Given this, the following guidelines are provided:

1. Recommendations for any interventions should be made based on an analysis of how well they address the assessment goals.
2. Interventions and other types of activities, even though they may be grounded in theory, should be results-oriented.
3. The results of any interventions should be both observable and measurable.
4. Any recommendations made must be cost-effective.

## PREPARING THE FINAL REPORT

The needs assessment final report is the official record of the project.[7] It documents all activities. Therefore, it should be comprehensive, accurate, and readable. The final report is the principal vehicle for communicating the findings, both quantitative and qualitative. It should clearly describe what was done (the assessment), why it was done (e.g., to address causality through problem solving, to improve performance and productivity, to explore and identify training needs or requirements, etc.), and how it was done, and it should include detailed descriptions of the data-gathering methods used. The final report should contain enough detail about the assessment's design so that it can be replicated at some future point in time. Specifically, the report should contain the following:

1. An introduction
2. A detailed overview of the the design strategy
3. A detailed description of the data-gathering methods that were used and why they were selected
4. A detailed description of the statistical methods used to analyze the data
5. A detailed presentation of the findings
6. The summary, recommendations, and discussion points

7. All administrative details associated with conducting the assessment, such as costs, logistics, personnel requirements, and so on

Moreover, the final report should be designed to motivate management or decision makers to take action.[8] It should specify alternatives to any recommended activities or interventions and should clearly communicate the consequences of inactivity. It should be thought-provoking and stimulate action.

### The Introduction

The introduction should contain a brief description of the assessment project. This normally includes (but is not necessarily limited to) a description of the identified causes and effects and how these contributed to the assessment goal-setting process. The introduction should also include details concerning administration and logistics. It should provide an overview of what was done and why by presenting a concise chronology followed by a detailed discussion.

### The Design Strategy

This section should contain a detailed explanation of the strategy used in the assessment's design. It should include information describing the sampling procedures that were used, how the assessment sample population was selected, the composition of the project team, a description of the data-gathering methods used and why they were selected, how the project was implemented, and any problems encountered. This section should also include a description of the methods used to set the assessment goals and an overview of all data analysis procedures (e.g., aggregate, correlational methods, and so on).

### Data-Gathering Methods

All information concerning the choice and use of the data-gathering methods should be described in detail. Specifically, information should be presented as to why a particular method was chosen. An explanation of how the data-gathering instruments were designed and administered should accompany information concerning each method's reliability and validity (assuming, of course, this information is available). All field-related activities involving personal contact with members of the assessment sample should be summarized. Any problems or irregularities that were encountered should be presented along with a brief explanation of how they were resolved or otherwise addressed. Most notably, this section should explain what procedures were used to handle missing or incomplete data.

### Data Analysis Methods

The relationship between each method that was used to analyze the assessment data should be fully detailed. The results of the analyses should be detailed with interpretations and explanations of each statistical procedure used. Each method should be fully explained and accompanied by a justification testifying to its particular suitability and utility.

### The Findings

This is the most critical part of the final report.[9] Its purpose is to present the findings and recommendations and to provide answers to questions. The findings must be clearly and succinctly presented. Both positive as well as negative outcomes should be discussed and all findings should be able to be substantiated (qualitatively and/or quantitatively).

### The Summary

There are basically two parts to the assessment report summary: the activity summary and the administrative summary. The activity summary condenses all events and findings into a few pages. Its purpose is to present an overview of the project in a detailed yet easily readable format. It is often placed at the beginning of the final report, yet, depending on the size and complexity of the project, it is usually one of the last portions written.[10] Because summaries are generally more widely circulated and read than are complete reports, they should be carefully prepared with respect to their content and accuracy. If the preparer's writing skills are only marginal, a professional writer or editor should be used.

The administrative summary should contain all logistical and budgetary information, including a condensed version of the project activity log. An important inclusion would be notes or comments on scheduling or other types of logistical problems encountered which may have archival importance. Some professionals prefer to exclude budgetary or cost-related information, while others feel it is necessary to provide a more rounded and comprehensive picture of the overall project. Those who prefer to exclude it from the report suggest that it should be included in the HRD departmental budgetary activity report. Whichever approach is taken, it is always necessary to conduct a reconciliation of expenses (i.e., a comparison of projected to actual costs). This is done for two reasons: (1) It provides a way to project costs more accurately for future assessment projects, and (2) it can be used to calculate any ROI the organization expects to receive.

A detailed example of a needs assessment budget reconciliation is included in Appendix B.

### The Executive Summary

An executive summary is usually prepared and included in part of the final report. It is similar to the final report summary except it is intended as a quick reference to be used in a formal, narrative presentation.[11] Executive summaries contain abbreviated yet concise discussions of the project findings, outcomes, recommendations, options, questions, and the predicted consequences on outcomes of the intervention activities suggested (e.g., training). It should be designed to stimulate thinking and should serve to motivate management to action, as previously noted.

Any graphs, charts, and other visual aids accompanying an executive summary should be included in the main portion of the text. The figures used to summarize any descriptive statistics (e.g., histograms, distribution curves, comparison charts and tables, etc.) should also be included.[12] Executive summaries do not usually contain the level of quantitative or qualitative detail found in the main report.

The executive summary generally has the greatest impact on decisions regarding the implementation of any recommended interventions or related activities. Therefore, it should be professionally prepared. Significant attention should be paid to details and mechanics. This includes checking for misspellings, errors in syntax, graphical misrepresentations, and so on. The information should be laid out in a concise, appealing, and easy-to-read manner.

The executive summary should be prepared on heavy stock or high-quality paper, include report covers, and be bound. It should be appropriately titled and contain a table of contents. In essence, it should reflect authority by imparting a sense of professionalism.

## PRESENTING THE FINAL REPORT

In preparing to formally present the final report to management, there are two main points to consider: planning for the presentation and the actual delivery.[13] Planning activities include developing an understanding of the audience, focusing the presentation to its level(s) of familiarity, and proactively anticipating its questions. Delivery details include fine tuning the presenter's style and presentation and matching these up with the audience requirements. The delivery also includes fine tuning the presenter's verbal as well as nonverbal presentation skills, how they answer or otherwise handle tough or complex questions, and the level of group-to-presenter involvement and interaction.

### Planning the Presentation

Planning for the final presentation involves three distinct yet critical areas: audience profile, topic or background research, and the physical environment where the presentation will take place.[14]

*Audience Profile.* To make an interesting and compelling presentation, the presenter must first know who will be in the audience. Most professionals will generate a composite profile of known audience members, which includes their educational backgrounds, current job titles, responsibility levels, age, gender, and even cultural orientations. The composite profile can also include information about interests—personal as well as professional.

*Topic/Background Research.* Background information on the subject matter, in this case on needs assessments in general, and, specifically, on any assessments that have been previously conducted in the organization, is compiled and studied. Additionally, any available information on previous assessments which may be related to the current one (e.g., similarity in topics, findings, etc.) should be investigated by paying particular attention to outcomes, problems, successes, failures, and so on. A significant amount of historical or archival information can be obtained from a comprehensive review of an organization's HRD records and by conducting literary searches in libraries for case studies, examples, and research that is relevant to the current assessment project. The following is a list of activities to consider when conducting topic or background research:

1. A decision must be made on what approach will be used in the presentation. This includes reinforcement of important points with case studies or research that is obtained from articles having appeared in respected journals.
2. A presentation plan around the audience profile should be prepared. Jargon that is not common to the audience should be avoided. The presenter must be cognizant of the amount of time available. For example, if the audience is composed of senior managers, then time will be a very important factor. With this in mind, the presentation should be focused, direct, and to the point.
3. A detailed plan for the presentation should be drafted and should include an agenda, time allocations for each section or segment of the presentation, an outline of each topic and subtopic, and a description of any graphical supporting material.
4. Audio-visual requirements should be determined. All equipment ordered should be used correctly and appropriately.
5. The presenter should rehearse the presentation at least three times, if possible, in front of a live audience. Criticisms should be constructively focused and, if relevant, should precipitate substantive changes to the presentation plan.
6. The executive summary should be reviewed by checking for accuracy, neatness, and consistency. The formal presentation should complement and enhance the written summary and vice versa. Continuity between the two is very important and influences how well the presentation is ultimately received. A poorly planned presentation will appear fragmented, while one that is well planned will flow seamlessly from one issue to another.

*Physical Environment.* The most dynamic presentation can fail in a poorly planned facility. For example, a warm or hot room with inadequate ventilation or one that is subject to frequent outside interruptions will have a negative effect on the most immaculately prepared presentation. The following are some factors to consider when choosing a suitable presentation environment:

1. Ensure that furniture (tables, chairs, etc.) is comfortable.
2. Ensure that there is adequate ventilation and that climate controls are functioning properly.
3. The room should be large enough to comfortably accommodate the size of the group.
4. Audio-visual equipment should be used in a manner that best complements the presenter's style.
5. The presenter should be aware of any individuals in the audience who are experiencing problems between them. These persons should be positioned so that contact between them is minimized.
6. Room lighting should be abundant and illumination levels easily controlled.

Last, an agenda should be composed and circulated in advance to all audience members.[15] It should reflect the thrust of the presentation, explain what will be presented and discussed, and clearly state starting and ending times.

### Delivery

Perhaps the most crucial part of the formal presentation lies in the delivery style of the presenter. If the narrative portion of the final report is not delivered in a focused and well-paced manner, chances are the results, recommendations, and options the presenter is attempting to communicate will not be received clearly and understood by the audience.[16]

The formal delivery stage consists of four major areas: the introduction, verbal and nonverbal communication, the use of supporting graphics and visuals, and the closing.

*Introduction.* The introduction should be concise, capture the essence of the assessment project, and grasp the audience's immediate attention. It should focus on the central theme of the assessment (e.g., to determine causality, to pinpoint areas where performance and productivity improvement programs are needed, to determine levels of employee satisfaction, morale, etc.); it should stimulate the audience's thought processes by focusing on why the assessment was undertaken; and, moreover, it should prepare them for decisions about the recommendations which they will eventually be asked to make.

*Verbal Communication.* How well the presenters' message is received is critically dependent on how well the report is verbally delivered. Voice projection (volume, pitch, and tone) is crucial to a successful presentation.[17] The speakers' tone and pitch should be varied. They should raise as well as lower their voices in order to emphasize important points. A voice that is monotone and unvaried in pitch will cause rapid degeneration in the audience's attention and interest levels. Presenters should always remember to whom they are speaking: Usually, where communicating needs assessment results are concerned, the audience will be senior managers—decision makers who are themselves accustomed to making formalized presentations. An audience like this can be very critical because consciously or subconsciously they will be comparing their own delivery styles to the one being presented. Because of this, presenters should work to quickly establish rapport. This can be done by communicating on a formal level. Using repetitive words and phrases like "Now . . . ," "O.K., now . . . ," "Think about this for a moment . . . ," and "Do you know what I mean . . . ?" should be avoided. Also, long pauses between statements should never be filled with phrases such as "Well, let's see . . . ," "Ummmm . . . ," "Uh, well . . . ," and so on.

Presenters should always talk to and not down at the group.[18] They should work to present an image of expertise. Important material such as the assessment outcomes, recommendations, and requests for action will help to mobilize the group to action. Abrupt transitions between topics should be avoided. Rather, transitions should be logically oriented and sequenced.

*Nonverbal Communication.* Nonverbal communications are equally important in formalized presentations. What is inferred through physical actions can sometimes say more than spoken words. Because audiences normally form an immediate first impression, presenters should be appropriately dressed. For example, presentations to senior management normally call for formal business attire. Anything less gives the visual impression that what is being presented is not critical or important.

Presenters should maintain eye contact and position themselves in front of the group. They should be able to read the audience's reaction to their presentation. In particular, they should look for signs of boredom, a lack of comprehension or understanding, as well as for any signs that portray a lack of enthusiasm for what is being said.[19]

Body language or physical actions such as hand gestures should be used frequently for emphasis. Energetic movements can call attention to important points.[20] They should not, however, be mechanized or predictable because they will appear to have been orchestrated. Movements such as walking or pacing can be used effectively as long as the stride is altered and used to enhance or emphasize salient points. All physical movements and gestures should be coordinated with voice inflections, tone, and pitch. When combined, they can be very effective in maintaining a high degree of audience interest and attention. Alternatively, presenters should be observant of any body language shown by their audience. For instance, slouching, heavy sighs, loss of eye contact, and constant fidgeting are signs of boredom or disinterest. These motions should send a clear signal to presenters to alter or speed up the pace.

Overall, presenters should impart a sense of expertise and authority. Recommendations or suggestions should be reinforced with pertinent facts and relevant examples. Most important, presenters must be prepared to succinctly respond to any questions posed by the audience. They must also be prepared to handle disagreements or challenges to the position(s) they are advocating. In order to do this effectively, presenters should try during the planning and rehearsal stages to anticipate any possible objections or challenges and devise a strategy to defend their position.

The delivery can be greatly enhanced through the use of audio-visuals (e.g., graphics and charts). Summarizing information by using descriptive statistics and presenting results through graphs are very effective presentation techniques. Visuals should be varied, engaging, and easy to read. If professionally prepared and properly used, they can make technically oriented or difficult information easier to understand.

The delivery should logically proceed toward a closing. This should incorporate and summarize the major findings, recommendations, options, and any alternative actions.[21] In particular, the closing should place emphasis on actions or decisions needed from the management group. It should contain a suggested time frame for making decisions. Any suggested interventions (e.g., training) should be accompanied by a topical outline, course objectives, evaluation methods, instructor information, implementation times, and estimated costs.

Presenters should allow adequate time for questions and answers. Questions that are technical in nature (such as those centered around specifics of data collection and analysis methods) can best be handled by referring the individual to the contents of the formal written report. Finally, the presenter should conclude the formalized presentation by thanking the group for their time, patience, and attention.

## POSTASSESSMENT PROJECT REVIEW

Many analysts make the mistake of assuming that once the final report is written and presented to management, the assessment project formally ends. Actually there is one final step that is often overlooked: the postproject review.[22] This is an important stage in the needs assessment process because systematic problems can be identified and strategies on how to best manage them (or avoid them altogether) can be openly discussed. The postproject review can provide an open forum where solutions to problems can be explored, particularly for future assessments.

A good postproject review involves each team member's input. A good technique is to conduct group debriefing sessions that focus on the project activity log, time lines, and each person's notes and narrative input. Issues such as how well the team performed, the level or spirit of intergroup relations and cooperation, and overall group communications can be discussed along with issues related to data processing (e.g., computer hardware and software, data handling, entry, or input procedures), logistics, and the overall project administration.

### Logistics/Administration

A comprehensive review of all assessment logistics and administrative elements including project time lines, budgeting factors, scheduling of data-gathering activities, details of data handling and processing, rescheduling activities, and so on should be undertaken by the project group. Specifically, the group should seek to answer the following questions:

1. What were the major problems?
2. How were they addressed?
3. Could they have been handled more efficiently or managed more effectively?
4. Was the project time line realistic?
5. Were the project cost estimates accurate (in comparison to the actual costs incurred)?

Frequent reference should be made to the program activity log in order to identify any logistical and administrative problems. Recommendations should be noted as to how such problems can be addressed or avoided altogether. Since problems of a logistical or administrative nature usually occur during the assessment implementation stage, it is advantageous to employ the same reasoning processes that were used to determine the project goals to solve problems by exploring any cause and effect relationships.

### Group Performance Evaluation

Determining how the project group performed is an important part of the postassessment review. Special care must be taken not to single out individuals by highlighting their mistakes or errors. Rather, the evaluation should focus on problem areas and on rating the team's cumulative efficiency level(s). Each member should be evaluated on a one-to-one basis by the team project leader. This evaluation should focus on individual performance and contribution to the overall effort. Each person's performance can and should be subjectively evaluated. Any criticisms should be constructively offered. In team or group evaluations, the same rules and procedures used in assessment focus groups apply.

When evaluating the performance of any contractual personnel or consultants, the following questions should be considered:

1. How well did they participate in the overall effort?
2. How insightful and valuable were they in their defined roles?
3. How well did they integrate into the project?
4. How effective were they in executing the specific function(s) and task(s) they were hired to perform? In other words, what measurable results did they produce?

Evaluation communications should be objective and unbiased. Any criticisms should be made in a constructive and nonthreatening manner. Equally, exemplary or above average performance should also be acknowledged.

## SUMMARY

Two methods used for summarizing needs assessment data are formative and summative evaluation. Formative evaluation is used primarily as a means for evaluating and changing the project in process. Summative evaluation is used to make decisions and formulate recommendations. Both have valuable application in needs assessment research, as do intuition and good judgment.

A major objective for evaluating data is to identify any existent relationships between various data sets. This is done by applying programmatic significance evaluation techniques. Programmatic significance is a means for logically organizing data. It also can be useful for pinpointing deficiencies in the assessment strategy.

One way to summarize quantitative data is to first organize them into clusters and perform a ranking based on the frequency of like or similar responses. Next, a threshold point is established. Scores falling at or below this point could be indicative of a need area. Because of their abstract nature, qualitative data should be evaluated on content and context. The conditions or circumstances under which the data were collected must also be taken into consideration. Influential yet outlying factors (e.g., environmental, political, economic, etc.) can significantly influence qualitative data. Also, because of its open-ended nature, it is more susceptible to misinterpretation and biasing. To properly analyze qualitative data requires time and rigor. One useful technique is to employ a process known as pattern analysis. This involves computing the statistical significance between responses and then comparing the results for differences as well as for similarities. Qualitative feedback that does not directly reflect back on the goals of the assessment should be treated as being peripheral. Peripheral information can also be valuable because it can and many times does contain information that is important to the organization's state of being. Peripheral information should never be discarded or treated as unimportant.

Problems due to scheduling conflicts as well as those associated with response misinterpretation can be managed through follow-up interviews. These should be structured to focus only on responses that are considered to be ambiguous or unclear. Questions should be specific but never posed in a threatening manner.

Because summarizing aggregate data can be time consuming, the use of a computer and software is highly recommended. Where these are not available, pen, paper, and calculator methods may be used. However, because of the complexity involved in summarizing and evaluating the qualitatively based portion of aggregate data sets, this technique is only recommended for use with small groups.

Outcome recommendations can be formulated in an operative or in an environmental context (or both). They may be tactical (immediate), intermediate, or long-range (ultimate). Since all recommendations will carry a certain element of risk, all aspects and consequences associated with them must be considered. Many times recommendations can be made by group consensus, where each member of the assessment team provides feedback on the results of the data analysis and evaluation.

The project final report should be accurate, truthful, and readable. It should clearly state what was done, why it was done, how it was done, and what results were obtained. It should summarize the findings and recommendations and provide archival documentation of the project.

Presenters should familiarize themselves with who will be in attendance (the audience) when presenting the final report to management. Topic and background research on the assessment subject matter and content should be conducted. Presenters should plan and rehearse the presentation. A concise and focused executive summary designed to motivate management to action should be prepared and included as part of the formal presentation.

One of the most overlooked phases of the needs assessment process is the postproject review. This is conducted to identify and document problems relating to the project's logistics and administration. The postproject review should also include an evaluation of the assessment team's performance. Each team member should be evaluated on a one-to-one basis by the team leader. This can be very useful—even critical—in planning for future needs assessment projects.

## NOTES

1. M. Scrivens, "The Methodology of Evaluation," in *Curriculum Evaluation*, R. Stake, ed., American Educational Research Association Monograph Series on Evaluation, No. 1 (Chicago: Rand McNally, 1967).
2. J. Kosecoff and A. Fink, *Evaluation Basics: A Practitioners Manual* (Beverly Hills, Calif.: Sage Publications, 1982).
3. G. Box, W. Hunter, and J. Hunter, *Statistics for Experimenters: An Introduction to Design, Data Analysis, and Model Building* (New York: Wiley & Sons, 1978).
4. Kosecoff and Fink, p. 207.
5. D. Miller, *Handbook of Research Design and Social Measurement Methods* (Newbury, Calif.: Sage Publications, 1991).
6. T. Gilbert, *Measuring Performance at Work*, in *Assessment for Decision*, D. Peterson and D. Fishman, eds. (New Brunswick, N.J.: Rutgers University Press, 1987).
7. Kosecoff and Fink, p. 209.
8. R. Zemke and T. Kramlinger, *Figuring Things Out: A Trainer's Guide to Job and Task Analysis* (Reading, Mass.: Addison-Wesley, 1984).
9. Kosecoff and Fink, p. 215.

10. W. Borg and M. Gall, *Educational Research: An Introduction*, 4th ed. (New York: Longman, 1983).

11. J. Phillips, *A Handbook of Training Evaluation and Measurement Methods*, 2nd ed. (Houston: Gulf Publishing, 1991).

12. Zemke and Kramlinger, p. 249.

13. J. Jeffries and J. Botes, *The Executive's Guide to Meetings, Conferences, and Audio-Visual Presentations* (New York: McGraw-Hill, 1983).

14. J. Wircenski and R. Sullivan, "Make Every Presentation a Winner," in *Infoline*, M. Callahan, ed. (Alexandria, Va.: American Society for Training and Development, 1986).

15. W. Cannes, *Effective Meetings for Busy People* (New York: McGraw-Hill, 1980).

16. M. Kenny, *Presenting Yourself* (New York: Wiley & Sons, 1982).

17. Wircenski and Sullivan, p. 5.

18. Ibid.

19. S. Bixler, *Professional Presence* (New York: Perigee Books, 1992).

20. D. Hon, *Meetings That Matter* (New York: Wiley & Sons, 1980).

21. J. Reith, "Meetings, Workshops, Seminars, and Conferences," in *Training and Development Handbook: A Guide to Human Resource Development*, 3rd ed., R. Craig, ed. (New York: McGraw-Hill, 1987), pp. 398–413.

22. C. Thompson, "Project Management: A Guide," in *Infoline*, B. Darraugh, ed. (Alexandria, Va.: American Society for Training and Development, 1990).

PART V

# The Role of Needs Assessments in Training and Managing Organizational Change

CHAPTER 9

# Designing and Developing Training Programs

One of the myths surrounding organizational needs assessments presented in Chapter 1 emphasized that needs assessments are not predisposed to recommend training as an outcome or as a possible intervention activity. However, the results of an assessment often highlight areas where training may be the most appropriate means for addressing gaps in KSAs. Therefore, it is important to understand how training programs are developed from needs that have been defined through an assessment process, and, further, how to design systems by which these programs can be effectively managed and delivered.

## TRAINING AS AN ASSESSMENT OUTCOME

As discussed in Chapter 2, organizational assessments are fundamentally oriented to identifying needs. These often can be met through formalized training. However, in situations requiring behavioral change, other types of interventions are often recommended because of the interpersonal dynamics involved. When deciding whether training is appropriate, the following questions should be carefully considered:

1. Is training an appropriate way of addressing any observed or measured performance discrepancies?[1]
2. Are the resources necessary to design, conduct, evaluate, and continually monitor the training's effectiveness available?
3. Is management committed to supporting the training being proposed?
4. Are the employees committed to participating in the training?
5. Will the goal of the training be to resolve problems, to fill KSA gaps, or both?

If it is uncertain whether training will yield the desired results or if training is not considered to be an appropriate approach to addressing the defined needs, alternate intervention strategies (e.g., behavioral or process consultation) should be investigated.

## WHY TRAINING PROGRAMS FAIL

According to some estimates, the annual expenditure on formalized training and development activities exceeds $45 billion.[2] Considering the enormity of the amounts involved, it should come as little surprise that many managers have begun to question the costs and worth of training.[3] In other words, what kinds of returns are being produced for the amounts being expended? With increasing pressure applied on HRD managers to become more accountable for the ROI involved in training and development activities, many creative ways for measuring results and returns have been devised. These involve in-depth analysis of the direct and indirect costs associated with developing and presenting training. Items such as instructor fees, logistical arrangements and support, HRD staff overhead, materials development, salaries paid to employees while they undergo training, equipment downtime, and lost production are all examples of direct as well as indirect costs. These are calculated against the returns a training program is expected to produce. In reality, the value that is sometimes received is significantly different from what was originally anticipated. The reasons as to why training sometimes produces little in terms of ROI can include the following: (1) Employees, for whatever reasons, failed to apply what they learned back on the job; (2) the course failed to meet its objectives; (3) it was poorly designed and presented; (4) it focused only on individual effectiveness rather than on increasing an individual's contribution to enhancing organizational performance; and (5) there was a lack of organization-wide commitment and support.[4]

One of the most prevalent reasons for training programs failing to deliver what was anticipated is that many are not designed to attain defined objectives that were derived from needs identified through a comprehensive needs assessment process. Further, individuals who are responsible for designing training may not understand how to formulate a training curriculum using an instructional design process that is driven by needs that were defined through a systems-oriented needs assessment.

## A NEEDS-DRIVEN INSTRUCTIONAL DESIGN MODEL

Designing and developing effective training is a core objective of instructional design. It is also a complex task. Since there are no universally recognized blueprints to follow, many experts have developed their own unique approaches and models.

Good instructional design emphasizes procedure and a systematic approach. There are three principal characteristics which virtually all types of instructional design models share: Each stresses comprehensiveness, each uses a systems-oriented approach, and each is objective and needs-driven.[5] These factors are critical if the training is to provide consistent results throughout successive offerings. Training specialists use a variety of approaches to instructional design. One of the most notable is the "Motorola U" approach, which includes additional steps such as precourse validation where the proposed curriculum is reviewed and approved by a team of SMEs.[6]

An example of an instructional design model that uses an objective-driven approach is presented in Figure 9.1.

**Figure 9.1**
An Objective-Driven Instructional Design Model

**Objective-Driven**
**Instructional Design Model**

Establish Training/Learning Objectives (Goals)
*Set Goals Relevant to Defined Needs
*Appraise Participant Learning Styles

▼
▼
▼

Instructional Strategy:
*Design/Select Instructional Methods
*Design and Sequence Course Content
*Develop Instructional Materials, Delivery systems, and Instructional Techniques
*Select/Train Instructors/Facilitators
*Design Evaluation Systems

▼
▼
▼

Optional:
*Pilot Test program if it is to be conducted on an on-going basis
*Revise curriculum, format, and content based on results of Pilot Test

▼
▼
▼

EVALUATE: Short- and Long-term

▼
▼
▼

Continually Monitor to Determine Necessity for Changes and/or Modifications

## Establishing Instructional Objectives

Just as goals and objectives were the major factors driving the design, facilitation, and analysis phases of the needs assessment process, they are also critical for designing and developing effective training curriculums. In order to have a clear understanding of what will be required to prepare a sound instructional strategy, one must first decide on what the outcomes of the training will be.

There are three major categories of learning outcomes. They are (1) the acquisition of new knowledge, (2) the development of new skills (or the enhancement of existing ones), and (3) the facilitation of changes in attitudes and behaviors.[7]

Instructional objectives are written expressions representing the intended results of a training program.[8] Their principal purpose is to establish criteria (outcomes) that participants will be expected to know or be able to do at the program's conclusion. They are important for the following reasons:

1. They set the direction for the training's curricular design.
2. They establish consistency in the instructional design process.
3. They set the standard for what participants are expected to learn.
4. They provide a reference point for all subsequent phases of the instructional design process.
5. They establish a direct link between the results of the needs assessment and the training program and, therefore, reflect directly on the outcomes or results produced by the needs assessment process.

There are two primary classifications for instructional objectives: primary and derived. Primary objectives are those which, first and foremost, the training is designed to attain. They are the dominant goals of the instructional design process because they provide meaning, clarity, and unity to all training program activities.[9] Derived objectives highlight the additional KSAs and behavioral changes that will be needed in order to support the attainment of the primary objective(s).[10]

One of the most useful ways for establishing sound instructional objectives is to state them in terms of performance. This can be broken down into three components: (1) increasing performance related to improvement (e.g., productive output that is measured against a predetermined standard), (2) the conditions under which improved performance is expected to occur, and (3) performance levels as they relate to individual and organizational achievement.

Instructional objectives must be clearly stated and understandable. They should focus on the learner outcomes and clearly communicate what will be gained. They should be written using action-oriented language and not be vague or obscure. Above all, instructional objectives must be realistic and attainable. In other words, they should stress measurable results.[11] Instructional objectives that are logically constructed and concisely stated provide the foundation for training course development. In addition, they allow trainees the opportunity to formulate individual expectations about what they will learn.

### Matching Instructional Objectives to Defined Needs

Instructional objectives are extensions of the needs that were identified through an assessment process. Each objective need should reflect an identified need. Sometimes a single need may produce multiple objectives. For example, if a need to improve interdepartmental communications was identified, one objective might focus on improving written communications (e.g., internal memorandums, reports, etc.), while two others could focus on improving interpersonal communications (e.g., one-on-one discussions, presentations in meetings, etc.) and on streamlining the organization's communication channels (e.g., making substantive changes and improvements to the quality, quantity, and timeliness of all narrative or written communications). In this example, a single defined need produced three instructional training objectives.

An important factor to consider when writing instructional objectives is what types of prerequisite knowledge, skills, experience, or formalized learning (if any) is required of prospective participants. If a learning goal is established without any consideration or regard to what trainees are bringing with them into the training program, it is unlikely that the primary or the derived goal(s) will be attained. This is especially true where technical skills training is concerned. For example, in developing a course on servicing aircraft avionics, the designer would first need to assess the present knowledge and skill levels of prospective trainees. This helps to ensure that the course content would be conceived with their present KSA levels in mind.

A systematic needs assessment also can be useful for prescreening participants' qualifications to be considered as potential training candidates. In the preceding example, it would make little sense to design and conduct training for individuals who have only a fundamental knowledge of how avionics systems work.

### Appraising Participant's Capacity to Learn

The preceding example raises an important issue—namely, how does one decide exactly what should be included in a training program? Since people possess varied skill, knowledge, and experience levels, at what level should the training begin; and, equally important, at what point or level should it end? In other words, how much information is too little and how much information is too much?

To answer this question requires that the level of trainee preparedness be defined. This includes (1) employees' present skill and knowledge levels and (2) their learning capacities.

*Qualifying Training Candidates.* In order to qualify potential trainees, one would first need to compose a list of learning prerequisites. Information obtained from any interviews or on-site observations would be very valuable here. Needs assessment data such as this can help the needs analyst decide whether to qualify trainees on the basis of job description, levels of responsibility, advancement potential, technical expertise, depth and span of knowledge and experience, or any other attributes which the designer considers important or necessary.

Using prerequisites derived from needs assessment data is an effective way to select and qualify potential training candidates. Because they can help to ensure that the right individuals are selected for training, prerequisites should be developed only after a thorough analysis of the needs assessment outcomes and training objectives has been completed.

Using needs assessment data to establish participant prerequisites presents a number of factors which merit consideration. Some of the more important ones are the following:

1. The extent to which training would assist employees in improving their job performance
2. The employees' potential to learn or to acquire new skills/knowledge
3. The extent to which employees have demonstrated an interest in applying what they have learned
4. The extent to which the employees' experience, skills, knowledge, abilities, and/or behaviors are to be improved
5. What ROI the organization expects to receive from its investment

Needs assessment information is also valuable for examining the context of each individual's job. It can provide indications as to how the training would be of benefit to each participant. For example, job and task analysis data can be helpful for deciding what measurable results or improvements are needed (see Chapter 1). To effectively accomplish this requires that

1. Each participant's job and job-related tasks must be carefully analyzed.
2. A summary of each person's present skills, knowledge, and experience levels must be prepared. This provides a way for identifying the levels where the training should begin and also indicates how much information should be included.
3. A summary of any specialized requirements, such as physical abilities, language skills, and the like, be prepared.
4. Each person's aptitude and interest levels (as can best be determined from the results of any interviews used in the job and task analysis) be examined and the results recorded for future reference.

Depending on the specific needs, it is often necessary to design custom training programs for homogeneous groups. Group homogeneity can be based on seniority, specificity to a particular job, levels of authority and responsibility, gender, job classification, issues regarding security, and so on. Designing training along homogeneous lines has certain advantages as well as disadvantages. One major advantage is that in courses where boss-to-employee relationships are to be openly discussed, employees are more prone to "open-up" when they are in the company of their peers as opposed to having their supervisor present.[12] A major disadvantage is that training such as this may be viewed as being elitist by employees who are not scheduled to participate, or it may send a signal that there are problems concentrated only within a certain group of employees. Therefore, when considering homogeneous group training, one should first define the nature of the training (e.g., behaviorally based) and then structure the group's composition, based on the needs assessment data. The proposed training group should be comprised of individuals who participated in the original needs assessment. It makes little sense to present custom training whose design was not based on employee needs defined through the assessment process. This illustrates one of the primary reasons for undertaking organizational needs assessments.

*Assessing Trainee Learning Styles*. For a number of years, the question of how people learn has been a central focus of HRD. Moreover, how people learn in an organizational setting has received particular attention.[13] Questions like these present a formidable challenge to defining and categorizing individual learning capacity so that relevant and effective training can be designed and delivered.

In order to understand how and under what conditions learning occurs, one must become familiar with and develop an understanding of traditional learning theories, the most dominant of which are Sensory Stimulation theory, Reinforcement theory, Facilitation theory, and Andragogy.

Sensory Stimulation theory suggests that in order for people to learn, they must be able to see, hear, touch, and do in the classroom or in the learning environment. It emphasizes a hands-on approach to learning by actively involving participants through the application of a variety of sensory stimuli. Its major criticisms are (1) that participants assume a purely responsive role which will eventually become passive and (2) the instructors bear the burden of presenting activities, thus forcing them to become "entertainers" rather than managers of the learning process.

Reinforcement theory is based on research that has its roots in the behavioral sciences. It suggests that people learn from experiences and that positive as well as negative ones serve to reinforce certain forms of behavior. Reinforcement theory promotes active involvement between the instructor and the trainee and places significant emphasis on positive trainee reaction. One of its major criticisms is that at some point the reinforcement process becomes more of a mechanical action–reaction process which eventually provides less and less motivation to both parties. Also, Reinforcement theory does not encourage debate or challenge, rather, it only rewards the trainees continued participation.

Facilitation theory contrasts both the Sensory Stimulation and Reinforcement learning theories. It places emphasis on the facilitative role of the instructor as opposed to that of being a stimulator or reinforcer. It also relies on individuals' level of self-motivation because its principal intent is to place the burden of learning on both the trainer and trainees. It provides for the learners to set the learning pace and to select the sequence in which they will acquire new skills. Further, Facilitation theory emphasizes self-evaluation. Its major criticisms are that it assumes too high a degree of self-motivation by the learner and that it takes control of the learning process out of the hands of the instructor. Its major value is that it provides a means for instructors (and designers) to identify behaviors that have the potential to produce the desired outcomes.

Andragogy, on the other hand, studies how adults learn and how this differs from the ways in which children acquire new behaviors.[14] It requires one to identify and to categorize the maturity of the learner. In training, it is problem-centered as opposed to being content-centered because it permits—indeed, encourages—active participation by the learner; it relies on the learner to introduce past experiences in order to impose them on new learning situations; it promotes a collaborative (instructor-to-trainee and vice versa) learning process; and it emphasizes experientially centered activities that are intellectually challenging. Thus, the designer focuses on presenting a personalized and motivational approach to learning new behaviors through active involvement of both the instructor and the learner.

Using theories such as these to identify learning capacity may appear, in a practical sense, to be somewhat hypothetical. In light of this, many experts recommend using a more universal approach; that is, (1) borrowing what each feels to be the best from all of the learning theories, (2) applying them in an environment that stresses relevancy and meaning to the jobs which the training is designed to enhance, and (3) emphasizing active participation and involvement by which results can be observed and measured.[15]

## Designing an Instructional Strategy

Once training objectives have been developed and the designers are satisfied that they have a good understanding of trainees' learning styles, the next step in a systematic instructional design process is to integrate this information into a strategy involving the methods of instruction, the selection of trainers, the development of instructional materials, the design of effective delivery systems (logistics and media selections), and the development of training course evaluation methods. This is the most complex phase of designing custom training programs. Too often, instructional strategies are selected on the basis of expediency, which ultimately produces inefficiency in attaining training objectives, or worse, results in a failure to achieve them altogether.[16]

There are three critical components in the instructional strategy design stage. They are the following: (1) determining content compatibility to the training objectives; (2) establishing continuity in the course design and development process (which necessitates constant reference to the outcomes of the needs assessment as well as the training objectives); and (3) determining variations in the training course delivery and in the design of evaluation systems and methods.

*Instructional Methods.* There are a variety of instructional methods available. The question is which are the most appropriate to use for the type or types of training being considered? In order to select appropriate instructional methods, designers must have information on the primary course objectives, the course content, participant KSA levels, behavioral characteristics, and learning abilities and traits of prospective trainees, along with the instructors' qualifications, time constraints, and, of course, cost factors.

Some instructional methods commonly used are lectures, conferences (seminars), demonstrations, self-instruction (also known as programmed instruction), performance-based (learning-by-doing), assignment methods, and tutoring. Some of the more advanced methods include the critical incident method, sensitivity training, case studies, role playing, and gaming and simulations. Table 9.1 contains a summary description of each along with notes on their uses, advantages, and disadvantages.

Needs assessment data can provide valuable indicators about which type or types of instructional methods to use. For example, job-related and peripheral information collected through the needs assessment can be used to help select the instructional method(s) that best suit the composition of the training group while emphasizing attainment of the course objectives. Because this composition will often require the use of more than one method, designers can obtain job-related criteria from the needs assessment data which can help to define the primary method, or rather, the one that is considered to be the most effective for attaining the training objective(s). Secondary or supporting methods that are considered to be essential components of and complementary to the primary method can also be identified from needs assessment outcomes. Last, alternative methods are chosen for those instances where the primary or the secondary methods are proven to be unsuccessful.

Whatever combination is ultimately chosen, the designer must also be concerned with the instructional techniques that are incorporated into each method. Various types include the use of audio-visual aids and associated equipment, how participant responses and questions are handled, and testing.

Once the parameters of the strategy have been defined, the next step in a systematic instructional design process is concerned with course delivery mechanisms: namely, the selection (and training, if required) of qualified instructors, the design and development of the instructional and participant ref-

**Table 9.1**
Uses, Advantages, and Disadvantages of Various Types of Instructional Methods

| Method | Use | Advantage(s) | Disadvantage(s) |
|---|---|---|---|
| Lecture | Instructor transmits information by means of oral communication | Time saving - considerable amount of information can be transmitted in a relatively short period of time; class size is limited only by size of meeting facilities; can focus on major points and related items because content is solely determined by instructor | No interchange of ideas between instructor and trainees - all ideas originate with instructor; not an appropriate means for teaching skills; lecture approach is mainly auditory - very little in the way of instructor awareness to trainee reaction or understanding |
| Conference | Group discussion - information transmitted through active interchange of ideas; types are open or directed discussion, seminars; used to develop solutions to problems, to stimulate thinking, to emphasize points, to supplement lectures, and to introduce new methods, theories, etc. | Active participation and interaction by both instructors and trainees. | Requires a significant amount of advance preparation, skillful and knowledgeable instructors; instructor has limited control over trainee preparedness; may require significant time and cost commitment |
| Demonstration | Used to show how something should be done; to teach operations and/or procedures; to illustrate how something works, etc. | Gives visual and hands-on meaning to spoken words; gives illustrative examples that can serve to clarify ambiguities between procedural steps; has wide appeal because instructor's can transmit a large amount of technical information through a visually based medium; can incorporate the use of models to illustrate proper operation, maintenance, etc. | Instructional design must be technically correct - little room for errors; where equipment is being demonstrated instructor's must insure that they have extensive knowledge and experience with it; the demonstration room or facility must be logistically accommodating to a demonstration; can be costly and time consuming in the preparation stage(s). |

| | | | |
|---|---|---|---|
| Self-instruction (programmed instruction) | Used to take trainee's through a carefully designed sequence of steps and procedures toward the attainment of skills and knowledge. | Trainees work at their own pace and receive feedback at each step; high completion and pass rate because of constant instructor monitoring and feedback; predetermined instructional content focused on learning objectives; can accommodate a wide variety of applications (e.g., machine and equipment repair, maintenance, etc.). | Requires a high degree of instructor monitoring and intervention; requires trainees to have a high degree of comprehension ability; creates numerous administrative problems such as scheduling, logistical arrangements, monitoring procedures, testing, etc.; many times must be facilitated on an individual basis; can be costly and time consuming. |
| Performance-based | Used as a means for permitting the trainee to perform a particular procedure or operation or demonstrate a certain skill or competency under observable, measurable, and controlled conditions. | Provides the trainee with the opportunity to apply learned skill or knowledge; feedback is immediate; corrective actions can be immediately implemented; maximized trainee participation and involvement; instructor can readily identify trainee's who are having problems or difficulties; excellent method for emphasizing the proper way of doing things or for giving hands-on instruction; excellent method for providing safety-related training. | May require several instructor's to constantly monitor and provide feedback simultaneously even to small number of trainees; requires each trainee to fully participate which can be a motivational or an incentive-based challenge; costly and time consuming. |
| Assignments | Used primarily to set the stage for some form of lecture or hand-on demonstration; used to prepare for in-class reviews or to provide supplemental knowledge or enrichment. | Relies on instructor assigning readings, the completion of a project or study, or otherwise imposing a task which, upon conclusion, will be evaluated as to its correctness and/or applicability; can cover a great amount of material and detail in a relatively short period of time; is a good substitute for lecture method. | Relies entirely on individual trainee self-motivation; very little in the way of instructor-to-trainee feedback; little way for instructor to know how much information trainee has actually acquired unless outcome is accompanied and measured by some form of testing; concerns about long-term retention as compared to the demonstration or self-instructional methods. |

**Table 9.1** *(continued)*

| Method | Use | Advantage(s) | Disadvantage(s) |
|---|---|---|---|
| Tutoring | Used to teach complex, highly technical skills and procedures; primarily used on a one-on-one (one instructor to one trainee) basis. | The most effective means of individualized instruction; can be designed to identify and exclusively address individual employee training needs; course design and delivery systems are matched to individual needs and/or requirements; performance is continually monitored and feedback is immediate, resulting in a high degree of learning acquisition and retention. | The most demanding and expensive type of instructional method. |
| Critical Incident and Case Study | Used for in-depth study, analysis, and group discussions of real-world incidents and situations; it's primary use is to promote open discussion and critique of situations and further to develop and improve participants problem-solving abilities. | Actively involves participants in interchange of ideas and analysis of case situations and critical incidents in organizational environment; raises awareness of individual perceptions and promotes greater self-understanding of group analysis and decision-making processes. | Requires considerable amount of time for trainees to read, comprehend, discuss, and formulate opinions and/or strategies and present critiques; group discussions can be manipulated by the more extroverted members of the group, sometimes making intervention by the instructor(s) necessary. |
| Sensitivity Training | Used primarily as a means for developing awareness and raising sensitivity to other's feelings and beliefs through behavioral training; usually conducted in small, unstructured groups. | Gives participant's new insights into how their behavior and actions affects others and how by modifying their behavioral patterns they can sometimes generate more effective results. | Can be costly; requires an instructor who is well versed in behavioral training techniques (usually a psychologist); possibility of limited application on the job due to organizational politics or cultural or other environmental factors. |

| | | | |
|---|---|---|---|
| Role Playing | Used to make simulation or business games more realistic and to highlight the potential for interpersonal problems; used to promote the necessity for increased understanding of other's points of view; To properly develop insights into personal attitudes, values, and behaviors. | A controlled method involving spontaneous interaction or the acting-out of a situation between two or more individuals; when used correctly, can result in a greater understanding of human behavior without taking real-world risks; promotes interpersonal communication; trainee's have opportunity to observe themselves and others in a simulated yet controlled, environment. | Requires considerable time; can degenerate into a confrontational situation unless closely monitored, mediated, and controlled; requires experienced instructor(s) who are well versed in behavioral situations; Requires some "acting" by participant's, some of whom may be too reticent or reluctant to participate; has the potential to be destructive, especially where two opposing personalities are involved. |
| Gaming and Business Simulations | Favored by many business as well as the military; includes a number of structured decision-making tasks which simulate real-world environment; used primarily to develop leadership skills, to build effective work teams, to foster spirit of cooperation, and to sharpen decision-making skills. | With proper facilitation and monitoring, participant's become actively involved; considerable experience can be gained in a relatively short period of time; allows integration of other disciplines such as behavioral psychology, finance, accounting, marketing, operations, etc., so that participants can observe without risk the impact that certain decisions and actions can have on the organization as a whole. | Costly, particularly if the simulation or game is self-developed; requires experienced and expert facilitator(s) who are well-versed in all aspects of the simulation or game; |

erence materials, the design of the training delivery system (e.g., training room, audio-visual media, logistical considerations, the integration of instructional methods and techniques, etc.), and developing postprogram as well as long-term evaluation and monitoring systems.

### Designing and Sequencing Course Content

Training course content is defined as what will be taught. It comprises all phases of the course which trainees will be exposed to and is directed at establishing focus and continuity in the training process. It consists of subject matter that is logically arranged into units and sequentially linked so that, as each unit is presented, the trainees are moved closer to the attainment of the objective(s). In this manner, learning is produced in a step-by-step process with trainees being exposed to and eventually acquiring the KSAs and behaviors that the training is designed to provide.

Developing a detailed outline of the course subject matter is the first step in designing and sequencing course content. This is gradually expanded outward until a detailed statement of the content along with its contribution to the attainment of the objectives is produced.

Throughout this process, any subject matter experts who were used in the needs assessment process should be regularly consulted about the accuracy and completeness of the course content. This helps to ensure that each unit will be matched to a corresponding training objective. It also provides a way for comparing course content to the projected outcomes (e.g., acquired learning).

Sequencing is the process of developing and logically arranging the course content. Its purpose is to increase the amount of learning within the allotted time frames. It maximizes continuity because each learning component is fully explored and developed, which helps to ensure that trainees will make a successful transition between the various course segments. For example, if a course on servicing computer monitors was being designed, it would make little sense to teach the intricacies involved in the servicing phase without first covering the techniques of how to disassemble the unit, how to use the various types of diagnostic instruments, and how to perform the various diagnostic tests. Thus, the sequence serves to organize, arrange, and present each prerequisite step in the learning process.

There are various types of sequencing techniques. Some of these are logical order, performance order, psychological order, descriptive order, and problem-centered order.

In a logical order sequence, the designer is mainly concerned with particulars as they relate to specific content items and in selecting the best instructional methods and techniques by which these particulars are presented. Performance order sequencing is based on how a job, task, procedure, or operation is actually performed. Psychological order sequencing involves the development of course content that is based on past experiences or "older" learning in order to establish precedence for the introduction and acquisition of new knowledge or skills. Descriptive order sequencing involves first identifying the best approach to developing a learning methodology and then supplementing it with a clearly stated description of what is to be learned and how it is to be learned. Finally, in problem-centered sequencing, a generalized problem is presented along with various means of solving it. Where there is no absolute solution, problem-centered sequencing provides a means of identifying contributing problematic factors so that alternative solutions can be explored.

Needs assessment data are valuable for selecting the best sequencing method. For example, assume that an assessment identifed the cause of a measured or observed effect and that this cause was behaviorally based. Further, this outcome suggested that training would be useful to prevent the cause from reoccurring. The instructional designer may want to first consider using the problem-centered approach to course sequencing or, depending on the nature of the problem (e.g., its causality), may also consider using psychological order sequencing.

### Instructional Materials, Instructional Techniques, and Delivery Systems

Instructional materials are developed for use in a training program and are intended to facilitate the learning process. Some examples of instructional materials are participant workbooks and manuals, texts, articles, books, pamphlets, instructional sheets, models, specimens, examples, charts, graphs, diagrams, audio tapes, video tapes, pictorial slides, computer-generated visual programs, and any other item whose purpose is to supplement the course presentation and to enhance the transfer of learning.

Instructional materials should be designed or acquired based on the contribution they make to the attainment of the training objective(s). They can be custom developed solely for use in a specialized course, or they may be acquired commercially, either as principle reference materials or for use in conjunction with and in support of custom developed ones. In either case, special consideration must be given to how materials are developed and how they will be used in the delivery of the training program.

Instructional materials should be designed to be used not only during the formal training session(s), but they should also provide long-term reference value. Therefore, they should be designed with both their present and their future applicability in mind.

To be able to develop excellent participant reference materials is as much an art as it is a science. It requires excellent composition and analytical skills. It is always helpful to have any and all materials reviewed by SMEs, particularly those who served as observers during the needs assessment phase, so that feedback regarding the conciseness, thoroughness, applicability, and clarity of the materials can be obtained.

### Developing Custom Workbooks and Manuals

A basic requirement for developing good reference materials begins with the development of an outline that coincides with as well as complements the training objective(s). The contents of the manual should closely mirror the course content and sequence. It should contain information and examples that not only explain relevant concepts in detail but also reinforce and clarify any points made. Since workbooks and manuals often contain worksheets, case studies, explanatory notes, and other types of reference materials, they should be organized in a manner that assists in establishing and maintaining course continuity. Workbooks should contain only materials that are required to facilitate the learning process. All materials should, in one way or another, serve to address the program's primary and secondary objectives.

Workbooks should be logically organized and free of clutter or filler. The materials should be carefully arranged to provide seamless continuity between the subject matter sections. This helps to ensure both clarity and consistency. Many experts also prefer to include paper copies of any and all overheads and graphics to attain maximum coverage.

### Instructional Delivery Systems

The term *delivery system* is used to describe the various types of equipment that are required to conduct a training program. This includes (but is not limited to) overheads, graphs, charts, flipcharts, chalkboards, tape recorders (audio and visual), microphones, room set-ups, seating arrangements, room lighting and climate controls, and any other equipment and logistics whose purpose is to contribute to the enhancement of the actual course presentation.

The mix of instructional methodologies, course content, and sequencing should be used to determine the mix of delivery and support equipment that is considered essential in order to effectively present the program. These should be selected, developed, and used to supplement, clarify, explain, and enhance the narrative portion of the presentation. A well-thought-out delivery system should incorporate all of the aforementioned components of the instructional strategy in that it should accentuate the selected instructional methods. The components selected should also complement as well as enhance the course content and sequencing. The combination of methods, techniques, and equipment should be the best options available so that the mix between material, delivery systems, and course presentation is optimized. Last, instructors must be familiar with this mix so they will be able to use it to provide as stimulating and thought provoking a learning experience as possible.

### Developing a Lesson Plan

A lesson plan is a detailed document that establishes objectives for each phase of the course content. It specifies what lessons are to be learned and includes pertinent and detailed information on how the content is to be taught. It serves as a point of reference to guide instructors in their facilitation of all training-related activities. It also establishes a link between the results or the outcomes of a needs assessment, the course content, and its delivery and evaluation system. A detailed lesson plan provides a way for standardizing instructional content throughout subsequent offerings. As such, it becomes a blueprint for other instructors to follow by summarizing the course content in terms of what is taught and how to teach it.

Some principal considerations to keep in mind when writing lesson plans are the following:

1. The type of content involved (e.g., technical skills, knowledge, behavioral, etc.)
2. The amount and complexity of detail included in the course content
3. The levels of difficulty associated with the various segments of the course
4. The amounts of time that are allocated to the various segments
5. The number of instructors and trainees each presentation requires and can accommodate, respectively

Finally, a lesson plan should include a complete package of actual course instructional materials, including all workbooks, manuals, overheads, graphics, and other forms of handouts or reference materials.

### Selecting and Training Instructors

The guidelines for selecting training instructors or course facilitators are essentially the same as those used for selecting assessment consultants, albeit with slightly different emphasis. Since course instructors play a pivotal role in determining how well the course is delivered and received by the participants and, thus, in determining how well the training meets its objectives, instructors should be screened and evaluated carefully.

First, a decision must be made as to whether to use internal training staff (providing, of course, such resources are available). If internal trainers are to be used, the person or persons selected must be familiar with all aspects of the instructional design strategy as well as with the outcomes and recommendations that resulted from the needs assessment. In addition, they should have experience with the selected instructional methods and have established credibility within the organization.

When it is necessary or otherwise desirable to hire external trainers, their backgrounds, previous work experience, and credentials (academic as well as work-related), should be reviewed to make certain that they are qualified and capable of delivering the training in an efficient and focused manner.[17] The training consultants should be made aware of how the instructional strategy was devised, exactly what is expected of them, and how they will be evaluated not only by the trainees but also by the instructional designer and any other persons who may be involved in the evaluation, monitoring, and ROI determination process. In short, the performance criteria for the training consultants should be clearly stated so that there are no misinterpretations or misunderstandings.

Most of the aforementioned requirements can be addressed through the provision of formalized training to the training consultants. This train-the-trainer activity includes familiarizing them with the intricacies of the instructional design strategy, the process used to select as well as qualify training candidates, aspects of how the need for training materialized (e.g., derived from the results of the needs assessment), and so on. It may be necessary to allow the training consultants access to the needs assessment final report and also to the assessment project activity log. A meeting between the training consultants and the assessment analyst or project leader (if he or she is different from the instructional designer) is mandatory so that any peripheral information that was not formally included in the assessment's final report can be discussed. This can add additional insight to the consultants' knowledge and perspective.

As was the case with the hiring of needs assessment consultants, using internal and external trainers has both advantages as well as disadvantages. The advantages to using internal training staff are that (1) they are less costly; (2) they usually have a more intimate familiarity with the organization's culture and operational environment; and (3) depending on the focus, scope, and context of the training, they may possess unique expertise regarding the application of the training within the confines of the organizational structure. The disadvantages to using internal training consultants are that (1) regardless of their experience and knowledge levels, they may not have significant internal recognition or credibility; (2) they may not be the best choice when compared to what is available externally; and (3) using internal trainers may send a signal to prospective trainees that the organization does not consider the training to be important enough to hire an outside "expert." In this case, using an internal trainer may be demoralizing and an inhibitor to the learning process.

The advantages to using outside training consultants are that (1) most possess experience that has been gained through contact with other organizations; (2) they often bring an additional degree of credibility to the training course by virtue of the fact that they are experts; (3) they can use their work-related experience—gained through assignments and projects with other organizations—to provide additional perspectives to the training program; and (4) they can use their experience to pinpoint any weak areas in the instructional design strategy that otherwise may have gone unnoticed.

The disadvantages to using external training consultants are that (1) the costs associated with hiring them will almost certainly be higher as compared to using internal staff; (2) the organization's management may be reluctant or even resistant to allowing an outsider access to what may be considered sensitive company information; (3) they may be unfamiliar with the internal workings (e.g., culture, politics) of the organization (this can also be an advantage); and (4) they may not be as flexible in regards to their availability and scheduling as might otherwise be required.

The following guidelines can be useful in qualifying and selecting external training consultants. External training consultants should

1. Possess excellent platform presentation and communication skills (e.g., speaking, listening, use of audio-visual aids)
2. Be experienced in the training course subject matter and should have a proven track record of conducting like or similar training in the areas they are being considered for (i.e., they should be experts)
3. In the case of technical training courses, be able to translate and present complex material in a clear and concise manner
4. Command an intimate mastery of the course subject matter (which can be enhanced further through a train-the-trainer process)
5. Be open to and not resentful of constructive criticism regarding their performance
6. Be willing to commit to a stated fee structure for their services, which should be tied to some form of performance-related criteria (the basis of which should be determined in consultation with the designer)
7. Be experts in using the selected instructional methods and their accompanying techniques
8. Be able to adjust their formal presentations and their group facilitation strategies if necessary to better accommodate the trainees' needs while maintaining focus on the attainment of the primary and secondary (derived) objectives

*Instructional Technique*. The term *instructional technique* refers to how the instructional methods and delivery systems are effectively integrated into the course presentation. The importance of perfecting instructional techniques cannot be overemphasized.

The instructors' presentation style is as much a part of the instructional strategy as are the methods, the materials, and the delivery systems. Without a well-organized and coordinated presentation, even the most meticulously designed instructional strategy will be mediocre. Most professionals, regardless of whether they are internal staff or external consultants, have developed mature, effective, teaching styles. Therefore, instructors must be familiar with the outcomes of the needs assessment and how this contributed to defining the course content, its sequencing, the selection of the instructional methodologies, and the delivery systems.

## Designing Evaluation Systems

The evaluation stage is a subsystem of a systematic instructional design process. Its primary purpose is twofold: (1) to gather trainee feedback and reactions to the formal course presentation and (2) to gather information on how well the course contributed to the attainment of its primary and secondary objectives.[18] Due to the complexities involved in addressing both functional as well as behavioral objectives, various evaluation methods—short term as well as long term—have been developed. A model of a systematic evaluation is illustrated in Figure 9.2.

In a tactical sense, the evaluation system is intended to measure how well the material was organized and presented, how relevant it was to the participant's job or tasks, and how well the training was logistically organized. In a more strategic sense, a well-designed evaluation system is designed to measure what impact the training has had on organizational as well as individual performance, and, further, what measurable effect it has had on the bottom line. Perhaps the best and most well-known example was originated by Kirkpatrick, who approached the concept of training evaluation as a four-step process that measures

1. Immediate trainee reaction
2. Learning by determining if learning has actually occurred and, if it has, if the extent of this can be identified so that improvements in knowledge, competencies, and skills can be measured
3. Behavioral changes by attempting to answer the following questions: (a) Has the training changed or otherwise altered the trainee's behavior and (b) has this learning or behavioral change been transferred to the workplace?
4. Business objectives by examining the financial impact the training has had and whether it has contributed to meeting the organization's business objectives. In other words, to what extent has the training affected the bottom line?[19]

Kirkpatrick's original work has since been refined into more systematic and applications-oriented models.[20]

Designing a meaningful and applicable evaluation system is, in itself, a very complex task. From a theoretical point of view, evaluations are aimed at determining if learning has occurred and, if it has, of what value it is toward improving employee as well as organizational performance.

A well-designed training evaluation system seeks to answer five basic questions. They are the following:

1. Were the course objectives (and, hence, the original needs assessment outcomes and recommendations) realistic?

**Figure 9.2**

**A Model for Evaluating Short- and Long-Term Training Effectiveness**

Assess Training Needs

▼

Develop Short and Long-term Objectives

▼

Conduct Observations/measurements to Determine Pre-course Conditions and to Establish Standards

▼

Present Course

▼

Conduct Post-course Short- and Long-term Evaluations

▼

▸ Analysis: Short-term

1. Were needs correctly Defined?
2. Were short-term objectives realistic?
3. Was curriculum designed around needs to address short-term objectives?
4. Was course presented in a manner which focused on attainment of short-term objectives?

▼

▸ Analysis: Long-term

1. Were long-term objectives realistic?
2. Were long-term objectives attainable?
3. Has behavior changed and/or skills/knowledge improved?

▼

Summarize and Record for Future Reference

*Source:* Adapted from Samuel B. McClelland, "A Model for Designing Objective-Oriented Training Evaluations," *Industrial and Commercial Training*, Vol. 26, No. 1, 1994, p. 6. Reprinted with permission from MCB University Press.

2. Did learning occur as a result of the training and, if it did, to what degree?
3. What are the short-term effects (gains)? Are these compatible with the primary training objectives?

4. What are the long-term effects (gains)? Are these compatible with the primary objectives as well as with the organization's strategic objectives?
5. Overall, is there measurable improvement and a positive ROI?

Like a needs assessment, training evaluation systems use a variety of data-gathering methods. Examples of these are survey questionnaires, tests (to compare and measure posttraining results against pretraining standards), interviews, observations, and performance records and reviews.[21]

One popular method for testing the validity of training evaluations is to use control groups in comparison to experimental groups. The requirements for the composition of a control group include equivalency in both groups' jobs, skill levels, abilities, and demographics. Experimental groups are composed of trainees who participate in the training program, while members of the control group do not. The control and experimental group approach is used to compare the performance levels of each group prior to and then after the training. Ideally, the performance levels of the experimental group will be higher than that of the control group.[22]

A well-designed evaluation system will generally have most of the following characteristics:

1. It is learner and not trainer centered.
2. It contains provisions for taking precourse, immediate postcourse, and long-term measurements.
3. It stresses attainment of the training's primary objective(s).
4. Trainees and other personnel, such as co-workers, supervisors, subordinates, and even external personnel such as customers, suppliers, and vendors, become facilitators in the evaluation process via their roles as both formal and informal performance evaluators.

The immediate postcourse evaluation phase for most kinds of training programs will usually employ survey questionnaires whose items reflect directly back on the course's delivery systems and on the performance of the instructors. Questions are usually closed-ended answer or ranked response types, which expedites quantitative tabulation (see Chapter 4). Many experts also require qualitative feedback because it usually contains information on outlying issues that may not have been covered in the quantitative questions.[23] Qualitative questions can be used to obtain feedback on the quality, applicability, and readability of the instructional materials, the instructors' performance, and the training delivery systems. In addition, an immediate postprogram evaluation may also include some probing questions such as (1) how the training will contribute to changes (improvements) in participants' knowledge, skills, competencies, behaviors, or abilities; (2) what specific actions or changes the participants will make in their work habits and the like; (3) what overall benefits or value can the organization expect to receive; (4) what were the most valuable and the least valuable components of the program; and (5) how to better the program's content and delivery systems.

Informal debriefing sessions are often conducted as a means for gaining feedback that may not have been requested in the survey questionnaire. This is important because such sessions can produce valuable information about the course structure, the instructional methods and techniques, the course content, the instructors' performance, and the efficiency and utility of the delivery systems. This information can be critical for making future changes and updating the instructional design strategy.

The long-term evaluation phase is generally conducted at predetermined intervals after the training and the immediate postcourse evaluation has concluded. Depending on the complexity of the course content, these intervals could span as little as a few days to as much as six months to a year. The main purpose of the long-term evaluation is to link the results of the training to measurable results on the job.

Interviews and observation techniques are generally preferred over the use of survey questionnaires. Interviews can be conducted with trainees as well as with their co-workers, supervisors, and subordinates. Observations are generally conducted by SMEs who are familiar with the trainees' jobs, tasks, and behaviors in the pretraining environment and are focused on identifying quantifiable or otherwise observable posttraining changes and improvements. In any case, long-term indicators directed at determining if performance and productivity have improved should also seek to identify whether such improvements can be directly linked to and have resulted from the training.

Once the data from both evaluation phases are collected and summarized, the results are then compared to the training objectives and, if applicable, to pretraining conditions or standards. Any reasons for partially attained objectives should be closely examined. This can be done by first reviewing the goal-setting process and its relationship to the recommendations that were derived from the needs assessment. In addition, the outcomes can also be compared as well as contrasted to the design, development, and implementation of the instructional strategy.

Evaluation results are eventually compiled into a composite format and retained for future reference. This is an important yet often overlooked component. Short- as well as long-term evaluation information can be useful both as a reference for future training projects and for initiating changes to the existing instructional design format.

### Pretesting

Assuming that funds are available, all newly developed training courses should be pretested before they are formally implemented. Pretesting training programs has a number of significant advantages:

1. It provides a way for determining if the program's primary and secondary objectives are realistic as well as attainable.
2. It enables the designer to simulate the instructional strategy and evaluation systems under real-world (not hypothetical) conditions.
3. It provides a means for assessing and evaluating the applicability of the course content.
4. It provides a way for determining if the course sequencing is appropriate.
5. It is useful for evaluating the effectiveness of the instructional methods selected.
6. It provides a means for evaluating the instructional skills of the trainers and for evaluating the effectiveness of the training delivery systems.
7. It provides a good indication of how well the course will be received by the trainees.
8. It will indicate whether the outcomes of the needs assessment and the subsequent recommendations are valid. It also can provide indications of whether additional training or some other form of intervention is required.

Pretesting should be carried out under controlled conditions. Ideally, the pretest training group should be comprised of individuals whose jobs and responsibilities are very similar or identical to those who have been selected to participate in the training course. Pretesting is very similar to the control group method used for designing and testing evaluation systems.

Once the training program's instructional strategy and evaluation systems are considered to be sound, the course is then formally scheduled, implemented, and evaluated.

### Course Presentation

How a course is presented has a tremendous impact on how it will be received and subsequently evaluated. The formal presentation will also impact on whether (and how) learning has occurred (e.g., the transference of skills, knowledge, changes in behavior, etc.). In essence, how the training is presented will determine its effectiveness in both the short and the long term. Given the importance of a well-planned, smooth, and professional presentation, careful consideration should be given to the following components as well as to the subsequent effect they have on the postcourse as well as the long-term results.

*The Training Facility.* The environment or the setting where the training is to be presented affects not only the actual delivery but also the degree to which the transfer of knowledge and skills takes place. Training rooms should be selected based on how well they contribute to facilitating the learning process. Participant seating should be comfortable, and there should be ample space between people so that they have room to perform the tasks that are required of them. For example, adequate work space should be provided if the training requires participants to work through exercises that require frequent reference to a variety of instructional materials. This would mean larger work tables accommodating not more than two persons per eight-foot table, and so on. Supplies (e.g., pencils, paper, calculators, rulers, erasers, etc.) should be placed at each seating position. Where audio-visual equipment is to be used as part of the delivery system, participant seating should be arranged so that each person has an unobstructed view of any screens and video monitors. Where the instructional strategy calls for role playing exercises, a special area should be provided where these can take place uninterrupted.

Training facilities should have ample lighting, the intensity of which can be controlled. Most facilities that have been designed specifically for training have a combination of both incandescent as well as fluorescent lighting and allow for each system to be controlled independently of the others. There should be adequate ventilation and climate controls. Audio systems such as microphones and loudspeakers should be controllable. Sound levels should never be excessive; rather, amplification should be set and maintained at a comfortable listening level. If the training room has windows, then curtains or some form of shades or blinds should be used to shield participants from any external distractions.

*The Instructors' Presentation.* The instructors should introduce themselves at the opening of the training session. They should quickly establish rapport with the group and set the tone and pace. Adequate time should be provided for question and answer sessions (providing, of course, that the instructional methodology allows for this). Instructors should work to engage participants in an interesting and thought-provoking manner. They should always maintain a professional presence and never let the group get out of control. This is particularly important where the training is designed to result in behavioral change. If trainees are to be tested at the conclusion of the program, they should be informed of this at the onset. Moreover, they should be made aware of what will be required of them throughout the duration of the course and what the expected outcomes will be.

Trainers should be well versed in the instructional design strategy and in the use of the instructional methods employed. They should be able to effortlessly interact with the trainees. They should present the material in a clear and coherent manner and be able to handle questions—even dissention—while maintaining the participant's focus on the program's objective(s). They must be able to integrate and use any and all audio-visual support equipment and related materials in a manner that enhances the learning process. In short, instructors must be professional in their preparations as well as in their presentations.

## Evaluation and Long-Term Monitoring

An extended phase of the course evaluation system that is external to the formal classroom training involves long-term monitoring. This is used to identify the long-term effectiveness of the instructional design strategy along with its value and applicability in the work setting.[24] Long-term monitoring provides a means for following up on what participants are doing with the KSAs they acquired during the formalized program. It also provides a means for measuring the ROI of the training. This information is extremely valuable for three reasons:

1. It serves as a basis for initiating future changes to the course instructional strategy.
2. It serves to reinforce what trainees have learned through on-the-job application and evaluation.
3. It provides useful information for future needs assessment projects.

Long-term feedback is generally collected through survey questionnaires, individual interviews, and on-site observations.

*On-Site Follow-Up.* On-site follow-up includes direct observation of trainees by SMEs, co-workers, supervisors, or managers. On-site follow-up activities can also include direct interviews in which at least a sampling of the original trainees are included. Narrative follow-ups have very distinct advantages. First, trainees are generally more willing to discuss things they would not normally take the time to write down. Thus, the depth of the feedback obtained is greater. Second, indicators of long-term effectiveness are more reliable because both the observers and the trainees have had the opportunity to evaluate the effectiveness of the training in the actual work environment. Third, on-site observation and follow-up interviews give the instructional designer as well as the needs assessment analyst the opportunity to validate the original assessment findings and design strategies under real-world conditions. Last, measurements of what ROI the organization is actually receiving as compared to what was originally expected can be taken.

*Survey Feedback.* Unlike the needs assessment process, survey questionnaires are used as a secondary data-collection method in long-term evaluation and monitoring. Their primary purpose is to supplement information obtained through the on-site observation and interview methods. Questionnaires can be custom designed to focus on the objectives of the training program and how well these are being met. The advantages to using survey questionnaires in this manner are that (1) a high sample rate of trainees as well as co-workers, supervisors, and other personnel can be obtained; and (2) they are less time-consuming and, therefore, are less costly to implement.

### The Final Report

A final report of the training activity should be prepared for presentation to management. It should contain background information on how the training program was designed in response to the outcomes of the needs assessment. It should explain what the objectives of the training were and how well they have been achieved. It should focus on the results that have been obtained as opposed to presenting generalized findings. It should also specify what type of return the organization is receiving (e.g., increased productivity, improved performance, lower rates of absenteeism, higher employee morale, positive behavioral changes, changes to policies and/or procedures that are resulting in greater efficiency, lower overhead costs, etc.).

## SUMMARY

Training is not a predisposed outcome of a needs assessment. However, it is often recommended as a means for filling skill or knowledge gaps or as a means for changing behaviors that are thought to be problematic or are barriers to improving organizational performance.

Training programs will fail to attain their goals for a number of reasons. These range from a lack of support by senior management (as well as employees) to a failure to design and develop training that adequately addresses the needs that have been identified through a needs assessment process. Further, training programs often fail due to poorly conceived instructional design strategies.

Effective instructional design models stress comprehensiveness. They are systematic in both their approach and their execution and are driven by training objectives that have been developed in response to identified needs.

A sound instructional strategy begins with first identifying training objectives. These are written expressions of intended training outcomes. Instructional objectives are results-oriented and can be classified into two types: primary and derived (or secondary). Primary objectives are the ones which the training is specifically designed to attain. They represent the main reason for the design, development, and delivery of the training program and should be directly linked to needs that were defined via the needs assessment process. Derived or secondary objectives are developed based on their relationship to the additional skills, knowledge, behavioral traits, and characteristics that will need to be improved or changed in order for the training to attain its primary objective(s). Thus, each training-related need that is identified in the assessment process provides a basis for the development of a separate instructional objective.

The outcomes of a systematic needs assessment can be useful for developing and identifying trainee prerequisites. These can be defined as any skills, knowledge, experience, abilities, competencies, or behavioral traits which trainees possess that qualify them to become potential training candidates. As part of the prerequisite identification process, thoughtful consideration must be given to the training candidates' learning capacities. The extent to which training would be useful in improving employee performance must be evaluated. Further, the individuals' potential to acquire new skills, the extent to which they (the employees) can implement the skills and knowledge in the workplace, and what degree of ROI the organization should receive must also be explored. In order to define individual learning capacities, an analysis and summary of the potential trainees' jobs and their present skill and knowledge levels should be prepared.

Each person has a unique learning style which will determine how he or she acquires new skills, knowledge, and behaviors. Although there are a variety of theories regarding how people learn (and thus how the transfer of learning takes place), most experienced instructional designers will employ a more universal approach as opposed to focusing on a single theory. These approaches usually stress active participation and involvement by both the instructors and the trainees.

The plan by which the participants' learning styles are integrated with instructional methods is called an instructional strategy. A well-conceived strategy involves the selection of appropriate instructional methods that best match the course content and participants' learning styles. The strategy must also address issues such as the selection of qualified instructors, the design of efficient delivery systems (presentations), the development of appropriate course materials (e.g., workbooks, manuals), and course topic sequencing.

A critical stage of the instructional strategy involves the development of a lesson plan. This contains a detailed description of the training, how and why it was developed, and what its objectives are. It is used to introduce order and continuity in the design and delivery of the training as well as in the systems used to evaluate its effectiveness. Last, it allows for standardizing the course content and is useful for modifying the course curricula.

The selection of qualified instructors is also a critically important factor in the formulation of an effective instructional design strategy. Regardless of whether instructors are drawn from internal or from external resources, they should have intimate knowledge and experience with the course content as well as with its sequencing and instructional methods. More important, instructors must have the flexibility to adjust their presentation styles and instructional techniques to the learning needs of the group. Their presentation techniques should complement the instructional methods as well as the course content, sequencing, and delivery systems. Overall, instructors need to be more than just course facilitators: They must be able to effectively manage the learning process.

Evaluation systems should be designed and developed to measure both short-term (immediate postcourse) as well as long-term (strategic) actions and results. A well-designed evaluation system will illustrate whether the course objectives were realistic and attainable (and, hence, reflect back on the outcomes of the needs assessment) and whether learning actually occurred. It will also illustrate the short- as well as the long-term effects (gains) and whether there were any measurable increases in performance. Last, well-designed evaluation systems will show what ROI the organization is receiving. Evaluation results should be compiled and retained for future reference in the event that it becomes necessary to modify the existing course format.

Before the course is formally presented, it should be pretested on a sample of employees. This sample should be composed of individuals who have identical or, at least, similar jobs and responsibilities as the group targeted to receive the formal training. Pretesting provides an opportunity for the course to be evaluated on a relatively low-risk basis.

Once all aspects of the instructional strategy have been developed, the training is then formally presented. Finally, an often overlooked but critically important factor is the necessity to prepare a final report on the training activity and outcomes. This should include information about how the course was designed (in response to needs that were identified through the assessment process), the development of the instructional strategy, the delivery and evaluation systems, and what results and benefits the organization is receiving.

## NOTES

1. D. Laird, *Approaches to Training and Development*, 2nd ed. (Reading, Mass.: Addison-Wesley, 1985).
2. *Training Magazine*, Vol. 30, No. 10, pp. 29–34.
3. J. Phillips, *Handbook of Training Evaluation and Measurement Methods*, 2nd ed. (Houston: Gulf Publishing, 1991).
4. G. Dangot-Simpkin, "How Come Nothing Changed?" *HR Magazine*, Vol. 36, No. 11, pp. 66–68.
5. G. Gropper and P. Ross, "Instructional Design," in *Training and Development Handbook*, 3rd ed., R. Craig, ed. (New York: McGraw-Hill, 1987), pp. 195–216.
6. W. Wiggerhorn, "Motorola U: When Training Becomes an Education," *Harvard Business Review*, Vol. 68, No. 4, pp. 71–83.
7. W. Tracey, *Designing Training and Development Systems*, rev. ed. (New York: AMACOM, 1984); L. Nadler, *Designing Training Programs: The Critical Events Model* (Reading, Mass.: Addison-Wesley, 1982); R. Cafferella, *Program Development and Evaluation Resource Book for Trainers* (New York: Wiley & Sons, 1988).
8. R. Mager, *Preparing Instructional Objectives* (Belmont, Calif.: Fearon, 1962).
9. I. Goldstein, *Training in Organizations: Needs Assessment, Development, and Evaluation* (Monterey, Calif.: Brooks/Cole, 1986).
10. Ibid., pp. 207–208.
11. Ibid., pp. 394–398.
12. S. McClelland, N. Harbaugh, and S. Hammett, "Improving Individual and Group Effectiveness," *The Journal of Management Development*, Vol. 12, No. 3, pp. 48–58.
13. P. Senge, *The Fifth Discipline: The Art and Practice of the Learning Organization* (New York: Doubleday/Currency, 1993).
14. M. Knowles, *The Adult Learner: A Neglected Species* (Houston: Gulf Publishing, 1973).
15. R. Gagne and L. Briggs, *Principles of Instructional Design* (New York: Holt, Rinehart, & Winston, 1979).
16. Tracey, p. 245.
17. P. Lewis, "Eight Steps to the Successful Appointment of a Training Consultant," *Journal of European Industrial Training*, Vol. 15, No. 7, pp. 25–29.
18. S. McClelland, "A Model for Designing Objective-Oriented Training Evaluations," *Industrial and Commercial Training*, Vol. 26, No. 1, pp. 3–9.

19. D. Kirkpatrick, "Techniques for Evaluating Training Programs," *Journal of the American Society of Training Directors*, Vol. 13, pp. 3–9, 21–26; Vol. 14, pp. 13–18, 28–32.

20. Phillips, pp. 211–246; S. Shelton and G. Alliger, "Who's Afraid of Level 4 Evaluations?" *Training and Development*, Vol. 47, No. 6, pp. 43–46; S. Dyer, "Kirkpatrick's Mirror," *Journal of European Industrial Training*, Vol. 18, No. 5, pp. 31–32; P. Bramley, *Evaluating Training Effectiveness* (New York: McGraw-Hill, 1991).

21. Phillips, p. 80.

22. Goldstein, pp. 144-148.

23. Cafferella, pp. 195-197.

24. Tracey, p. 466.

CHAPTER 10

# Needs Assessments in Organizational Change and Performance-Improvement Programs

A continual theme of this book has centered around the role needs assessments play in providing front-end information and in-process feedback that is critical for improving individual and organizational performance. In Chapter 1, needs assessments were defined as a composition of analytical methods comprised of various diagnostic instruments and procedures whose purpose is to investigate performance deficiencies (obvious as well as not so obvious) and to pinpoint areas where an intervention strategy may be developed and applied to correct the deficiency or fill the knowledge gap. Within this context, comprehensive needs assessments are useful for identifying organizational change, development, and transformation opportunities. They also provide feedback and background information that is useful for designing and implementing other performance-enhancement processes, such as TQM and CQI (Continuous Quality Improvement) programs. Finally, needs assessments also can provide valuable front-end information for designing systems to successfully link management development programs to strategic planning processes.

## IDENTIFYING PERFORMANCE-IMPROVEMENT NEEDS

It is natural to think of improved organizational performance as being the result of improved employee performance. It is possible, however, to improve organizational performance without collectively improving individual employee performance. For example, the results of a needs assessment could indicate areas where the organization may need to consolidate its staff or outsource jobs or activities which could be handled more cost effectively by external vendors. Although disruptive and socially damaging, activities such as these are unfortunately sometimes necessary in order to return the organization to a more stable financial position. Over the long term, however, it is unlikely that increased levels of organizational performance can be sustained without improving individual employee performance. Increased levels of employee performance can take the form of increased KSAs brought about through training, effective employee mentoring programs, updating organizational systems and technologies, or any number of other efforts. However, one thing is certain: In order to increase and maintain long-term organizational performance improvement, it is necessary to concentrate on identifying and addressing organizational as well as individual employee needs. This is one of the fundamental reasons for conducting organizational needs assessments. From this perspective, the concepts of improving organizational and individual performance are not mutually exclusive.

A comprehensive assessment aimed at identifying individual performance-improvement needs can uncover a wealth of information. It can highlight areas that, heretofore, may have gone unnoticed. For example, as discussed in a previous chapter, an organizational needs assessment could be used to identify policies or rules that actually inhibit individual performance. Some of these inhibitors could be a lack of understanding on behalf of employees as to what is expected of them; a lack of formal education or on-the-job experience; an unsuitable working environment; poorly maintained, broken, or outdated equipment; disinterested management; prohibitive work rules and policies; and so on. Each of these can contribute to poor performance on an individual as well as on an organization-wide level.

A well-planned needs assessment also can highlight individual performance problems that are behaviorally or psychologically related and, moreover, call attention to their causes. Some of these are easily identifiable. For example, problems related to drug or substance abuse, marital or social problems, personal financial problems, and so on, have the very real possibility to manifest themselves in the form of poor or substandard performance. Alternatively, there are individual performance problems that are objective in nature and, therefore, are more difficult to identify. For example, an employee who engages in "busy work" that produces little to no tangible returns or has inconsistent results may actually be exhibiting signs of confusion or signs of stress which could lead to eventual burnout. Symptoms such as these are recognizable, especially through interview and observation methods. Even though an assessment may not have been directed at identifying performance obstacles, when they are encountered, they should be noted and resources directed toward correcting them.

Another example of a case where organizational needs assessments are useful for improving individual employee performance is job analysis. In many instances, employees who would otherwise be productive are not because they are unfamiliar with the job and, worst of all, unfamiliar with what is expected of them. The result is frustration, a loss of interest and initiative, and eventual collapse in performance. As part of a comprehensive organizational needs assessment, a job analysis can help to uncover ambiguity in job (and task) performance standards and expectations. This can be used to clarify or to restructure the job completely. It can also identify job prerequisites which can be useful in qualifying potential job candidates.

Organizational needs assessments can provide excellent feedback that is necessary in order to establish performance standards. Through various types of data-gathering methods, assessments produce quantitatively based data that can be used, for example, for setting production standards, for establishing minimal employee performance standards, and for setting rules of conduct.

A question that HRD analysts continually wrestle with is how to quantitatively measure performance improvement. Some experts suggest that performance improvements can be made only when there is sufficient data available on current performance levels. Others suggest that one of the main purposes of needs assessments is to establish baseline performance criteria against which future performance measurements can be subjectively applied. When one looks at the true essence of organizational needs assessments, it would appear that both positions are correct. Needs assessments can pinpoint areas where, in the case of performance standards, a performance deficiency may exist. Likewise, the results of a needs assessment can also contain information that could be used to develop a variety of options to deal with the deficiency effectively. Thus, needs assessments can help to define and establish performance standards and, more important, illustrate what needs to be done to exceed them.

## CHANGE: CHALLENGES, UNCERTAINTIES, AND OPPORTUNITIES

The information provided through a comprehensive needs assessment can play a vital role in organizational transformation. In contemporary organizations, change is brought about by a variety of factors such as competition (foreign as well as domestic), shifts in the political, economic, and social environments, changes in attitudes and behaviors, changes in demographics and technology, and the advent of new societal trends. All of these contribute to creating a need for changing organizational structures, particularly in the ways in which organizations make the most efficient use of their human resources.[1]

The results of needs assessments can be a catalyst for developing a strategy by which change (and improvement) can be introduced into the organization's management, structure, and operations. Assessments can provide an indication of where the organization can improve its effectiveness, enhance its productive output, create higher ROIs, improve the quality of work life, and better motivate its employees. However, before examining the role that needs assessments play in the process of organizational change, it would be beneficial to first examine the concept of change on a humanistic as well as an organizational level.

Traditionally, organizational structures have emphasized maintenance and control. Thus, bureaucratic hierarchies had evolved to the point where, in the 1980s and particularly in the 1990s, it became obvious that if organizations were to successfully compete in an increasingly competitive and globalized marketplace, they were going to have to radically alter—in some cases completely dissolve—the structures which, heretofore, dominated their very existence.

### Human Fears

The concept of change, organizationally as well as personally, evokes a wide range of emotional and behavioral responses. These often manifest themselves in the form of fear, uncertainty, stress, suspicion, and resistance.[2] Change is rarely welcomed, even by those who view it as a necessity and are primarily responsible for introducing it into the organization. It can raise anxiety levels to the point where dysfunctionality—or rather, the breakdown in linkages between various units (and employees)—occurs.[3] At the onset, the effects of change are unknown and, therefore, are unpredictable. Thus, the uncertainties that accompany change can have very negative effects on employee morale.

When an organization undergoes change, regardless of whether it is planned or unplanned, a negative by-product is employee alienation.[4] This is often exhibited in passive withdrawal behavior such as tardiness, absenteeism, depression, high anxiety, frustration, and a lack or loss of interest that will, eventually, adversely effect organizational performance and productivity. If left untreated, passive withdrawal behaviors can lead to open conflict and result in a fragmentation of the organization's social networks and operational structures. Under these circumstances, the social as well as financial costs can be tremendous.[5]

In the minds of many corporate managers, change is inevitable. Likewise, employee resistance to change—which is also viewed as inevitable—must be overcome if the change processes are to be implemented and produce the desired results. In this respect, change is viewed as necessary though problematic. How an organization deals with the human problems it encounters in change scenarios will determine whether the outcome is favorable or unfavorable. For instance, take the case of Procter and Gamble (P&G), who, for years, institutionalized a hierarchical, top-down, management structure. It was not until the mid-1980s that P&G actually acknowledged that its once revered structure was in disarray and in need of a dramatic overhaul. Through a planned change effort, the resulting structure was made more streamlined and efficient. P&G embraced the concept of employee empowerment in its structure, policies, and rules that govern the conduct of its day-to-day business. It also adopted new management methods and philosophies that focused on quality, customer service, and competitive strategic planning. Consequently, the new structure yielded higher degrees of employee job satisfaction and improved organizational performance.[6]

### Change in an Organizational Perspective

Change can either be planned or unplanned. Planned change occurs when the organization recognizes a need to improve its competitive position. In this sense, it is proactive because conditions—either internal or external—have created circumstances in which the organization realizes it must transform and, in some cases, renew itself in order to take advantage of new challenges and opportunities. Some examples of a planned change process could be found in the introduction of new products or services, entry into a new market, planning for new or pending government regulations, and corporate mergers and acquisitions.

Alternatively, unplanned change, although driven by many of the same factors as planned change, is more reactive because the organization may find itself in a position where it must change in order to meet new demands being placed upon it. For example, unplanned change can occur when banks suddenly raise their commercial loan interest rates or when weather conditions or other phenomena (e.g., hurricanes, tornadoes, floods, and so forth) necessitate plant closings. Factors like these surface abruptly with little or no warning. In order to offset and compensate for the sometimes negative effects that unplanned change produces, an organization must have formulated proactive contingency plans.

Whatever the catalyst, change is an ever present factor in today's global business environment. In order to remain competitive, however, organizations must formulate plans to effectively and efficiently manage it. A historically favored approach to managing change is through the design and implementation of OD strategies.

## CHANGE THROUGH ORGANIZATIONAL DEVELOPMENT

When confronted with the prospect of change, organizations have traditionally relied on developing a systematic approach for managing it—namely, through the implementation of an OD process. Such strategies are designed to introduce change in a planned, orderly, and systematic manner.

### An Overview of OD

The term *organization development* first appeared in the mid to late 1950s. Although it is not clear who first used the phrase, it is thought to have emerged simultaneously out of the works of Robert Blake, Jane Mouton, Herbert Shephard, Douglas McGregor, and Richard Beckhard.[7]

OD is composed of various theories that are based upon human as well as organizational values. It focuses on people and their work within organizational settings. It investigates the reasons for as well as the effects of change. In effect, OD's primary objective is to plan for ways to manage human behavioral reactions to organizational change.

OD is process oriented. It consists of data-gathering methods that are used to diagnose organizational problems and, if necessary, to formulate intervention strategies to offset any possible negative effects. It seeks to identify problems associated with change and to develop manageable solutions. Its most prominent activity is in the collection of feedback that provides connecting links to those parts of the organization undergoing change. It involves self-assessment on the part of the organization and its employees. Its primary and overriding objective is to improve organizational efficiency, which many times involves the integration of multiple organizational goals that reflect directly on output (productivity), on the quality of work life, and on the job satisfaction of employees.

The following are some characteristics of contemporary OD thinking:

1. OD is problem oriented. It draws on theory and research stemming from a variety of disciplines and applies these through a behavioral sciences approach to solving organizational problems.
2. OD involves planning through goal-setting processes, through the design of intervention strategies and techniques, and through the initiation of corrective, in-process actions.
3. OD is mainly concerned with and, therefore, focuses on improving organizational performance. It stresses human involvement, contribution, and participation in change processes.
4. OD is systemic and systematic. It seeks to improve the linkage between human resources and technologies and the organization's culture and operational environment(s) and processes.
5. OD focuses on accomplishment and results. It not only describes how change takes place but it focuses on ways to facilitate and manage change.
6. OD is continuous and ongoing. The process must be adopted and integrated into the organization's day-to-day activities.

### Processes and Activities

OD is viewed by many as being both a continuous process and a continuous activity.[8] As is the case with needs assessments, it involves a number of unique yet interrelated steps. Each represents an important part of the overall process, yet, like needs assessments, there are no clearly defined or universally agreed-to models. What does exist is a variety of concepts that can be integrated into a system of processes and activities.

*Prework.* Prework involves the building of the relationship between OD consultants and the client organization. Since most major OD efforts will require the services of outside experts whose job it is to design, implement, and facilitate the change process, the basis for establishing this relationship is very important. As discussed in previous chapters, the client–consultant relationship, whether focused on needs assessments, training, or, in this instance, OD, must progress from a basis of mutual trust and cooperation.

Prework activity involves action research in which consultants seek to better understand the existing organizational structure so that they can assess potential sources of information that are critical to successful OD design and implementation. The main focus of prework activity involves assessment of the organization's readiness to change.[9] This usually involves educational activities that are designed to help employees address and understand the fundamental reasons for change (e.g., why it is necessary), to cope with stress and anxieties, and to provide information on what strategies have been developed to assist in the overall change effort.

*Data Collection.* Data collection involves collecting feedback for the purpose of identifying obstacles and barriers to change. As is the case with needs assessments, data gathering is both fundamental and critical to the OD process because it requires the involvement of many people from different levels and groups throughout the organizational spectrum. Through data collection and analysis, consultants are able to generate a clearer picture of what problems currently exist as well as what problems have the potential to exist at some future point in time.

As with organizational needs assessments, there are a number of strategic decisions consultants must make regarding the data-gathering process. They are (1) determining who will participate; (2) determining the nature (type) and amount of data that will be required to provide an accurate representation of the current state of the organization as well as to give indications of what will be needed to facilitate the change process; (3) determining what data-collection methods (and instruments) to use; and, (4) how these methods will be designed and implemented.

*Analysis and Evaluation.* OD data analysis and evaluation is primarily concerned with identifying problems and formulating recommendations and solutions. Data analysis and evaluation is conducted jointly by the consultants and knowledgeable personnel from within the client organization.

Data analysis and evaluation focuses on the need to identify obstacles to change. These may be physical or conceptual, static or dynamic, or real or imagined. Whatever the form, it is important for both the consultants and the organization to acknowledge their existence and potential. One way this is done is through the construction of models designed to display and communicate the parameters of the findings in relation to the existing organizational structure and climate. The underlying value in adopting this approach is that it permits the consultants and the client organization to conduct minimal-risk intervention experiments. It also provides a basis for developing in-process action plans and revisions.

*Interventions.* Interventions are activities that are designed to develop and reinforce desired behavior(s) and performance and to apply these in-process so the organization's structure will be in a continual state of transformation and refinement. Intervention methods include team development, job redesign, training, individual coaching and counseling, structural reorganization, policy revision and refinement, the development of more effective communication strategies, and other activities whose purpose is to change, refine, and enhance the existing structure, processes, and systems. Although OD touches all organizational levels, managers become the key players in communicating, facilitating, and championing the change processes.[10]

### Similarities and Dissimilarities between OD and Needs Assessments

As has no doubt become obvious, there are many similarities between needs assessments and OD, in terms of the various types of processes and techniques each employs as well as in their general purpose and use. Some experts argue that needs assessments are by their very nature integrative components of the OD process because there is relatively little difference between the two and whatever difference does exist is mainly a case of semantics and jargon.[11]

Logically, the argument could be made that needs assessments and OD are two similar means that are geared toward producing identical outcomes; that each employs similar data-gathering methods for investigating and diagnosing organizational problems; and, further, that each uses the data it collects to make decisions and to formulate recommendations regarding intervention methods. Such arguments are, however, only partially accurate. Although there are many similarities between their methods and techniques, the main differences are separately rooted in both their individual purpose and intent. The intent of a needs assessment is to focus primarily on identifying gaps in skills, knowledge, behaviors, and competencies, and, further, to identify what techniques, methods, and processes (e.g., training) can be used to address them.[12] In essence, the needs assessment process, among other things, can provide a means for identifying change opportunities, which can then be addressed through a comprehensive OD effort. Thus, in this context, the needs assessment is essentially a front-end diagnostic process that can be used to identify OD opportunities. For example, many times the results of a needs assessment indicate a need for educational or training programs that are designed to address change on a personal (humanistic) as well as on an organization-wide level. The information obtained through the needs assessment can identify potential obstacles to change that can be addressed through training or some other form of intervention. Therefore, it could also be logically argued that there are distinct relationships between the intent and purpose (and even some of the techniques) of needs assessments and OD.

For many different reasons, an organization may not readily see—or it fails to acknowledge—a need to change. As outlined in Chapter 1, it may have a need to investigate its operational environment (e.g., the efficiency with which it delivers it goods and services), the attitudes of its personnel (e.g., its culture and how it affects employee morale), or its market position with respect to its competitors. In effect, an organization may not be actively seeking to investigate a need to change. Rather, it may want to inwardly examine itself to determine how well its systems are functioning, how well it makes use of its resources (human as well as material), and what, if anything, needs to be done to improve organizational performance. Thus, the organization may seek to identify its needs, one of which, it may come to find, is the need to change—change in the way it is structured or in defining its culture, mission, or policies. It also may discover, as P&G did, a need to massively transform and reorganize to improve its competitive position.

## ASSESSING THE ORGANIZATION'S READINESS TO CHANGE

A continual theme of this book has emphasized the utility and use of needs assessments to obtain feedback on issues of concern to the organization. In this context, the task of designing, developing, and implementing needs assessment systems has generally fallen into the domain of the HRD department, who are and should continue to be the organization's key players in centralizing and coordinating all needs assessments as well as all OD activities.

As part of its usefulnesses as an identifier of change needs, assessment can provide valuable insights into the organization's state of readiness to accept and undertake change. To illustrate, assume that a company was about to be merged with another. In an attempt to identify and understand employee concerns, a needs assessment was conducted. The results showed that there was a significant amount of uncertainty about future employment security. During the individual interview phase of the assessment, this concern became more and more apparent as many employees were displaying high degrees of anxiety. In this situation, the organization, through the conduct of a needs assessment, discovered that some form of intervention was necessary to counter the negative behavioral effects that the pending merger was producing. Thus, the organization not only identified an area affected by change; it also obtained valuable feedback about its readiness to change.

This is a crucial factor in the change process. Because an organization consists of interrelated technological systems as well as interrelated social networks, employee anxieties have the potential to derail even the most meticulously planned change process.[13] Therefore, consultants or HRD analysts must take appropriate steps to address behavioral dysfunctionality as part of their effort to prepare employees for the changes that are about to take place.

Even though an organization may not have acknowledged a need to change, the probability is that, at some point in time, change will become inevitable. In preparing for this, the organization can adopt a proactive position by assessing its state of readiness to undergo comprehensive transformation. A systematic and well-organized assessment can be useful for determining this state of change readiness by examining the following criteria:

1. Determining the need to change: As discussed earlier, change can be driven by a number of factors. These can be internal and/or external and can range from a loss of market share or a shift in competitive positioning (both external) to a rise in absenteeism (internal).
2. Defining change parameters: Parameters for change can be described as those areas within the organization's structure that need to be transformed or will be the ones most affected by change that is driven by internal and/or external factors.
3. Examining alternatives: A needs assessment can provide feedback on what alternatives to change, if any, are available. For instance, an organization may seek to improve employee performance through incentive systems or through some other motivational means as opposed to initiating any structural or procedural changes.
4. Predicting outcomes: Needs assessments also can be useful as predictors of any outcomes of planned organizational change. The information obtained through an assessment, particularly qualitatively based feedback, can give a good approximation of how any pending changes may or are being viewed by employees, and, further, can indicate what kind of results are most likely to appear. These data can provide consultants not only with a broader perspective on what the outcomes could be but also with insights on employee behavioral reactions and how these can either facilitate or hinder the change process.

## NEEDS ASSESSMENTS IN TOTAL QUALITY MANAGEMENT PROGRAMS

Within the last fifteen years, the term *quality* has become part of virtually every organization's vocabulary. The emphasis on quality of service, in the goods produced, and in focusing on the customer's needs has inspired new managerial thought and philosophies. In concert with the emergence of quality at the forefront of business and industry, a significant number of efforts have taken root. These include training, management and leadership development programs, changes in organizational culture, an emphasis on empowering employees to make decisions that were once in the domain of senior management, and designing internal systems that focus on servicing markets and customers. All these have given rise to a term that many see to be the embodiment of competitive strategy formulation: total quality management (TQM).

### Defining TQM

In a broad sense, TQM is seen as a holistic process in which the organization seeks to continuously improve its performance through continual transformation. It is centered on producing quality goods and services through changes in the organization's culture and in its management styles, production methods, education, and employee relations.[14] It requires developing a plan for equipping employees with multiple skills, the flattening of management and bureaucratic structures, and implementing systems and methods to improve the delivery of goods and services. Fundamentally, TQM promotes a broader view of the concepts of quality. It relies on employee empowerment, participation in decision making, the introduction and refinement of consultative management styles, the development of leadership skills and abilities, and imparting a vision as a means for focusing on continuous process and product improvement.

Although the concept of TQM is easy to understand, defining exactly what it is and how to implement it poses problems for both researchers and practicing managers alike. While most academicians and business professionals have expressed differing views of what comprises a TQM program, most agree that, fundamentally, TQM is a philosophy based in the organization's culture.[15] Many agree that, fundamentally, the organization's culture must be changed in order to successfully implement the concepts of TQM. This requires a change in management practices, the redesign of work efforts, a redefinition of management roles, and the reformulation or reorientation of organizational goals and business objectives.

The successful implementation of TQM was, for a time, considered to be revolutionary in its approach because it often runs counter to the traditional norms which view the organization as an economic and financially driven enterprise. TQM, on the other hand, departs from this normative view by promoting the concept of the organization as an enterprise driven by people, all of whom share a common vision of quality. Thus, employee empowerment and involvement are at the heart of TQM and are critical components of the cultural change that must take place throughout the organization if TQM is to be implemented successfully.[16]

Perhaps one of the best attempts to define TQM was presented by Kanjii, who stated that quality is what satisfies customers' requirements and needs on a continual basis; that total quality is to meet customers' expectations, again, on a continual basis, but with lower costs; and that TQM is to obtain total quality through commitment and involvement by all employees on a daily basis.[17]

## Requirements

A well-designed TQM program requires a number of components, most of which are instrumental for introducing fundamental cultural change. Among these are the following:

1. Group problem-solving activities in which teams are encouraged to explore solutions to routine as well as nonroutine problems with maagers acting as group facilitators rather than taking the more traditional roles of organizers and directors
2. The use of hard data as opposed to guesswork for making informed decisions
3. The use of quality-improvement teams to empower employees to make critical decisions that, in more traditional organizations, were entrusted only to more senior managers
4. The implementation of employee and management training programs stressing quality throughout all organizational levels

Moreover, there are a number of complementary factors that must be firmly in place in order for TQM to be implemented. Some of these are the following:

1. A firm commitment to, complete involvement in, and total support of the TQM philosophy by all employees
2. Clearly defined quality-improvement goals
3. Action-oriented planning
4. A span of focus that addresses both narrowly defined work processes as well as entire organizational systems
5. The compilation, analysis, and use of benchmark data for comparing the organization's performance to its competitors
6. HRD resources to design and facilitate the TQM process as well as to continually monitor it by identifying problems and exploring solutions

*Cultural Change.* As mentioned earlier, cultural change is at the heart of any TQM program. To successfully implement TQM requires more than installing or modifying existing procedures and systems.[18] Many academicians and professionals alike support the view that a cultural shift is first required before any attempts are made to introduce new systems, methods, and procedures. Others argue that since cultural change does not occur quickly, a more adaptive in-process approach is preferable. This view acknowledges that, as change progresses, its effects must be arduously monitored and corrective actions must be devised and implemented in-process. This view allows the organization to undergo change in an incremental manner and, further, it identifies and compensates for resistance factors and other barriers. This gives the organization the time it will need to address these as well as other in-process issues.

*Training.* Another requirement for the successful implementation of TQM is the need to design, develop, and deliver effective training. There are a number of training-related variables and issues that must be factored into the implementation plan, the very least of which is designing training that makes employees aware of what the organization's approach to TQM will be and, more important, how it will be introduced. Another training issue centers on gaining employee input, support, involvement, and commitment to the effort. Other factors that training will be required to address are the need to equip individuals with the knowledge, tools, and techniques associated with any quality-improvement effort, the design of quality teams, training in new technologies that may be required to support the TQM effort, and a concerted emphasis aimed at building employee technical, administrative, and interpersonal skills.[19]

Overall, HRD's role in TQM training is to (1) understand the concepts and philosophies of TQM, (2) design and conduct training that is based on the needs of the organization as well as the needs of individual employees, and (3) implement and practice the concepts of TQM themselves.

### Assessing Organizational TQM Needs

The role that needs assessment plays in the successful implementation of TQM is multifaceted. A needs assessment can be initiated prior to the implementation of TQM to identify barriers to the change process, some of which are (1) lack of management and employee commitment, (2) resistance or suspicion, (3) improper planning and timing, (3) lack of proper training, (4) lack of vision that is needed to guide the effort, and (5) a lack of resources and effective monitoring and measurement systems.

Second, a front-end needs assessment can identify where funds can be most appropriately allocated during the implementation stages. This is critical because, as the process continues, various phases will compete for available funds. A comprehensive needs assessment can establish priorities for the allocation of limited resources.

Third, a needs assessment will highlight skill and knowledge gaps where training will most certainly be required. Through the various methods presented throughout this book, HRD specialists and consultants are able to identify those gaps and to formulate recommendations on how they can best be addressed.

Fourth, needs assessments can identify which organizational systems will need to be adjusted or altered to make them more compatible with the TQM program. This could include virtually anything from formal communication systems to work processes and procedures, from the introduction of new technology to new planning and implementation models.

Fifth, behavioral interventions that have been designed to address some of the barriers to TQM can be implemented through information provided from needs assessments. Since these barriers can be formidable and potentially volatile, it would be necessary to assess the organization's culture and employee attitudes on an ongoing basis.

Sixth, needs assessments can also pinpoint areas where the organization's training is inadequate to meet the tasks at hand. For example, in Deming's Fourteen Points for managers, two that specifically relate to training emphasize that workers learn their jobs from other workers (Point Number 6) and that both employees as well as management should be educated in new methods, including teamwork and statistical process techniques (Point Number 13).[20] These can be acquired through vigorous education and training programs redesigned to specifically address organizational needs (inadequacies) that have been identified through a well-planned needs assessment.

### Debate over TQM's Effectiveness

It should be noted, however, that there has been widespread debate recently about the concept of TQM and Continuous Improvement (CI) programs and whether these programs, over the past ten years or so, have produced the kinds of results that they were originally heralded to produce. Some experts believe that TQM has not been successful because empowerment was a term that no one was familiar with and, therefore, could not adequately describe. Thus, the results produced nothing more than confusion and frustration when there seemed to be no control over the TQM system. Others see nothing different in the approach to quality improvement other than simply a change of names (e.g., from Quality Circles, to TQM, to CI programs). Still others see value in any concept where quality and the maximization of employee talents are the end products of change, restructuring, reengineering, and a continual focus on improving quality in the production and delivery of goods and customer service.[21]

## USING NEEDS ASSESSMENTS IN STRATEGIC MANAGEMENT DEVELOPMENT PROGRAMS

Within the last decade, considerable emphasis has been placed on integrating management development programs into the strategic and competitive planning process. Driving this emphasis is the increased pressure that is being brought on contemporary organizations by relentless global competition. The need to be able to quickly respond to constantly changing demands from competitors and customers alike has resulted in massive reorganization efforts. Yet, pressures to reduce overhead and increase the ability to produce and deliver quality goods and services has intensified. Thus, in today's business environment, organizations are faced with the certainty of "doing more with less." As global competition continues to increase, a significant question remains unanswered: How can an organization increase profitability, continually lower its overhead costs, and strategically integrate its resources to respond to the challenges and opportunities being presented?

As part of its plan to predict for the challenges ahead, an organization must formulate a competitive strategy in which it seeks not only to maintain but to increase its market share. Given the limited number of resources which contemporary organizations have at their disposal, they continually are seeking ways in which they can improve their internal structure(s), work processes, and systems in order to be more responsive to their customers' demands and expectations. Efforts such as these have given rise to an increase in the use of technology and in the design and implementation of TQM and CI, organizational reengineering, and other quality-centered programs. One outcome of all of this is a heightened attention to the role that management development plays as an integral component of competitive strategy formulation.

### The Concept of Strategic Management Development

Many organizations have come to find that the traditionally functional management roles where managers were educated and trained to work only within defined areas of specialty (e.g., marketing, finance, operations, information systems, etc.) are luxuries they can no longer afford. Rather, the concept of specialists within the managerial ranks is becoming more and more obsolete. Pressures are mounting on academic business institutions to modify and realign their academic programs to more accurately reflect the environment in which today's managers must operate.[22] However, since this will undoubtedly take time, organizations that are facing an immediate and critical need to train and educate their managers to assume broader roles on more generalized and less specialized levels are turning to their internal HRD staffs to guide them through this transitionary period. In response to this, HRD has been charged with the task of assessing the organization's management staffing needs and developing programs to assist managers in making the transition from specialist to generalist. This transition must not only focus on breaking managers out of their functional roles, it must also provide them with a means to look beyond maintenance and functionality and to focus more on the "big picture." Thus, management development is emerging as an increasingly important weapon in competitive strategy formulation.

Strategic management development (SMD) is essentially a process whereby capable managers are immersed in career-pathing programs that emphasize the development and refinement of leadership skills. Such programs focus on developing an understanding of the corporate vision, organizational capacity, renewal, and change.[23] This signals a radical departure from the more traditional training-based concept of management development that tended to concentrate on maintenance by doing specified things correctly while ignoring whether the things being done are the right things to do in the first place.[24]

### Implementation by Assessment

Fundamentally, SMD requires a change in the perception of what management development is and what purposes it serves. It stresses a rethinking of the ways that managers accomplish tasks. It signals a departure from a focus on functionality and a refocusing on development of institutional capacity and growth. It also requires, as does TQM, a sense of commitment to its philosophy, which may produce conflict between the old and the new ways of thinking in traditionally hierarchical organizations. As part of the cultural change required by SMD, management must move away from emphasizing individual effectiveness and concentrate on the individual's contribution to organizational effectiveness. SMD requires intervention in order to change behaviors and attitudes. It requires that needs assessments aimed at gathering information on the organization's culture and readiness to change and on identifying the availability of managers who are capable of guiding the organization through transitionary periods be designed and implemented. The mind-set of many traditional managers will require a refocusing on the concept that, in order for the organization to grow, an understanding of the new corporate vision and long-term strategies must be introduced through an organizational change and a philosophical renewal process.[25]

Needs assessments are valuable—indeed, vital—to the design and implementation of a successful SMD program. They are used to identify what prerequisite skills will be required and to identify potential candidates for career-pathing programs. Needs assessments also provide feedback on which organizational systems are in need of adjustment and, moreover, how these can be modified to better function in the changed organizational structure.

As in organizational change and TQM programs, the needs assessment process uncovers potential obstacles to the implementation of SMD efforts. Two of the more notable ones are the following:

1. The mind-set of senior management may be focused on maintenance as opposed to change. Therefore, the culture and philosophy of the organization probably will have evolved accordingly. In these types of organizations, all management development efforts—from training to career path selection to mentoring—must be changed to focus on the individual's contribution to and the enhancement of organizational renewal, growth, and the expansion of organizational capacity.
2. Organizations that have the desire to integrate management development into their competitive strategies but lack the ability (knowledge) and/or internal expertise (personnel) should seek assistance from qualified organizational change and management development consultants who can provide critical input on the design and implementation of a SMD strategy. Professionals such as these also can continually monitor its progress.

A competitive SMD strategy requires that all management development and training-related activities be closely integrated with the organization's business objectives. This necessitates that needs assessments be ongoing throughout the organization in order to understand how the implementation of SMD is proceeding and what changes need to be made in order for it to achieve its goals.

Just as an organization implements a competitive strategy to become proactive rather than just reactive to change, the concept of SMD is aimed at personal growth and development, which, in turn, provides continual organizational growth and development. Through systematic and continual in-process implementation, the organization adopts a proactive approach to forming its competitive strategies and enhancing its ability to improve its competitive position.

## OTHER USES FOR ORGANIZATIONAL NEEDS ASSESSMENTS

While needs assessments are useful for improving organizational performance, introducing change, and designing and implementing TQM and SMD programs, they are also applicable for investigating and identifying needs in a variety of other areas.

### Employee-Involvement Programs

Employee-involvement (EI) programs are very similar to TQM and other quality-oriented programs in that each focuses on improving organizational performance by increasing individual employee performance. Where they differ slightly is in their approach. EI programs tend to focus more on employee involvement through team efforts where TQM does not specify any particular type of activity, rather, it focuses on philosophical change, on training, and on changing the organization's culture and systems. EI seeks to involve employees in decision making and problem solving throughout all organizational levels. Within this context, needs assessments can be used to identify problem areas within the organization's systems, which can then be posed to EI teams that can collectively work toward a solution.

### Employee-Assistance Programs

Employee-assistance programs (EAPs) are designed to help employees deal with personal matters and problems before they surface as performance inhibitors in the workplace.[26] They are essentially a strategy for improving employee performance. Examples of the types of personal problems which EAPs are set up to address are alcohol and substance abuse, marital problems, behavioral or psychological dysfunctions, stress, financial problems, and so on. They provide counseling and a variety of other services that are designed to assist employees in dealing with problems before they become manifest as on-the-job performance inhibitors.

Needs assessments, particularly those focused on identifying performance problems through behavioral observation, can be used to identify which employees are experiencing personal problems that are or have the potential to negatively affect their performance. From this information, a determination of which EAP services may be effectively used to intervene or to otherwise help the employee deal with these problems can be made. However, since needs assessments are not usually specifically intended to isolate individual behavioral problems, particularly those that originate outside of the workplace, and being that guarantees of confidentiality and anonymity usually accompany needs assessment data-gathering processes, extreme care must be taken to safeguard identities. In instances such as these, needs analysts should first consult with the employees' supervisor about the problems. It then becomes the supervisor's responsibility to refer the employee to the EAP unit for assistance.

### Organizational Reengineering

This term has been used to describe activities that are designed to address and to initiate fundamental changes to an organization's work systems and structures. Also referred to as work redesign, organizational reengineering focuses on designing new systems or changing older ones to enhance the delivery of quality goods and services and on changing or eliminating those systems that are found to be unproductive, counterproductive, redundant, or repetitious. Within this framework, needs assessments (particularly those emphasizing operational audits, job and task analysis, and benchmarking activities) can be used to identify and isolate which systems are functioning properly and which ones are in need of repair or elimination. In addition, a needs assessment can produce valuable front-end information that can be used to identify redundancy in existing systems and work processes. Last, assessments can provide valuable feedback on collective ideas about how to design new systems within the organizational structure to enhance the organization's ability to deliver quality goods and services.

### Measuring Knowledge Value Assets

Needs assessments can also be used to help measure the value of knowledge in a company. In more specific terms, knowledge is what employees carry with them and, more important, what they take home with them at the end of the day. In essence, any knowledge that is added to a process or a system that makes that system better (e.g., increases its utility or worth), produces value. If knowledge is introduced yet nothing changes as a result of its introduction, no value in output is provided. However, if the input of knowledge produces a better product or service or if it creates economies of efficiency, then output value is received.[27]

A systematic needs assessment can identify pockets of untapped knowledge (e.g., dormant KSAs) in the organization that, for whatever reason, may have gone unrecognized and, therefore, are untapped sources of economic value. Although feedback of this type is usually obtained as peripheral information in an organizational needs assessment, it has enormous potential. Only now are some organizations such as Hewlett-Packard and Skandia AFS beginning to realize the potential importance of this untapped source of economic value.[28]

## SUMMARY

In addition to providing information that is valuable in designing and developing employee training programs, needs assessments provide feedback that is useful in organizational development efforts, developing and implementing TQM and SMD programs, and undertaking other performance-improvement initiatives. Needs assessments provide information that is critical to improving organizational as well as individual performance and are useful for undertaking organizational change efforts.

Change can be predicated by a variety of needs and can be initiated through a variety of processes. One is through comprehensive OD interventions. A core component to successful OD is the collection and analysis of data. Through their data-gathering and analytical components, needs assessments can play a critical role by providing OD consultants with feedback on the organization's readiness to change. They can also help to identify barriers to the change process.

Organizations have focused on flatter, more responsive, and more efficient structures and on delivering quality goods and services. This has led to various approaches. One of the best known is through the design and implementation of TQM programs. Although there is no exact definition for TQM, it can be hypothetically described as a process that seeks to improve organizational performance through employee empowerment and continual transformation. As such, TQM is process- as well as change-oriented. Its underlying philosophy is somewhat radical when compared to more traditional organizational philosophies in that it depends on a number of factors, not the least of which is the necessity to alter or change the culture in which it is to be implemented. TQM incorporates group problem-solving techniques, the use of hard data to make informed decisions, the design and implementation of empowered quality-improvement teams, and comprehensive management and employee training programs. In addition, it requires a firm commitment to quality improvement by all employees, clearly defined improvement goals, action-oriented planning, and knowledgeable individuals who take primary responsibility for its design, implementation, and continual monitoring.

Needs assessments can provide important feedback on the organization's culture and what changes will be needed in order to successfully implement TQM. Assessments also provide information on employee behavioral characteristics and what will be required in order to design effective TQM work teams. A well-designed and systematic needs assessment provides insight into where the organization's funds can be most appropriately allocated, particularly during the implementation stages, so that barriers to successful implementation can be identified and overcome. Last, needs assessments provide feedback on critically needed training requirements once the organization undergoes transformation and change. In concert with these, behavioral barriers can be identified and means for appropriately addressing them can be explored.

The value of TQM has come under serious debate and criticism. Organizations that once heralded it as a means for delivering quality goods and services to their customers are now questioning whether TQM is as viable as they once thought it was. Some have abandoned it in favor of organizational reengineering and other activities designed to streamline organizational processes while still focusing on quality. Others see value in TQM or any other type of program that focuses organizational talents and resources on quality in products as well as in service delivery.

Needs assessments provide important information that is germane to the design and development of an SMD effort. As the need to become more competitive using less resources has increased, needs assessments can be used to identify what types of education and training will be needed to move organizational management away from functionally specialized roles and into the role of generalists. Thus, information provided through a well-designed systematic needs assessment can provide guidelines on how to integrate management development efforts and competitive strategy formulation processes. As a result, organizations adopt a proactive approach to accepting and planning for change as opposed to waiting for and then reacting to it.

Finally, needs assessments can be used to identify employee performance obstacles through the implementation of EI programs. They can also identify chronic employee performance problems that can be referred to and handled through effective EAPs. Needs assessments also are useful for gathering information on which organizational systems and work processes are in need of repair or elimination in organizational reengineering efforts.

## NOTES

1. J. Naisbitt, *Megatrends: Ten New Directions Transforming Our Lives* (New York: Warner Books, 1982).
2. N. Marguiles and A. Raia, *Conceptual Foundations of Organizational Behavior* (New York: McGraw-Hill, 1978).
3. Ibid., pp. 356–358.
4. Ibid., pp. 356–359.
5. Ibid., p. 359.
6. R. Griffin and G. Moorhead, *Organizational Behavior* (Boston: Houghton Mifflin, 1986).
7. W. French, "The Emergence and Early History of Organization Development with Reference to Influences upon and Interactions among Some of the Key Actors," *Contemporary Organization Development*, D. Warrick, ed. (Glenview, Ill.: Scott, Foresman, 1985), pp. 18–19.
8. Marguiles and Raia, pp. 138–139.
9. M. London and R. Wueste, *Human Resource Development in Changing Organizations* (Westport, Conn.: Quorum Books, 1992).

10. J. Aguilar, *General Managers in Action* (New York: Oxford University Press, 1988).

11. W. Tracey, *Designing Training and Development Systems*, rev. ed. (New York: AMACOM, 1984).

12. R. Miribile, "A Simple Approach to Skills Assessment," *Training and Development*, Vol. 45, No. 12, pp. 19–22.

13. D. Kirkpatrick, "Riding the Winds of Change," *Training and Development*, Vol. 47, No. 2, pp. 29–32.

14. A. Brown, "TQM: Implications for Training," *Industrial and Commercial Training*, Vol. 25, No. 1, pp. 20–26.

15. R. Grant, R. Shani, and R. Krishnan, "TQM's Challenge to Management Theory and Practice," *Sloan Management Review*, Vol. 35, No. 2, pp. 25–35.

16. E. Lawler, "Total Quality Management and Employee Involvement: Are They Compatible?" *Academy of Management Executive*, Vol. 8, No. 1, pp. 68–76.

17. A. Patel, "Total Quality Management (TQM): Paving the Way for Future Training?" *Industrial and Commercial Training*, Vol. 25, No. 2, pp. 23–32.

18. L. Morris, "Organizational Culture and TQM Implementation," *Training and Development*, Vol. 48, No. 4, pp. 69–71.

19. R. Ripley and M. Ripley, "Empowerment: The Cornerstone of Quality," *Management Decision*, Vol. 30, No. 4, pp. 20–43.

20. M. Walton, *The Deming Management Method* (New York: Perigee Books, 1986).

21. C. Goldberg, "TQM: At the Crossroads," *Workforce Training News*, Vol. 2, No. 8, pp. 16–19.

22. J. Neelankavil, "Corporate America's Quest for an Ideal MBA," *Journal of Management Development*, Vol. 13, No. 5, pp. 38–52.

23. S. McClelland, "Gaining Competitive Advantage through Strategic Management Development," *Journal of Management Development*, Vol. 13, No. 5, pp. 4–13.

24. R. Fulmer and K. Graham, "A New Era of Management Education," *Journal of Management Development*, Vol. 12, No. 3, pp. 30–38.

25. D. Hussey, "Implementing Corporate Strategy: Using Management Education and Training," *Long Range Planning*, Vol. 18, No. 5, pp. 28–37.

26. S. Smits and L. Pace, *The Investment Approach to Employee Assistance Programs* (Westport, Conn.: Quorum Books, 1992).

27. T. Stewart, "Your Company's Most Valuable Asset: Intellectual Capital," *Fortune*, Vol. 130, No. 7, pp. 68–74.

28. Ibid., p. 72.

CHAPTER 11

# A Needs Assessment Case Study: DM Technologies

This chapter contains a case study of an actual organizational needs assessment project. It has one major purpose: to provide a real-world example of the events that led up to the decision to conduct a needs assessment, how it was designed and implemented, and what its results and outcomes were. The organization's name and the names of the people involved have been changed as a means for safeguarding confidential and proprietary information.

## HOW TO USE THIS CASE

There are a variety of ways in which this case can be used. First, it can be used as a guide to illustrate the complexities involved with conducting a comprehensive organizational needs assessment. Second, it can be used by practitioners as well as HRD and OD students as an illustrative simulation. Third, it can be used as a basis for discussing what can go right, what can go wrong, what outcome(s) can be realistically expected, and how things can be done more efficiently.

The case begins by presenting background information and an overview of the current situation. All salient steps leading up to the assessment's design, facilitation, analysis, and recommendations are detailed and presented. It concludes with an explanation of the actual outcome and explores various issues and problems through questions and accompanying discussion points.

In any organizational needs assessment, there are a number of events—internal as well as external—that have significant influence on the outcome(s). Some of these events are strictly business related and deal with decision making and other types of organizational issues. Others are related to personalities, opinions, and differing points-of-view, while still others are directly related to interpersonal and behavioral issues. All of these factors are presented in the case.

## CASE STUDY: DM TECHNOLOGIES

DM Technologies was founded in 1980 by David Meyers, a talented aviation electronics and design engineer. DM designed and manufactured advanced aeronautical guidance and control systems that were used primarily in U.S. Air Force and Navy fighter planes. In this capacity, DM was a major subcontractor to one of the largest aviation defense contractors in the United States.

The company had a reputation for designing and manufacturing quality avionics components and systems. It was considered by many in the industry to be in the forefront of the aerospace high-technology manufacturing segment. With the U.S. military buildup that had taken place during the early 1980s, DM's business grew considerably. By 1987, the company had three separate plants: one each in California and Texas, which were mainly concerned with manufacturing the control and guidance systems and related components, and one in Florida, which housed some manufacturing elements and all of the research and development (R&D) and corporate functions. The company employed over 1,400 people. Profits and future business prospects, it seemed, were so good that Meyers considered taking the company public.

In 1987, the Pentagon announced cutbacks in defense appropriations. DM's largest customer, Hardin Aerospace, notified Meyers that, as a result of the pending cutbacks, they were canceling all of their outstanding as well as future orders. Almost simultaneously, two of DM's other major customers canceled their orders as well. Within twelve months, DM's business and profitability fell by almost 40 percent.

Meyers knew that the guidance and control systems his company designed and manufactured would have commercial applications as well as military use. He contacted several domestic commercial aircraft manufacturers and began a program to market the systems directly. However, since many of these organizations were also feeling the effects of the cuts in military spending, orders were very small and slow in coming. Moreover, because DM's systems had been previously used solely in defense-related manufacturing, the company was prohibited by law from marketing the products to prospective customers outside of the United States.

In late 1987, DM's Florida plant had just developed a new type of microwave weather radar system that could be used to increase a pilot's ability to detect windshears, a deadly type of downdraft that was considered responsible for a number of commercial plane crashes. Before being able to manufacture and market the system, however, DM would have to have the Federal Aviation Administration (FAA) test and approve it. Meanwhile, with all three plants now operating at less that 50 percent capacity and facing the prospect of a continued decline in profits, Meyers postponed his plans to take the company public and sought the assistance of a consultant, George Simmons, who was well known for helping to "turn companies around" and return them to profitability.

After a comprehensive three-month examination of DM's operations and current market position, Simmons made the following recommendations:

1. In order for DM to remain profitable, it would have to close its California and Texas plants. This meant making room for and then transferring all manufacturing operations along with some key employees with specialized areas of expertise to the Florida facility. It also meant laying off over 1,000 people.
2. The Florida plant would have to undergo major restructuring to accommodate the consolidation of the company's manufacturing capacity, and it too would have to undergo staff reductions.
3. DM would have to concentrate mainly on obtaining FAA approval for the new windshear detection system while also cutting manufacturing costs. Simmons reasoned that, in doing so, DM could reduce the sales price of the guidance and control systems, which would make the company's mainstay product(s) more attractive to potential customers.
4. Once the consolidation was completed, the company would need to implement major cost-cutting measures. On the manufacturing side, Simmons recommended that DM invest in new manufacturing and production methods (including increasing their use of robotics to replace laid-off workers). Overall, it would need to increase its production efficiencies. He also recommended that the company concentrate its R&D assets on developing products for consumer markets. On the administrative side, the recommendations included a restructuring of the compensation and benefits program, new purchasing and approval policies, a reduction in health-care benefits coverage, and overall tighter controls on all expenses. The recommendations also called for increasing sales expense allowances, which Simmons felt would be necessary for the company to promote its products more aggressively. This would allow DM to continue operations without seeking additional financial assistance by reducing its overall cost of goods sold. However, the company's immediate future rested on reducing the manufacturing costs of its guidance and control systems, on stepping up its efforts to gain FAA approval to sell its systems to foreign manufacturers, and on successfully developing and marketing its windshear detection system.
5. Knowing that the effects of the downsizing would be painful and have a deteriorating effect on employee morale, he also recommended that DM hire an expert to conduct an organizational assessment that would focus on identifying the needs of the organization and its employees at the Florida facility. The principal objective of the assessment would be to identify what organizational systems would need to be changed, what negative effects the downsizing had on behavior and employee morale, and what changes or other types of interventions would need to be made to restore employee confidence and build a more efficient and productive work force. This could include introducing changes into the company's management structure and in its operations.

Simmons's findings and recommendations were unwelcome news to Meyers. He had long taken pride in building a company where the culture was based in a "family environment," and he was fully aware that the announcements to close the California and Texas facilities would be painful for the employees and their families. Therefore, he delayed implementing any of Simmons's recommendations for another six months and instead implemented a staff-reduction plan based on attrition as a means of reducing the company's overhead costs. The strategy offered incentives for employees to resign and did not fill vacant positions unless they were key ones that the company felt it could not do without. It also contained a plan for offering early retirement to a select number of employees who were within ten years of retirement age (which, at present, was sixty-five years). He reasoned that the attrition program would send a message to the company's employees and give some of them the motivation or incentive to resign. He also gambled that in taking this approach the company could buy valuable time to obtain permission to market its guidance and control systems to foreign manufacturers and would also buy time to secure FAA approval to commercially market its windshear detection system. He did, however, implement tighter spending controls. Further, he reduced sales staff per diem allowances and used the savings to boost expenditures on the research and development of new products. He also boosted expenditures on marketing research, advertising, and product promotion in an effort to increase future sales leads.

The next six months were disastrous for DM. To begin with, the FAA had not yet given them permission to market their guidance and control systems to foreign manufacturers. However, a competitor announced that they had received permission to market a similar system. In fact, not only had they received permission to sell their systems, they had previously implemented cost-cutting measures similar to ones that Simmons had recommended, and, as a result, they were able to produce and sell their system at what it cost DM just to manufacture theirs. Next, only a small percentage of eligible employees had opted to take advantage of the retirement plan. Furthermore, because of the severity of the defense-related cutbacks in both California and Texas, only a few of DM's employees had resigned to take other positions. The defense-related cutbacks had produced severe job shortages, particularly in the aerospace industry. In effect, those in the industry who had jobs were staying put.

In early 1989, DM received permission to market their guidance and control systems to foreign aircraft manufacturers, and even though the company's sales strategies were starting to show promising signs, there were still no firm commitments. To add to the troubles, production costs had increased to the point where they were higher than they had ever been. On top of that, the new windshear-detection system was still in its preliminary testing stages. Meyers recalled Simmons to immediately assess the company's financial, operational, and market positions. After an intensive two-week review, he concluded that if the company was to have even a chance for survival, a forced downsizing would have to take place immediately.

Meyers called a meeting between Simmons and the company's officers: Gary Banks, the vice president, Don Strong, director of Operations, Sid Harrison, director of Sales and Marketing, and Ellen Craft, director of Human Resources. He announced that within forty-five days, the California and Texas operations would close. He instructed Strong and Harrison to work together with the plant's managers to identify key engineers and technical, sales, and marketing personnel who might need to relocate to Florida. He also instructed Strong to identify all nonessential exempt as well as nonexempt personnel at the Florida plant and announce to them that they too would be laid off within the next forty-five days. He assigned Craft the task of selecting and working with an outplacement firm to set up an assistance program for all affected employees. Last, all company officers as well as managerial personnel were going to be subjected to a 10-percent cut in pay. The only employees who would now be eligible for any bonus or incentive programs would be the sales and marketing staff—and even those were to be cut in half. These measures, Meyers explained, were necessary for the very survival of the company and would remain in affect until such a time when DM was in a stronger financial and market position. He instructed Banks, Strong, and Craft to oversee the plant closings. Specifically, he charged Banks and Strong with the task of cutting production costs and with getting the windshear detection system ready for FAA testing. He and Sid Harrison would concentrate on aggressively marketing the control and guidance systems and pursuing FAA approval of the new windshear-detection system. Meyers concluded the meeting by firmly stating that all other matters were secondary. The company's primary objective now was to cut costs, concentrate on securing FAA approval of the windshear-detection system, and effectively market the company's existing guidance and control systems.

## THE DOWNSIZING

Banks and Strong worked closely in overseeing the consolidation of the California and Texas operations into the Florida facility. Craft took over the responsibility of dealing with all the human resource–related matters including making the formal announcement of the closings (which was a letter written by Meyers). She also selected and began working with the outplacement firm. Banks and Strong, after consultation with the California and Texas plant managers, worked with her to identify key personnel whom they believed were indispensable and should be offered the option of transferring to the Florida facility. Ten days after the meeting with Meyers, a total of 1,050 personnel had been identified as being nonessential and were given forty-five-day notices. An additional thirty-five people were given the opportunity to relocate to the Florida facility. Of those, twenty-eight agreed to relocate.

Even before the formal announcement had been made, news of the downsizing spread throughout the company and employee morale was collapsing. Production errors and cost overruns increased substantially and there was, overall, a general attitude of impending doom. Absences increased, even among some of the key employees who were scheduled to remain with the company. Frequent arguments between DM's managers over who should have authority over and control of the remaining functions began surfacing. On numerous occasions, Banks and Strong had to personally intervene just to keep things from getting out of hand.

Banks had managed to find a tenant for the Texas facility—a commercial printing company that wanted to expand. He arranged for them to lease the property with an option to purchase it at the end of a year. Both plants were gutted and all assets that were not to be transferred to Florida were liquidated at auction.

Craft hired a relocation firm to handle the details of the transfers from California and Texas to Florida. The outplacement firm was not having a great deal of success in placing DM's laid-off employees. Of the 1,050 who were scheduled to be laid off, the firm had only managed to place 90 of them. At the end of forty-five days, the California facility was permanently closed and the property put up for sale. The Texas facility was vacated and the printing company moved in. All of DM's business and operations had now been consolidated to Florida. A total of 105 of the 1,050 employees who had been laid off had secured other positions through the outplacement firm.

The Florida facility was in complete turmoil. Because they needed to concentrate on closing the California and Texas facilities, Banks and Strong had not had enough time to fully sort out all of the details of the consolidation into the Florida operation. As a result, arguments between the plant's management and even some of the remaining employees were getting worse because it was not yet clear who was supposed to be in charge of what. Production was getting bottlenecked, and quality was beginning to suffer. Meyers was absent from the facility, spending most of his time marketing the control and guidance systems and pursuing front-end arrangements with the FAA for testing the windshear-detection system. But because of the turmoil at the Florida plant, the detection system was already forty-five to sixty days behind schedule. As a result, Harrison's sales and marketing staff were virtually idle because they had nothing to sell. To compound matters, arguments between line employees were becoming more frequent and more severe. In a number of instances, Craft's assistant, Jerry Thomas, had to intervene in what had deteriorated into physical altercations between employees. The plant's equipment maintenance schedules were not being followed as they should have been, which resulted in longer equipment downtime. To make matters worse, the Florida facility used a different computer system than did the Texas and California plants. Therefore, vital company records were not being transferred, entered, and processed efficiently. This produced bottlenecks in the company's information and data processing functions which had, on two separate occasions, resulted in DM being three days late in processing its payroll.

Banks, Strong, and Craft worked furiously to bring the Florida plant under some sort of control. After a brief meeting with Meyers, they redrew DM's organizational chart and produced a new mission statement. They spent another two weeks rewriting the company's employee handbook and held regular meetings with department managers in an effort to deal with immediate and more pressing issues. Through these meetings, it became apparent that in order to get DM fully functional again, some major OD effort was going to have to be undertaken.

At the end of the first quarter of 1989 and shortly after DM had finally won approval from the FAA to market their guidance and control systems to foreign manufacturers, Meyers announced that DM had just won a major contract to provide the systems to a South American and a French aircraft manufacturer. Also, R&D had just produced a working prototype of the windshear detection system and was testing it for the FAA. The results of the test were positive and the FAA gave DM temporary approval to manufacture but not to sell it. All of this meant that production would have to increase immediately. However, in its present state, DM wasn't anywhere near being in a position to resume full-scale production, let alone begin even temporary production of the windshear detection system. Banks, Strong, and Craft met with Meyers and Simmons to discuss the situation. After summarizing what they saw to be DM's main as well as immediate problems, Simmons suggested that DM hire a team of experts to conduct what was one of his original recommendations: a comprehensive organizational needs assessment, the results of which would form the basis for an OD process that would be focused on reengineering the company and on identifying and solving DM's problems.

Meyers agreed. He assigned Simmons the task of identifying the needs assessment experts. Banks, Strong, and Craft would work with them to oversee the project. Simmons contacted John Harmon, an expert needs assessment analyst. After numerous discussions about recent events at DM and outlining the assessment strategy, it was decided that it would center on three major components: (1) An operational audit would be designed to identify what systems, processes, and procedures would need to be consolidated, changed, or eliminated; (2) it would contain a behavioral element that would be designed to identify barriers to improving employee as well as overall organizational performance levels; and (3) each job and its related tasks would be analyzed to ensure that they fit properly into the new organizational structure. Any redundant jobs and tasks would be consolidated, changed, or eliminated. This meant that further staff reductions could be necessary.

Harmon prepared a proposal that included the following primary objectives:

1. To conduct an organizational audit aimed at identifying any and all systems, processes, and procedures that, in the analyst's opinion, would need to be merged, changed, or under certain circumstances, eliminated completely
2. To design a behavioral component into the assessment whose goal would be to identify personality or other behavioral elements that would need to be changed in order to form more cohesive and productive work teams
3. To complete job and task analyses for each of the company's remaining 422 positions and to implement them—the goal being to redesign any and all positions where necessary

It was estimated that the entire assessment could be completed in thirty days. Meyers reviewed the proposal and, after receiving input from Simmons, Banks, Strong, and Craft, agreed but expressed some reservations about the behavioral and job and task analyses components. He gave Harmon the go-ahead with the option of changing the preliminary goals before formally implementing the assessment.

## THE NEEDS ASSESSMENT DESIGN

The proposal called for three types of data-gathering methods to be used. First, a survey questionnaire containing closed- as well as open-ended questions was designed. It was two pages long (back and front of one page) and contained items that were focused on obtaining feedback about employee morale, whether employees felt they understood their jobs, whether they felt they had the skills to successfully carry out their responsibilities, and what problems they felt the organization was facing. Certain questions that were considered mandatory in achieving the assessment's primary goals were identified and keyed. These were to provide a link to the other two data-gathering methods to be used: interviews and on-site observations. The questionnaires were intended to be anonymous but they were also to contain codes which would be used to contact nonrespondents in an effort to increase the overall response rate. They were to be sent to all of DM's employees. An expected return rate, based on a sample test, was estimated to be 75 percent. The survey questionnaire would be sent out with a cover letter from Meyers explaining that it was anonymous and that the code was only to be used to identify individuals who had not responded.

The interviews were intended to gather mainly behaviorally based feedback. A script containing questions dealing with behavioral issues, such as how individuals handled stressful situations dealing with both personal as well interpersonal conflict, was devised. Each question was open-ended. In all, 25 percent of DM's employees (approximately 105 people) were randomly selected to participate in the thirty- to forty-five-minute interviews.

The on-site observations were to be carried out by three employees who were experts in new manufacturing systems and processes. The objective of the observations was fourfold: (1) to observe work methods in-process and recommend changes where necessary, (2) to identify jobs and tasks that were not compatible with the skills of the incumbent, (3) to identify those jobs that were in need of redesign so that the incumbents were better matched to their individual responsibility levels within what was to be the new organizational structure, and (4) to identify any positions that were not considered to be essential. The observers also were to pay close attention to any behaviors displayed by job incumbents which they felt were (or could become) problematic. In all, 280 manufacturing (including management) positions were to undergo observation.

Harmon presented the assessment strategy and plan to Meyers, Simmons, Banks, Strong, and Craft. Meyers replied that he had some second thoughts about the interviews and job and task analyses. He felt that some employees would feel threatened and think the company was searching to identify more people to lay off even though, in reality, this was a real possibility. He also felt that the behavioral component was too intrusive. It might, he reasoned, send the wrong signal that the company was on a "witch hunt." He reiterated his primary goal: to raise DM's production capacity to a level where they could meet their quality standards and fill their standing as well as their incoming orders. Therefore, he wanted to conduct the surveys, and, in addition, he wanted them to be completely anonymous and not contain any type of respondent coding. He also wanted the observations to be conducted with each of DM's observers focusing only on work methods and processes. No feedback was to be collected on individual jobs or tasks, and, most important of all, he did not want a behavioral component included.

Strong and Craft raised serious objections. First, they argued, it was obvious that there were serious behavioral problems present, problems dealing with interpersonal relations that had manifested and were manifesting themselves throughout the organization. Second, the job and task analyses components were vital if the organization was to develop adequate job documentation in relation to the new organizational structure. This was necessary, they went on, to identify areas where DM would need to design and develop skills-based training for jobs that had been redesigned so they could fit better into the new structure. Last, they considered it necessary, as did Banks and Harmon, that the surveys be coded. Using codes, they argued, would increase the return rate and add validity to the results.

Meyers was not convinced. He countered that the company already had accurate job documentation even though it was based on the old DM Technologies. He was convinced, however, that any investigation initiated by management would only further weaken employee morale and make an already bad situation worse. Therefore, he asked Harmon to resubmit the proposal based only on using the noncoded anonymous survey questionnaires and observation of the work processes and methods.

After the meeting had concluded, Simmons, Banks, Strong, Craft, and Harmon met in private. Craft was outraged. She felt that not only were the behavioral feedback and the job and task analyses necessary, but that the company was missing an excellent opportunity to gain vital information that would be mandatory for a comprehensive OD effort. She thought that Meyers was not really in touch with what was actually happening within the company and that his focus was concentrated on external affairs, namely, the marketing of the control and guidance systems and on securing FAA approval for the windshear-detection system. Therefore, she suggested that Harmon resubmit the proposal based on Meyers's requests that the assessment contain only the uncoded survey questionnaires and the observations aimed at investigating the work methods and processes. However, she also suggested that any observations conducted be focused on obtaining feedback on behavioral and interpersonal problems as well. This should not, she stressed, be itemized in the new proposal.

Harmon objected on ethical grounds; however, he concluded by saying that any type of observation would naturally have a behavioral component to it. To try to purposefully exclude the behavioral aspect from any observation, he said, would be impossible to do. He suggested revising the proposal as Meyers had requested and, if any behaviorally based feedback "just happened to find its way into the observer's report . . . then it could be considered peripheral to the primary goals." To try to hide the job and task analyses and the interviews, he went on, would be impossible and, he concluded, unethical. Simmons, Banks, and Strong agreed, even over Craft's continued objections.

Harmon revised the proposal to specify using uncoded anonymous survey questionnaires. Because the data-gathering methods were to be implemented concurrently, he estimated that the time to complete the assessment would remain at thirty days. Harmon resubmitted the proposal to Meyers who reviewed and approved it.

## THE IMPLEMENTATION

Announcements about the assessment were sent through interoffice mail to each of DM's employees. Additional announcements were also posted on the company's bulletin and notice boards. They contained a statement from Meyers about why the assessment was being conducted and outlined its goals (i.e., to identify employee needs and to help redesign obsolete, nonfunctioning, or redundant work processes). Particular emphasis was placed on the importance of each person's participation. The announcements contained a request for employees to return the survey questionnaires within five working days after receiving them and emphasized that no identification with individuals was required. Therefore, employees were asked to be candid and frank in their responses. Additional information on the work observations that were to be conducted by three well-known employees of the company were also detailed. Everyone was asked to give the observers their full cooperation.

Craft arranged for one of DM's computer programmers who was familiar with the data base program Harmon was using to compile the assessment data to work with him. An associate of Harmon's, Terry Atkins, was given the task of reviewing the incoming survey questionnaire data for completeness and to work with the programmer to set up a system to deal with incomplete responses. Atkins was also to play a role in analyzing and evaluating the data, in developing recommendations, and in preparing the final report for Meyers.

The surveys were sent through interoffice mail and the observations were scheduled. Within a couple of days only a small number of surveys had been returned. Harmon and Atkins were puzzled by this—they had expected a much larger return early on in the process. Then, at the end of the first week, Atkins received a call from one of the production supervisors asking him, if no names or identities were required, then why was there a small number written on the lower left-hand corner of the first page of each survey questionnaire. Atkins was shocked and contacted both Harmon and Craft. Harmon was equally surprised, but especially so when he heard that Craft, in an effort to increase survey response, had coded the questionnaires at the last minute before they had been sent out. Harmon and Atkins were angry. Now, not only would each survey have to be recalled, but there was a real possibility that any employee trust had been completely lost. Harmon and Craft met with Banks to explain the situation. They agreed that the best way to handle the situation was to tell each employee to tear off the corner of the page that contained the number and then complete and return the questionnaire. They also agreed that a letter should be sent out by Craft explaining why the number was put there in the first place and apologizing for the error. The next day Craft sent memorandums to each employee. Two days later, the surveys were being returned, and by the end of the tenth day, Atkins had obtained a response rate of almost 70 percent.

Each of the observers was meeting with Harmon on a regular basis after each scheduled observation had concluded. Harmon conducted debriefings which focused on the observer's reactions to the work processes and methods and what they thought could be improved. During the course of some of the debriefings, the SMEs told Harmon that employee morale was very low; people were scared about the company's—and obviously their own—future. Many were, in the SME's opinions, more concerned with the company's future prospects than they were with carrying out their jobs. They also found that there was considerable friction between some of the production employees and management. It seemed that some supervisors were putting a great deal of pressure on employees to complete production runs and ship the systems before all quality-improvement checks had been completed and the products certified.

Harmon met with Banks and Strong to alert them to the production and quality control problem. Strong replied that he would meet with the production supervisors to discuss the issues. Harmon advised against doing it at this time because the observations were still going on. They would be finished within the next ten days at which time they should all meet again to discuss what actions to take. Banks and Strong agreed. They would also notify Simmons and Craft.

By the end of the twentieth day, the survey response rate was better than 80 percent. But then, a mishap occurred. The computer's hard drive, which was being used to store survey response data, crashed. The programmer had already made backups of 70 percent of the returns and tried to recover the other 10 percent, but he could only recover about 2 percent. When informed of the computer breakdown, Harmon asked the programmer and Atkins why backups were only being made at the end of each day as opposed to being made hourly. The programmer responded that Harmon had not specified when he wanted backups to be made, so he assumed that daily copies would be sufficient. Harmon studied the situation and concluded that they would just have to do without the other 8 percent of the data. However, when inputting the data, Atkins and the programmer had also failed to identify and record some of the responses to the keyed open-ended questions. This meant that they had to go back over all of the questions from the surveys, one-by-one, and compare the responses with what had been entered. Questions that were keyed but were not recorded as being keyed were corrected.

By the end of the twenty-fifth day, the observations had concluded. Harmon spent the rest of the day debriefing the SMEs and obtained a significant amount of qualitative information. Since time was now running short, he gave half of the SME's reports and copies of the debriefings to Atkins. He also instructed the programmer to start the data manipulation and statistical analyses on the repaired computer.

## ANALYSIS AND RECOMMENDATIONS

Various statistical tests were used on the survey questionnaires. As the data were being tabulated, Harmon and Atkins compared it to the qualitative information obtained through the observations. After a series of meetings, they both concluded that there were various items, each related to in-process operations as well as final quality control, that could be changed to make the processes more efficient and to increase the quality of each finished system component. In addition, they determined that ongoing quality control meetings between the production engineers, managers, and employees would be helpful. This would increase not only production efficiencies but could also facilitate group as well as intergroup communications. However, they were not able to come up with any concrete recommendations about what should be done to address employee job security concerns. They decided to discuss the problem with Banks, Strong, and Craft as part of the final report. They also felt that the company should design some sort of employee counseling program as part of their overall OD effort.

A thorough evaluation of the quantitative and the qualitative data verified that employees were concerned most with their own job security. Many felt that the recent downsizing had left the company vulnerable and in a much weakened state. There were very serious concerns that even though DM had recently secured major foreign contracts, the quality of their products was suffering because the company was in what many considered to be a completely disorganized state. Most respondents felt that they both understood and were able to carry out their jobs, but they expressed dissatisfaction with the way management was running the company. As a result of comparing the keyed survey questions and the information and comments obtained from the SMEs, Harmon and Atkins recommended that DM

1. Combine R&D and production under one person.
2. Clearly communicate and publish the company's mission, goals, and objectives.
3. Devise better quality control procedures by implementing quality control teams made up of production as well as managerial personnel.
4. Initiate a skills training program to update employees whose jobs were in the process of changing.
5. Conduct monthly company meetings (which some suggested could be accomplished more efficiently through the use of a newsletter) to keep employees informed of where DM was heading.
6. Design and implement programs to help employees cope with problems both on and off the job. In essence, employees were suggesting that the company design and implement an EAP.

As a result of the observations, an additional twenty-five positions in the manufacturing area had been identified as nonessential. Harmon recommended that these individuals be retrained to assume other positions, perhaps in quality control. He advised against laying them off because he felt this would have a devastating effect not only on employee morale but also on any future OD intervention effort the company might undertake.

Harmon also included some additional comments that were based on experiences he had had in similar organizations and under similar circumstances. He proposed, as part of DM's OD process, that the company consider restructuring itself into three divisions and that the head of each division report directly to Meyers through Banks. The three divisions he proposed were R&D/Production (to be renamed Operations), Marketing and Sales, and Finance and Administration. Harmon and Atkins prepared a draft of the final report and presented it to Banks, Strong, Craft, and Simmons for their review and comments before finalizing it for presentation to Meyers.

Banks and Simmons liked the idea of combining R&D and Production under one person. They had long thought that Strong would be the perfect individual for such a position. They also liked the idea of redefining DM's goals and rewriting its mission. Banks thought the idea of devising better quality control procedures would best be left up to Strong. Both he and Strong reasoned that this would be an excellent place to begin a comprehensive OD effort. He also liked the idea of designing and initiating a skills training program to update employee skill levels, particularly in those areas where jobs may change as a result of the production and operational changes. They all agreed that a monthly newsletter outlining the company's ongoing activities should be published. This would facilitate the recommendation about improving the company's internal communications process. Craft was undecided about the EAP. She thought it was a little too early to initiate a comprehensive one and thought also that it might interfere with any subsequent OD effort. Harmon, Banks, Strong, and Simmons agreed; however, they felt that the recommendation should stand and that Meyers should be the one to make the final decision.

Everyone agreed with Harmon's recommendation about restructuring the company. Banks also suggested changing titles: He would remain executive vice president of Finance and Administration; Strong's title would be changed to vice president of Operations; and Sid Harrison, the current director of Sales and Marketing, would be named vice president of Sales and Marketing. Craft's title would remain as director of Human Resources and she would continue to report directly to Banks. They made the changes and prepared the final report for Meyers.

The next day, before the final report was given to Meyers, DM's South American client called to complain that the first set of systems they had just received were delivered "brain dead," meaning that they were inoperable and could not, therefore, be used. They also complained about the quality. Strong, after close consultation with DM's engineers and quality personnel, assured the client that the problems would be fixed and that DM would provide them with new and thoroughly tested units.

Meyers had been away with Harrison and some of the R&D personnel and sales representatives preparing a final presentation of the windshear-detection system and had not been back in the plant for over two weeks. After successful testing of the new windshear-detection system, the FAA gave their final approval which permitted DM to manufacture and sell the systems commercially to domestic as well as foreign customers. He returned to the plant only to hear of the quality problems their South American customer had experienced. Strong told him that he had made arrangements for the systems to be replaced and had assured the client that this would occur within a couple of days. In the meantime, however, it was discovered that there were fundamental defects in some of the circuit boards used in the systems that had already been shipped as replacements. And now, on top of that, the same problems were showing up with the units that had been shipped to DM's French customer as well.

Meyers called a meeting between Banks, Simmons, Strong, Craft, and DM's quality control managers. During the discussion, Craft announced that the needs assessment had been completed and a final report was ready for his review. Meyers stated that, given the quality control problems and the number of orders for the new windshear-detection system he was expecting, now was not the right time to discuss any of that. All their efforts had to be focused on solving the quality control problems with the guidance and control systems and in gearing up for production of the windshear-detection system.

## THE OUTCOME

News of the FAA's approval of DM's windshear-detection system spread quickly throughout the aerospace industry and, within a matter of weeks, DM had received substantial orders from both domestic and foreign manufacturers. Yet, despite their best efforts, DM was still experiencing quality problems with the guidance and control systems. It seemed that the defects were stemming from circuit boards that were being assembled incorrectly. The issue was creating a major headache for Strong. While Meyers was reassuring both the South American and the French clients that the problem had been diagnosed and corrected, he was working feverishly to focus the operations managers' and employees' attention on assembling the circuit boards correctly. However, he was not having much success. Interpersonal conflicts were continuing to surface with ever-increasing frequency, and employee morale was at its lowest point ever. Simultaneously, DM was now experiencing start-up production problems with the windshear-detection system. Sporadic disagreements were occurring almost hourly between the R&D and Production departments. Quality control was now rejecting over 40 percent of the new windshear-detection units as well as the guidance and control systems as they came off the production line. Strong instructed his managers and engineers to decide how to correct the problems on a unit-by-unit basis. This, too, had little effect and was also very costly. Then, after intensive investigation, Strong traced the cause of the defects to those employees whose jobs Harmon had found to be redundant. Apparently, word of the recommendation had reached these employees who had interpreted it to mean that they, too, were going to be laid off. As a result, many were just going through the motions of doing their jobs correctly, when, in fact, most were not doing their jobs at all. Strong was furious and immediately discharged all twenty-five employees.

As news of the dismissals spread, Meyers, upon his return from a sales demonstration of the windshear detection system to a prospective major client, observed that employee morale was even lower now than after the downsizing. Absenteeism was running at its highest point ever and there was a general feeling among the executive group (Banks, Strong, and Craft) and Simmons that DM was now spiraling out of control.

Remembering that Craft had said the needs assessment he had approved was completed, Meyers retrieved his copy and read through it. He liked the ideas presented though he did have some reservations about the recommendation concerning the EAP. It then occurred to him that solutions to the problems that DM was currently experiencing had already been addressed to a considerable extent in the recommendations contained in the needs assessment's final report. He was now wondering if it was too late to implement them—specifically, whether it was too late for DM to begin an OD and reengineering effort in earnest.

## QUESTIONS AND DISCUSSION POINTS

The following questions and discussion points focus on some of the major aspects of the case study:

1. From a business perspective, was Meyers's decision not to immediately implement Simmons's first set of recommendations a prudent one?
2. Was Simmons's first set of recommendations justifiable?
3. Would there have been significant differences in the assessment's outcome (and recommendations) if Meyers had followed Simmons's first set of recommendations?
4. Were Harmon's assessment strategy and plan sound given the present conditions of the company?
5. Given the information and details provided, was the design of the assessment (e.g., the use of the data-gathering methods) appropriate?
6. Were Strong and Craft's arguments for wanting to include the behavioral component, the job and task analyses, and the coding of the survey questionnaires justifiable?

7a. Was Craft's view that Meyers was "out-of-touch" with what was really happening at DM correct or incorrect?

7b. How did this affect her decisions regarding the assessment's design strategy?

8a. Was the approach taken for countering the effects of using survey questionnaire codes appropriate and effective?

8b. What alternative approaches or other actions could have been used?

9a. Were the recommendations provided by Harmon sound ones given DM's current operational condition?

9b. Should Harmon have recommended eliminating the twenty-five positions he found to be nonessential? If so, what possible impacts could this have had on other employees?

10. If Harmon's recommendations had been fully implemented, would they have provided enough of a foundation to implement a comprehensive OD and reengineering effort?
11. What are some other types of assessment design strategies that could have been used?

12a. Would it have made any difference in the case outcome if Meyers had immediately implemented Harmon's recommendations?

12b. If so, why? If not, then why not?

PART VI

# Appendixes

## Appendix A
## Needs Assessment Estimated Budget Form

Project Name: Needs Assessment | Number of Salaried Employees: 20 | Number of Hourly employees: 75

Duration: 60 days

Overview: Identify Training Needs

Expense Itemization:

**HRD Department**

| Name | Title | % of time allocated | salary | hourly rate | ttl. est. cost |
|---|---|---|---|---|---|
| J. Davis | HRD Manager | 5 | 60 k | 30 | 812.50 |
| H. Jones | HRD Analyst | 100 | 40 k | 20 | 9999.00 |
| R. Long | Adm. Asst. | 90 | 20 k | 10 | 5400.00 |
| | | | | | |
| | | | | | |

**Consultant**

| Name | Hours | @ per hour | ttl. est. cost |
|---|---|---|---|
| D. Owens | 100 | 50.00 | 5000.00 |
| | | | |

**Data Gathering Costs**

| | Method | Est. time to complete | Est. # Employees Participating (salary) | (hourly) | Total |
|---|---|---|---|---|---|
| 1. | Questionnaires | – hr. 30 min. | 20 | 75 | 95 |
| 2. | | hr. min. | | | |
| 3. | | hr. min. | | | |
| 4. | | hr. min. | | | |

**Calculations: Hourly Employees**

| | | Highest rate | Lowest Rate | Average | Est. time to complete | avg.cost to complete | est. no. employees participating | cost |
|---|---|---|---|---|---|---|---|---|
| 1. | Complete Questionnaire | 18 | 6 | 12 | .5 | 6.00 | 75 | 450.00 |
| 2. | | | | | | | | |
| 3. | | | | | | | | |
| 4. | | | | | | | | |

**Calculations: Salaried Employees**

| | | | | | | | | |
|---|---|---|---|---|---|---|---|---|
| 1. | Complete Questionnaire | 48 | 15 | 31.50 | .5 | 17.25 | 20 | 345.00 |
| 2. | | | | | | | | |
| 3. | | | | | | | | |
| 4. | | | | | | | | |

**Other Costs: (itemize)**

| | | |
|---|---|---|
| 1. | Consultant and Staff Travel (4 days) | 2,000.00 |
| 2. | | |
| 3. | | |
| 4. | | |

**TOTAL ESTIMATED PROJECT COSTS:** 24,006.50

## Appendix B
## Needs Assessment Budget Reconciliation Form

Project Name: Employee Training Needs Assessment  Number of Salaried Employees: 20  Number of Hourly Employees: 75
Duration estimated: 60 days  Actual Duration: 60 days  (Under)/over: --

**Expense Summary:**
**HRD Department**

| Name | Title | % of time allocated | actual time | est. cost | actual cost | (under)/over |
|---|---|---|---|---|---|---|
| J. Davis | HRD Manager | 5 | 5 | 812.50 | 812.50 | --- |
| H. Jones | HRD Analyst | 100 | 100 | 9999.00 | 9999.00 | --- |
| R. Long | Adm. Asst. | 90 | 70 | 5400.00 | 4200.00 | (1200.00) |
| | | | | | | |

**Consultant**

| Name | Hours | @ | per hour | est. cost | actual cost | (under)/over |
|---|---|---|---|---|---|---|
| D. Owens | 100 | 50 | per hour | 5000.00 | 5000.00 | --- |
| | | | per hour | | | |

**Data Gathering Costs**

| Method | est. time to complete | actual time | est. no. employees participating | actual no. participating | est. total | actual total | (under)/over |
|---|---|---|---|---|---|---|---|
| 1. Questionnaires | .5 | .4 | 95 | 102 | | | +7 |
| 2. | | | | | | | |
| 3. | | | | | | | |
| 4. | | | | | | | |
| **Calculations: Hourly Employees** | | | | | | | |
| 1. Complete Questionnaires | .5 | .4 | 75 | 81 | 450.00 | 388.80 | (61.20) |
| 2. | | | | | | | |
| 3. | | | | | | | |
| 4. | | | | | | | |
| **Calculations: Salaried Employees** | | | | | | | |
| 1. Complete Questionnaires | .5 | .4 | 20 | 21 | 345.00 | 289.80 | (55.20) |
| 2. | | | | | | | |
| 3. | | | | | | | |
| 4. | | | | | | | |

**Other Costs:**

| | estimated | actual | (under)/over |
|---|---|---|---|
| 1. Consultant and Staff Travel (4 days) | 2000.00 | 2310.00 | 310.00 |
| 2. | | | |
| 3. | | | |
| 4. | | | |

TOTAL ACTUAL COSTS: 23,000.10

TOTAL ESTIMATED PROJECT COSTS: 24,006.50  ACTUAL PROJECT COSTS: 23,000.10  (UNDER)/OVER: 1,006.40

# APPENDIX C

# Sample Needs Assessment Survey Questionnaire

**SURVEY ON ORGANIZATIONAL CLIMATE**

Instructions: Please read each statement carefully and then provide your response. Note: Please check only one response!

| | |
|---|---|
| Strongly Agree | = SA |
| Agree | = AG |
| Disagree | = DA |
| Strongly Disagree | = SD |
| No Opinion | = NO |

| | SA | AG | DA | SD | NO |
|---|---|---|---|---|---|
| 1. I have confidence in management's ability to lead this organization. | [ ] | [ ] | [ ] | [ ] | [ ] |
| 2. Policies are administered fairly and uniformly. | [ ] | [ ] | [ ] | [ ] | [ ] |

| | | | | | |
|---|---|---|---|---|---|
| 3. Management generally sets a good example for employee's to follow. | [ ] | [ ] | [ ] | [ ] | [ ] |
| 4. The organization's mission, goals, and objective's are clearly understood. | [ ] | [ ] | [ ] | [ ] | [ ] |
| 5. The policies and rules are designed to foster productivity, encourage participation, and facilitate performance throughout the organization. | [ ] | [ ] | [ ] | [ ] | [ ] |
| 6. Employee's are encouraged to take initiative and make their own decisions. | [ ] | [ ] | [ ] | [ ] | [ ] |
| 7. Individuals who have performed well are routinely recognized and/or rewarded. | [ ] | [ ] | [ ] | [ ] | [ ] |
| 8. Task assignments and other performance-related criteria are well defined and understood. | [ ] | [ ] | [ ] | [ ] | [ ] |
| 9. Training and development of employee's is a high priority. | [ ] | [ ] | [ ] | [ ] | [ ] |
| 10. The goals set by the organization are unrealistic. | [ ] | [ ] | [ ] | [ ] | [ ] |
| 11. Raises, promotions, and other forms of recognition are provided relative to job performance. | [ ] | [ ] | [ ] | [ ] | [ ] |
| 12. This organization provides a *quality* product/service. | [ ] | [ ] | [ ] | [ ] | [ ] |
| 13. A lot of time is spent "putting out fires" and resolving crisis situations that could have been avoided in the first place. | [ ] | [ ] | [ ] | [ ] | [ ] |

| | | | | | |
|---|---|---|---|---|---|
| 14. The policies of this organization are designed to foster team spirit and cooperation. | [ ] | [ ] | [ ] | [ ] | [ ] |
| 15. There are some people in this organization who manage to get by with only marginal performance. | [ ] | [ ] | [ ] | [ ] | [ ] |
| 16. Promotional opportunities are good - there appears to be a lot of advancement opportunities. | [ ] | [ ] | [ ] | [ ] | [ ] |
| 17. There seems to be a lot of "in-fighting" between divisions, departments, etc. | [ ] | [ ] | [ ] | [ ] | [ ] |
| 18. Our high performance standards are reflected in the products we sell. | [ ] | [ ] | [ ] | [ ] | [ ] |
| 19. The organization provides clear communications about the policies and work rules. | [ ] | [ ] | [ ] | [ ] | [ ] |
| 20. I enjoy working here and am proud to be part of this organization. | [ ] | [ ] | [ ] | [ ] | [ ] |

## APPENDIX D

# Sample Interview Script

*Note: The following script was prepared for use during interviews that were used in conjunction with a survey questionnaire as part of a needs assessment that was designed to gather feedback on employee attitudes. Questions that are linked to questions contained in the survey questionnaire are indicated with an asterisk (*), while weighted questions or those carrying special significance are indicated with an exclamation point (!).*

Hello, Mr./Ms.____________. Thank you for taking the time to meet with me. As you know, we are conducting an organization-wide assessment that is aimed at gathering feedback on employee morale levels. The result of this information will be compiled and analyzed in an effort to identify barriers to improving employee morale which we believe will ultimately translate into improved performance and productivity. The results of this interview will remain confidential—in effect, I'm only interested in your opinion and in your responses to the questions I will be asking. Your identity will remain strictly confidential. If, at any time, I pose a question that you are uncomfortable with, please let me know and I will proceed on to the next one. At the conclusion of the interview, I will be glad to let you look over my notes if you would like.

Do you have any questions before we begin?

1. As part of the assessment process we have distributed survey questionnaires throughout the organization. Have you received one? Yes No

If "Yes," then ask: (!) Have you completed it and returned it? Yes No

If "No," then ask: (!) Could you please tell me why?

____________________________________________________________

____________________________________________________________

___________________________________________________________

2. (!)(*)Do you personally feel that employee morale at the company is:__
_____ Very Good _____ Somewhat Good _____ O.K.
_____ Could Be Better _____ Poor or Low

(!)If "Could Be Better" or "Poor or Low," then ask:
Could you please explain why you feel this way?

______________________________

______________________________

______________________________

3. (!)In what ways do you feel that employee morale could be improved?

______________________________

______________________________

______________________________

4. (!)(*)Are you satisfied with the progress that has been made in the areas of quality improvement? Yes _____ No _____
If "No," than ask: Why?

______________________________

______________________________

______________________________

5. (!)(*)What do feel could be done to improve the quality of the product/service?

______________________________

______________________________

6. (!)Have you noticed any behavioral changes in other employees which you feel need to be brought to attention? Yes _____ No _____
If "Yes," then ask: Could you please elaborate?

______________________________

______________________________

______________________________

7. (!)Do you believe that communications (interdepartmental, interorganizational, as well as interpersonal) could be improved? Yes _____ No _____
If "Yes," then ask: Could you please explain?

______________________________

______________________________

______________________________

8. (!)Are you, as an employee, satisfied with the benefits package the company provides? Yes _____ No _____

   If "No," then ask: What could be done to make it better?

   ______________________________________________

   ______________________________________________

   ______________________________________________

9. (!)(*)What major problems do you see coming up?

   ______________________________________________

   ______________________________________________

   ______________________________________________

10. (!)Do you see absenteeism as a problem? Yes _____ No _____

    If "Yes," then ask: What do you feel should be done about it?

    ______________________________________________

    ______________________________________________

    ______________________________________________

11. (!)(*)What organizational policies, rules, and/or regulations do you think need to be changed? Please be specific.

    ______________________________________________

    ______________________________________________

12. (!)(*)Please indicate your confidence level in management's ability to effectively lead this organization.

    Very High _____ Moderately High _____ Average _____

    Low _____ No Confidence ______

    If "Average," "Low," or "No Confidence," then ask: Could you please explain or elaborate further?

    ______________________________________________

    ______________________________________________

    ______________________________________________

    ______________________________________________

Thank you, (Mr./Ms.) for your time. Your feedback is important and valuable. I appreciate your candid remarks. (Ask respondent if he or she would like to look over this sheet.)

Date of Interview:_____ Time Interview Began:_____ Time Interview Ended:_____

Location where interview took place: ______________________________

Interviewer's comments: ______________________________

______________________________

______________________________

______________________________

______________________________

______________________ ______________________

Interviewer's Signature Reviewed by Assessment Team Project Leader

# APPENDIX E

# Sample Focus Group Script

*Note: The following script was prepared for use in a focus group discussion aimed at gathering feedback on procedural, behavioral, and organizational structural barriers to implementing a TQM program. Each of the participants in the focus group had already received information about the company's intention to implement the TQM program which had been designed based on extensive feedback that was obtained through a comprehensive needs assessment process. Note that many of the questions may elicit the same types of answers; therefore, some responses may overlap. The moderator must be aware of the potential for this to occur. If enough information on the current question under consideration has already been obtained and that information is also directly related to another question, please be careful not to pose the question in a like or similar manner as the first question. Under these circumstances, it may become necessary to skip over a question altogether.*

Good (morning, afternoon), everybody. My name is ________________ and I'm the moderator of this focus group discussion. The purpose of this group is to explore possible barriers which exist within this company to the implementation of the TQM program. Before beginning, I would like to lay a few ground rules down so that we, as a group, can make the most productive use of the time that's available (one hour). First, we are interested in everyone's opinion and feedback; therefore, if an individual does not respond willingly, then I will purposefully call on that person to gain their input. Second, we may touch on some subjects that people are very concerned with and have very strong opinions about. We will not let the discussion deteriorate into a conflict of opinions or attitudes. There are no right or wrong answers here. Third, please refrain from naming specific individuals. We are not interested in identifying any one particular person; rather, we are interested in identifying and isolating what could be (or have the potential of becoming) barriers to the TQM implementation process.

Each of you has already received comprehensive information concerning the TQM program. Therefore, we will dispense with an overview of the specifics of the program and move right to the issues. Please note that individual identities will remain confidential. This focus group discussion is not being either audio or visually recorded. Are there any questions before we begin?

1. What aspects do you feel have the biggest potential to impede the implementation of the TQM program as it has been designed?

______________________________________________

______________________________________________

______________________________________________

______________________________________________

______________________________________________

2. Is the fundamental philosophy and approach being taken to implement the program sound?

______________________________________________

______________________________________________

______________________________________________

______________________________________________

3. How do you feel employees will react to the changes being proposed? (The moderator may want to review some of these or have them written on a flip-chart for the participants to observe.)

______________________________________________

______________________________________________

______________________________________________

______________________________________________

4. Should any of the stages of the proposed implementation schedule be changed and, if so, why?

______________________________________________

______________________________________________

______________________________________________

______________________________________________

5. What outcomes do you expect to see from the TQM program?

______________________________________________

______________________________________________

______________________________________________

______________________________________________

______________________________________________

6. Are the incentives that have been incorporated into the TQM program adequate? Are there any that are not adequate?

______________________________________________

______________________________________________

______________________________________________

Why? __________________________________________

______________________________________________

______________________________________________

Closing: Thank you all for your time. I will be preparing a summarization of the feedback which I will distribute to each of you to review prior to formally submitting it to _____________. Are there any questions or comments?

Close.

Date Conducted: ________________ Time Started: ________________

Time Ended: ________________ Location: ________________

Moderator's comments (attach extra sheets if necessary). Please print:

______________________________________________

______________________________________________

______________________________________________

______________________________________________

______________________________________________

______________________________________________

______________________________________________

______________________________________________

______________________________________________

______________________ ______________________

Moderator's Signature Assessment Project Leader's Signature

APPENDIX F

# Sample Job Analysis Form

| | |
|---|---|
| **Position Title:** | Process Supervisor |
| **Department:** | Primary Assembly |
| **Classification:** | Exempt |
| **Minimum Formal Educational Requirement:** | High School |
| **Immediate Supervisor's Title:** | Assembly Operations Manager |

**Significant Job Segments or Key Results Areas:**

- Individual must have complete knowledge of primary component assembly operations and procedures including scheduling, inventory control, equipment operation, and maintenance procedures.
- Individual must have understanding of significance of primary assembly process in relation to secondary and final assembly processes and how the primary process impacts production process stages.
- Individual must have appreciation for in-process quality control procedures.
- Individual must have excellent record-keeping skills.

**Functional Abilities Required:**

- Individual must be able to perform all primary assembly operations to conform to quality control standards.
- Individual must have excellent eye/hand coordination.

**Special Equipment Required:**

- Mark IV Automated Assembly Unit
- Hausen Computer-Control Unit
- Various hand tools (soldering iron, hand grinder and polisher)

---

## ATTRIBUTES

Rating Scale: 0 = Not Important - No Knowledge Required - No Additional Training Required

1 = Somewhat Important - Some Familiarity - Training Required

2 = Important - Working Knowledge/Understanding

3 = Very Important - Expert/Demonstrable Knowledge

4 = Critical

| | Importance to Job | Knowledge Required | Training Required |
|---|---|---|---|
| **Technical Skills** | | | |
| 1. Understanding Basic Process Operations | 0 1 2 3 4 | 0 1 2 3 4 | 0 1 |
| 2. Operation of Assembly Equipment | 0 1 2 3 4 | 0 1 2 3 4 | 0 1 |
| 3. Maintenance of Assembly Equipment | 0 1 2 3 4 | 0 1 2 3 4 | 0 1 |
| **Decision-Making/Problem Solving** | | | |
| 1. Ability to Solve Routine Problems | 0 1 2 3 4 | 0 1 2 3 4 | 0 1 |
| 2. Ability to Solve Non-routine Problems | 0 1 2 3 4 | 0 1 2 3 4 | 0 1 |

### Leadership Skills

| | | | | |
|---|---|---|---|---|
| 1. | Ability to Build Effective Work Teams | 0 1 2 3 4 | 0 1 2 3 4 | 0 1 |
| 2. | Ability to Communicate Action Plans | 0 1 2 3 4 | 0 1 2 3 4 | 0 1 |

### Interpersonal Skills

| | | | | |
|---|---|---|---|---|
| 1. | Ability to Work Well with a Diverse Group of Employee's | 0 1 2 3 4 | 0 1 2 3 4 | 0 1 |
| 2. | Ability to Handle Potential Conflict | 0 1 2 3 4 | 0 1 2 3 4 | 0 1 |

### Managing/Adapting to Change

| | | | | |
|---|---|---|---|---|
| 1. | Ability to Lead Work Group Change Efforts | 0 1 2 3 4 | 0 1 2 3 4 | 0 1 |
| 2. | Ability to Identify Barriers to Change | 0 1 2 3 4 | 0 1 2 3 4 | 0 1 |

### Communication Skills

| | | | | |
|---|---|---|---|---|
| 1. | Excellent Verbal and Written Skills | 0 1 2 3 4 | 0 1 2 3 4 | 0 1 |

### Work Organization

| | | | | |
|---|---|---|---|---|
| 1. | Ability to Organize and Assign Work Efficiently | 0 1 2 3 4 | 0 1 2 3 4 | 0 1 |
| 2. | Ability to Delegate Effectively | 0 1 2 3 4 | 0 1 2 3 4 | 0 1 |

Date Analysis Written:______________ Date of Last Revision:______________

Signature of Current Job Incumbent:________________________________

Signature of Immediate Supervisor:________________________________

Signature of Departmental

Manager/Vice President:________________________________

APPENDIX G

# Sample Task Analysis Form

I. General Overview

1a. Job Title:______________________________________________

1b. General Description: ____________________________________

_____________________________________________________________

_____________________________________________________________

_____________________________________________________________

_____________________________________________________________

_____________________________________________________________

_____________________________________________________________

_____________________________________________________________

1c. Job Incumbent Educational Level:

High School _____ Vocational School _____

College _____ Graduate Level or Higher_____

1d. Experience Level of Job Incumbent:

0 to 1 Year:_____ 2 to 5 years:_____

6 to 10 years:_____ More than 10 years:_____

II. List the major components of this job in sequential order from *most* to *least important*:

_____________________________________________________________

_____________________________________________________________

_____________________________________________________________

_____________________________________________________________

III. List the primary tasks required of the job (number and list from most to least important):

________________________________________

________________________________________

________________________________________

________________________________________

IV. List the secondary tasks required of the job (number and list from most to least important)

________________________________________

________________________________________

________________________________________

________________________________________

V. For each primary task, list the steps and the knowledge, skills, and abilities (KSAs) required of the job incumbent:

1. Task: ________________________________

   Steps: ________________________________

   ______________________________________

   KSAs: ________________________________

   ______________________________________

2. Task: ________________________________

   Steps: ________________________________

   ______________________________________

   KSAs: ________________________________

   ______________________________________

3. Task: ________________________________

   Steps: ________________________________

   ______________________________________

KSAs: ______________________________

______________________________

VI. For each secondary task, list the steps and the KSAs required of the job incumbent:

1. Task: ______________________________

   Steps: ______________________________

   ______________________________

   KSAs: ______________________________

   ______________________________

2. Task: ______________________________

   Steps: ______________________________

   ______________________________

   KSAs: ______________________________

   ______________________________

3. Task: ______________________________

   Steps: ______________________________

   ______________________________

   KSAs: ______________________________

   ______________________________

Date Task Analysis Performed: ______________________________

Date of Last Revision (enter "None" if first time analysis has been done) ______________________________

Task Analyst's Comments: ______________________________

______________________________

______________________________

| | | |
|---|---|---|
| Task Analyst's Signature | Title | Date |
| Supervisor's Signature | Title | Date |
| Job Incumbent's Signature | Title | Date |
| Reviewed by HRD Dept. | Title | Date |

APPENDIX H

# Team Building Assessment for Increasing Organizational Effectiveness: Analysis, Summary, and Recommendations

*The following exhibit is a project report of an actual needs assessment whose objective was to identify barriers to building effective work teams. It is provided to give the reader an understanding of what a comprehensive final report generally includes. Because of proprietary requirements, the organization's name along with information specifically relating to its business and markets has been omitted.*

## PROJECT OVERVIEW

Two specific goals were established for this project:

1. To collect information and feedback about the current operational and attitudinal climate of the company's employees as they relate to team and individual performance and effectiveness
2. To design a systematic approach in which a strategy for increasing individual and team performance can be integrated into the current business and operational environment

The definition of these primary objectives necessitated that an assessment of current conditions—to include an analysis of the entire organizational structure—be undertaken. The purpose was to identify any barriers to achieving the stated goals. The process adopted to accomplish this is outlined as follows:

1. A written survey questionnaire was developed which would collectively characterize respondents' feelings through feedback regarding relevant issues that have a strategic impact on the future growth and competitive posture of the organization solicited through these questionnaires.

2. Interviews were conducted concurrently with a randomly selected sample of middle- and upper-level managers who were also selected to participate in the survey questionnaire feedback process. The purpose here was to parallel and correlate responses received through administration of the survey questionnaire.

Ideally, correlations between what is apparent on the surveys would be more clearly defined through the interview process. These correlations provide the base criteria for accomplishing goal 2. This process was agreed to by the company's officers and implemented during the second half of February.

## PROJECT IMPLEMENTATION AND DATA

The survey questionnaire portion of the project was developed utilizing acceptable methods of survey response tabulation. Given a base survey population of fifty prospective management-level respondents, a reliability factor of 82 percent was attained as calculated by the return of forty-one completed survey forms. This factor is considered acceptable when applied against a normalized random distribution of 75 percent or greater response rate to reliability.

The key areas defined for the survey questionnaire were determined from compilations of surveys previously conducted. The following criteria were identified as being germane to determining overall organizational effectiveness:

1. New Idea Encouragement
2. Channels of Communication (lateral as well as horizontal)
3. Quality and Productivity Improvement
4. Distinction between Management Levels
5. Conflict
6. Goal Setting and Task Prioritizing
7. Resistance to/Acceptance of Change
8. Problem Identification and Solving
9. Incentive Systems and Rewards
10. Interpersonal Relationships

The following criteria were applied in the section of the survey questionnaire dealing with individual effectiveness and job satisfaction:

1. Employee Expectations
2. Self-Conflict, Judgment
3. Task/Work Load Accomplishment
4. Lack of Time
5. Job versus Personal Life
6. Defining a Personal Sense of Direction
7. Extent of Authority versus Level of Responsibility
8. Communications (interpersonal)
9. Performance Feedback and Evaluation
10. Peer/Superior Reaction
11. Philosophical Conflicts

Responses were tabulated and grouped in clusters based on the significance of the feedback obtained in each of the categories listed.

Ideally, a "bell" distribution would normally apply whereas responses would appear in clusters. On the scale used in the survey questionnaires (e.g., Never, Seldom, Sometimes, Usually, Always), the proportion of response percentages should ideally fall between the "Sometimes" and "Usually" or the "Sometimes" and "Seldom" parameters. Response categories where percentages exceeded 13 percent were considered to be significant and indicate a need area. These are highlighted along with their percentage (score) values.

## INTERVIEW STRUCTURE

Individual interviews were conducted with a random sample of managers who were also survey respondents. The interviews were conducted within a thirty-minute time frame. The interview questions were linked to keyed questions in the survey questionnaires that were considered to be significant in addressing the project's primary goals. This was done to provide a basis for comparative analysis between the quantitative data that were obtained from the survey questionnaires and the qualitative information obtained from the interviews. The random sample interviewed consisted of thirty-three individuals, which represented 66 percent of the total survey population of fifty managers.

## ORGANIZATIONAL SURVEY QUESTIONNAIRE

The questions contained in the survey questionnaire, along with their response percentages, are shown in Table H.1.

## ORGANIZATIONAL SURVEY INTERVIEW

The following questions were asked during the interview phase:

1. In your opinion, what are the major problems you see that have the potential to block progress in team development within this organization?
   - In any organization there is always room for improvement in communications. Of late I have been concerned that each department is becoming more of an island and an "us against them" mindset is developing. When something goes wrong the first order of business is to assign blame to the other guy.
   - This is a fast-growing company. It is an exciting environment. However, most managers within the company find it impossible to complete their jobs in a normal workday. This results in stress not only on the job but in their personal lives as well. This is, in my opinion, probably the single most major problem encountered.
   - Inflexibility of our organizational systems—especially the data processing systems. They cannot cope with the challenges of a rapidly evolving business environment. Second, compartmentalization of responsibility as the organization grows places an increasing burden on communications between individuals. Communication is needed to inform us of changes and to make employees feel like they are more a part of the whole.
   - In order of importance, the three problems facing our company are prioritization, segmentation, and the existing organizational structure. First, our corporate priorities

**Table H.1**
Organizational Survey Questionnaire

## PART I

The following are the questions contained in the survey questionnaire along with their response percentages.

| STATEMENT | NEVER | SELDOM | SOMETIMES | USUALLY | ALWAYS | AREA |
|---|---|---|---|---|---|---|
| 1. New ideas are encouraged and welcome. | 0 | 0 | **23** (56%) | **14** (34%) | 4 | New idea encouragement |
| 2. Management openly encourages new ideas and techniques | 0 | 0 | **25** (60%) | 12 (29%) | 4 | " " |
| 3. A great deal of conformity to the status quo is required. | 0 | 0 | **20** (49%) | 8 | **13** (32%) | " " |
| 4. As managers we are openly encouraged to speak up and "tell it like it is." | 0 | 6 | 16 (39%) | **17** (41%) | 2 | " " |
| 5. Important information is shared in a timely manner. | 0 | **21** (51%) | 16 (39%) | **21** (51%) | 4 | Communications |
| 6. Communications are open and clear. | 0 | **19** (46%) | **17** (41%) | 4 | 1 | " " |

| | | | | | | |
|---|---|---|---|---|---|---|
| 7. Each employee has an important impact on costs, quality of service, and productivity. | 0 | 1 | **22 (54%)** | 11 (27%) | 7 | Quality/productivity improvement |
| 8. There are many opportunities available to us to improve the quality and delivery of our product and service. | 0 | 1 | 8 | **20 (49%)** | 12 (29%) | " " |
| 9. Employees are truly interested in performing quality work. | 0 | 1 | 3 | **30 (73%)** | 7 | " " |
| 10. There is a lot of class distinction between management levels and/or groups. | 0 | 7 | **21 (51%)** | 10 (24%) | 3 | Rivalry |
| 11. We, as managers, often consult our peers for assistance when faced with a delicate problem. | 0 | **21 (51%)** | **14 (34%)** | 4 | 2 | " " |
| 12. There is ongoing conflict between departments and the managers who head those departments. | 0 | 3 | **14 (34%)** | 11 (27%) | **13 (32%)** | " " |
| 13. Work goals and standards are clear, understandable, and adequately communicated. | 0 | 3 | 20 (49%) | **15 (36%)** | 3 | Goal setting |
| 14. Most goals are realistic and attainable. | 1 | 1 | **15 (36%)** | **22 (54%)** | 2 | " " |
| 15. Employees, including management, are given recognition when they perform at above-average levels. | 0 | 1 | 12 (29%) | **24 (58%)** | 2 | Recognition/ achievement |
| 16. Change is always welcome with little to no resistance. | 1 | 8 ) | **19 (46%)** | **13 (32%)** | 0 | Resistance to and acceptance of change |
| 17. New and useful ideas are openly solicited. | 0 | **15 (36%)** | **16 (39%)** | 7 | 3 | " " |

**Table H.1** (continued)

| STATEMENT | NEVER | SELDOM | SOMETIMES | USUALLY | ALWAYS | AREA |
|---|---|---|---|---|---|---|
| 18. We, as managers, always seek to find the causes of problems and jointly seek to resolve them. | 0 | **25** (61%) | 11 (27%) | 5 | 0 | Problem resolution |
| 19. One is rewarded for assuming greater degrees of responsibility. | 1 | **17** (41%) | **16** (39%) | 4 | 3 | Awards/incentive/ recognition |
| 20. I have problems relating professionally to other members of the management team. | 1 | 2 | 10 (24%) | **26** (64%) | 2 | Interpersonal relationships |

**PART II**

The following are statements contained in the survey questionnaire along with their response percentages. Participants were to complete the following sentence after reading each statement: **"This factor is a problem..."**

| Statement | NEVER | SELDOM | SOMETIMES | USUALLY | ALWAYS | AREA |
|---|---|---|---|---|---|---|
| 1. Not knowing just what the people you work with expect of you. | 5 | **25** (61%) | 7 | 3 | 0 | Fulfilling expectations |
| 2. Feeling that you have to do things on the job that are against your better judgement. | 4 | **27** (69%) | **22** (54%) | 1 | 0 | Self -conflict/ judgment |

| | | | | | | |
|---|---|---|---|---|---|---|
| 3. Thinking that you will not be able to satisfy conflicting demands of various people over you. | 3 | **15** (36%) | **22** (54%) | 1 | 0 | Task/work-load accomplishment |
| 4. Feeling that you have too heavy a work-load, one that you possibly cannot finish during an ordinary day. | 0 | 4 | **13** (32%) | **18** (44%) | 6 | " " |
| 5. Not having enough time to do your work properly. | 0 | 2 | **24** (59%) | 10 (24%) | 5 | Lack of time |
| 6. Having the requirements of the job impact on your personal life. | 0 | 4 | **18** (44%) | 10 (24%) | 0 | Job versus personal life |
| 7. Being unclear on just what the scope and responsibilities of your job are. | 7 | **21** (51%) | 11 (27%) | 2 | 0 | Authority and responsibility |
| 8. Feeling that you have too little authority to carry out the responsibilities assigned to you. | 5 | **17** (41%) | **14** (34%) | 4 | 1 | " " |
| 9. Not being able to get the information you need to carry out your job. | 4 | 12 (29%) | **22** (54%) | 1 | 2 | Communications |
| 10. Not knowing what your superiors think of you - how they evaluate your performance. | 11 (27%) | **19** (46%) | 9 (22%) | 2 | 0 | Performance evaluation and feedback |
| 11. Not being able to predict the reactions of people above you. | 1 | **19** (46%) | **19** (46%) | 2 | 0 | Superior's reaction |
| 12. Having ideas considerably different from those of your managers. | 1 | **21** (51%) | **17** (46%) | 2 | 0 | Philosophical conflicts |

need clarification. Currently we are making large inroads into our market. Our administrative efforts need to be enhanced just to keep pace with the growth and changes in the business. If a clear and reasonable list of priorities was set, we could be more effective and efficient in the delivery of service to our customers. Second, there has been an increased segmentation between work groups. In part this may be due to the lack of corporate priorities and the fact that not all the work gets done within an acceptable period of time. While some friction is normal and should be expected, it is difficult to perceive a concerted "team" effort underway. Third, the organizational structure itself is limiting. Each person's job is very demanding and requires a varied set of skills, yet the organizational structure does not facilitate recognition through advancement. There are only seven job levels between the president and entry-level management. As someone in middle management—pay grades 4 and 5—there is not much room for advancement. A higher number of job levels is needed to foster increased performance and rewards such as promotion, advancement, and the like.

- First, some individuals are more concerned with making sure that their personal career and position is protected than they are with admitting a mistake so that the mistake can be fixed and not repeated. This would benefit the company as a whole. Second, Finance and Operations sometimes seem jealous about the leadership role that is naturally taken by the Marketing Department.
- I see individual ambition being counterproductive to the company's business objectives. The vice presidents of Operations and Finance are jealous of the vice president of Marketing's promotion to a pay grade above them. This inhibits their ability to rationally and impartially address interdepartmental concerns. For example, the Operations vice president is extremely defensive. Lots of his time and energies are diverted to cover-up activities and behind-the-scenes manipulation. One of his subordinates has the very same style. Both are extremely ambitious and are not team players.
- I feel that there are two problems which have the potential to inhibit team development progress with the company. First, there is a lack of timely communication between departments. In all areas we are on an extremely fast-paced timetable. We often fail to realize the urgent needs that the next person might have in having access to the information you have in order that they can properly prepare for the next change or addition in customer service accounts. The second major problem is the lack of time—or perhaps better worded as the amount of responsibilities each manager has and the time required to carry them out correctly. I feel that the company could use more lower-level managers such as pay grades 1 and 2 to accomplish some of the more mundane day-to-day responsibilities and tasks.
- First, there is a very narrow vision of corporate goals by the employees. In a lot of cases, individual goals come first, company goals second. There is a virtual absence of team player spirit. Second, there are too many jobs laden with overwhelming responsibility and accountability with very little authority accompanying them. This creates huge problems and major bottlenecks.
- The most important departmental problems affecting organizational team development are the amounts of negative competition introduced between the Operations and Finance organizations. Also, the amount of empire-building by the vice presidents is to the extent that work groups end up reporting to the wrong departments. What is worse is that this problem has remained unresolved. For example, Distribution Services should belong to the Marketing Department and not come under Finance. Similarly, the Information Systems group should be resident in a neutral department—again, not in Finance. We have also had externalization of problems within individual work groups that has resulted in excessive finger pointing with no real honest attempt to address the overall philosophical problem ever coming to light. There is a real conflict between

those who want centralization and those who want decentralization. This has added fuel to the empire-building-and-keeping fire.

- The first problem I see is that people tend to look at situations in terms of the overall company. People appear in many instances to be interested solely in protecting their "turf" or building their "empires" rather than taking an interest in rolling up their sleeves and pitching in to solve the problems in the interest of the company. This causes friction between the departments and tends to cause the second problem, which is "I did my job so it must be somebody else's fault." This leads to more finger pointing and memorandums which, in turn, further increases friction. It is a vicious cycle that we must, as a company, overcome. Unless people focus on the company as a whole and not on their individual departments and careers, the company will always be struggling to reach its business goals.
- As a mere infant in a rapidly expanding market, it is my opinion that there are many strengths as well as weaknesses in the company that affect sound organization development. As an employee, the following items reflect what I see to be the company's strengths and weaknesses:

  **Weaknesses**

  a. Lack of a clearly defined mission statement (if one exists at all)

  b. Lack of competitive business experience in senior management

  c. "Invisible" long-range planning

  d. Departmental and executive in-fighting

  e. Lack of individual departmental direction

  **Strengths**

  a. Good technical expertise

  b. Good, talented personnel

  c. Good positioning in the marketplace

  d. Excellent working environment (physical)

  e. Good financial backing

  While these items are not all of the goods and bads, I believe that these are the ones that have the most profound affect on the company's organizational growth and team development processes.
- Some problems I see that inhibit team building within the company are

  a. disproportionate work loads between employees—some people work long and hard while others are strictly "9 to 5ers"

  b. a lack of trust and communication between departments and also up and down throughout the organization

  c. the promotion candidate system is inconsistent—the ground rules appear to be adjusted to the situation at hand. There seems to be insufficient effort to promote from within—especially across department lines (e.g., Operations to Finance, Finance to Marketing, Marketing to Operations, etc.).

  d. distinct "kingdoms" in Operations, Finance, and Marketing. This has fostered a "my problem, your problem" environment that negatively affects the smooth operation of the business by inhibiting problem solving and decision making.
- I see conflict between departments and unusually heavy work loads carried by a small percentage of people as being the biggest inhibitors to increasing team effectiveness. Other major factors that have the potential to inhibit team building progress are conflicting objectives between departments and the feeling of many field service

employees that the headquarters staff is unresponsive to their requests for support and assistance.

- The two most major problems which have the potential to inhibit progress in organizational team development are the lack of manpower and the lack of automation. The work load for each manager is much too heavy, and as a result, errors are made to many people simply being overworked. There also needs to be more automation within the company—the telephone system alone is evidence of the need for more efficient and effective support systems.
- The company has entered the full competitive stage of development which is new to many managers who lack this kind of experience. This change has and will continue to create substantial levels of stress and insecurity until everyone realizes that the team approach is the most effective way to compete in the real world. Additionally, priorities in the business appear to be disjointed. Many managers appear to always be fighting fires which I feel is a sign of poor planning or a lack of skill sets necessary to correctly perform the required tasks. From my point of view, everyone loses when managers are not given the liberty to perform their tasks over a reasonable period of time. Innovation and creativity are stymied because of short-term solutions being implemented in an effort to solve long-term problems.
- I think that a major inhibitor to building effective work teams in this company is that persons who are in daily contact with customers are usually the last ones to know about services and changes in pricing. These two factors combined negatively impact on our ability to service our customers. Another factor is that too many decisions are required at the vice presidential level. Authority should be more decentralized. Our planning for each market is done by persons who are not in these markets or have never been there. The local managers in our markets are seldom consulted about pricing, customer quotas, technological changes, advertising/media selection, or local municipal requirements. Our competition appears to be better positioned in localized markets and, therefore, they become positioned better and faster. I think our planning staff underestimated how aggressive our competition would be. Likewise, they underestimated the budget requirements that would be needed to simply maintain parity between us and our competition.
- I think that one of the biggest problems facing team development at this company is that there is too much paperwork. As the staff increases, the volume of paperwork increases and thus, the work load and the responsibilities of each manager increase commensurately. The result is that the local field service managers end up being facilitators and responding to the requirements of the staff rather than responding to the needs of the customers.
- The major problem that inhibits the company forming as a team is interdepartmental feuding. It has become Finance versus Marketing versus Operations. Employees are spending too much time defending their turfs and/or accusing other departments rather than cooperating on fixing problems and providing better service to our customers. Another problem is the mentality of many of the staff. We are a young, growth-oriented company that should be flexible enough to adapt to virtually any type of situation. We should not be resistant to trying out new things simply because many are comfortable with the way things have always been done—regardless of whether what was done was right or wrong.
- The biggest obstacle to team development is the rapid growth of the company itself. We are so focused on capturing market share that we cannot foresee problems that are right around the corner. As a result, we become reactionary and often implement "knee-jerk" solutions. When a company grows at a rate at which we have, personnel in all departments become stretched. They are forced to focus on completing their next project,

which creates a constant environment where output from departments is produced without focusing on how that output will affect other departments. No department stands alone. Everything that Operations does affects Marketing, everything that Marketing does affects Finance, and so on. We must each carefully consider how our work impacts the other departments. This can only be done by communicating more and fighting less.

- One problem with building effective teams in this company is employee burnout. Another is that senior managers appear to lack understanding of how to lose a battle in order to win the war. Many managers are, because of the culture of in-fighting, risk averse. They hedge their bets with slow deployment of resources and commitment. There are simply too many turf battles going on here. Each department tends to view itself as a self-sufficient feudal empire. There is also a big lack of trust between departments. The real problem, however, as I see it, is a lack of priorities. We tend to promote short-term gains rather than adopt strategies for long-term growth. These factors inhibit the company from coming together as a well-oiled and competitive team.
- In order to build effective teams there have to leaders. Our managers are simply spread too thin to concentrate on developing visions and then leading the company to goal attainment. Added to this, the lack of concern over hiring and adding more people at lower pay grades to do the daily, routine tasks causes people to become overworked—particularly managers. Not all departments pull in the same direction toward attaining the business objectives of the company. Many hide behind departmental policies which have grown underneath the company policies.
- The company policy is still focused on "lean and mean," which seriously curtails our ability to perform and respond to problems affecting our customers. Until we can begin to communicate intradepartmentally as well as interdepartmentally, our ability to service our customers as a team will continue to suffer. Because we are a new company, we must often do a lot of developmental work in support of administrative activities which have little to no positive impact on servicing our customers. Headquarters implements some new form, for example, and requires all field offices to complete it within a certain period of time without even explaining why the information is needed or, further, what it will be used for. As a result, many managers simply put anything down and send it in just to get it off their desk. This misinformation, as it were, can greatly inhibit our ability to compete and does little to engender headquarters to the field staff.
- There is far too much in-fighting and politics both inter- as well as intradepartmentally. This puts the brakes on any type of team-building effort. It is particularly noticeable at the more senior levels. More effort is spent on finger pointing and dynasty building than at solving problems. Consequently, organizational efficiency suffers and ultimately, this translates into poor service quality for our customers. There never seems to be enough time to do the job right but always enough time to do it over. The pace of the business inhibits proper training and development of management personnel.
- There are many talented, strong-willed managers working here. Most have career aspirations that are well beyond the ability of the company to meet. As the realization of the degree of competition for advancement becomes widespread, I believe that maintaining a balance between individual competition and teamwork will become increasingly difficult. As we have grown, communication problems have increased. Some interdepartmental attention to the problem of establishing and maintaining a regular flow of information is needed.
- A major inhibitor to team building is an unwillingness of many managers to accept responsibility when things go wrong, particularly at the more senior levels. There is too much rivalry between top managers, which has fostered a sense of "us" and "them" between their respective departments.

- One of the biggest things I see blocking effective team development is a lack of quality personnel. We use too many full-time "temps" to perform what I think are important tasks. Due to the lack of personnel, many people are often overworked and cannot devote the amount of attention to details which get swept under the carpet. This results in poor service to our customers. Further, many managers then begin to blame other managers for mistakes which have gone unnoticed in their own departments. This is a continuous cycle. I think that proper planning and working effectively in intradepartmental team units is the way to overcome these problems.
- Interdepartmental conflicts are the biggest obstacles to building effective organizational teams. Each department appears to be more interested in building their staffs and pointing fingers than they are in identifying and solving problems. Some departments appear to take the position that their individual needs outweigh those of the entire company. These attitudes are both demoralizing and counterproductive when trying to develop a team attitude and approach.
- One of the major inhibitors I see to building teams in the company is the now extensive use of temporary personnel. This directly impacts on how departments are staffed, organized, and how they respond to customer needs. It also impacts, negatively, I think, on how departments communicate with each other. For example, when work loads increase, many departments just add more people and try to smother the problem with bodies instead of addressing the problem and trying to figure it out using permanent staff. No matter how good or dedicated the temps are, you cannot build effective organizational work teams with temporary personnel.
- The major problems which I feel will inhibit progress in team development are
  a. The perception that more employees equates to more power and higher esteem.
  b. The cover-up and finger-pointing syndrome whereby employees and departments are more concerned with "covering up" or making someone else "look bad" than in concentrating on and solving problems.
  c. Procedures, policies, and rules are defined at the departmental level as opposed to the company level; thus, there are significant differences between the way the same items or situations are handled by different departments. This causes department loyalties and jealousies to override corporate loyalty and undermines the company's overall goal-setting processes.
  d. The example set by top management is, at times, not one of teamwork for the benefit of all but rather of teamwork within individual departments.
- Each department and, specifically, groups within each department, seem to always be trying to make themselves look good—often at the expense of others. There is a lot of covering up or trying to make problems look as if they were either caused or should be taken care of by another department. There also seems to be a lot of friction between the officers of the company and maybe even the president. Perhaps this is because they think that interdepartmental competitiveness is good. I do not agree with that.
- I think the level of employee morale has the greatest effect on building effective organizational teams. I also think that this level has gone down in the last year in spite of overall good performance. While all employees appreciated the healthy bonuses they received this year, this was not enough to improve morale. I think that morale is decreasing due to pressures and stresses of the job. A lot of this pressure and certainly the stress levels could be significantly reduced if departments and work groups within these departments would cooperate and especially communicate more. Also, in the early days, when the company was being formed, there was a great deal of talk about high risk/high reward. This has not turned out to mean anything. While we have received

good bonuses, we have not received pay increases, and it is apparent that similar levels of managers in competitors' companies make a lot more—salary-wise.

- Several organizations desire to develop their own specialized teams. Our specialists have developed out of in-fighting which has produced an "us" against "them" mentality.
- One thing that could be corrected through the building of more effective work teams would be a reduction in the administrative burden. With the pace of our growth, we need to streamline our administrative and procedural requirements and not require vice presidential–level signatures on routine forms to order such things as office supplies. This approach does not produce any savings.

2. List *two* outcomes which you would like or expect to see as a result of this assessment.
   - I would like for us to achieve the following:
     a. Raise the level of awareness between senior managers that we need to cooperate and not defend individual fiefdoms and turfs.
     b. Raise the level of trust among higher management to reduce friction and unnecessary stress.
   - The first outcome would be to call a truce between the departments and start working as a company, not as individual, self-contained kingdoms. The president needs to take a more proactive role in setting corporate policy, not simply entrust it to the vice presidents. Too many departments are setting their own playing rules. It is difficult for middle managers to try to cooperate when their superiors cannot get along. The second outcome I would like to see is higher levels of interdepartmental cooperation. It is imperative to develop teams where each team member knows specifically what his or her duties are and, more important, how their work impacts or otherwise affects people in other departments and in other teams.
   - I would like for this study to make us aware of what we have done and are doing to quality personnel and the frustrations that are felt by a great many people in this organization. We have a wonderful opportunity here to become the premier company in this market if we do not blow it by allowing turf battles to refocus our attention inward and away from the customer. I hope this study sends a message to "stop the finger pointing."
   - I would like the outcome to build trust and confident relationships between all management personnel. I would like to see an efficient information and communication system established that would help, not handicap, the flow of vital information between departments.
   - That senior management emerges as a "team" and as an example for the rest of us to follow. That the focus be set toward a common goal and the destruction of these little power-hungry fiefdoms.
   - That the company become stronger as a result of this project. That emphasis be placed on the company's strongest and most valuable asset—its employees.
   - I would like to see the organization structure changed to capitalize on our strengths collectively (e.g., technical acumen, marketing savvy, and so on).
   - I would like to see us focusing more on the customers' needs and less on our own. We have to realize that we have a significant investment in our customers and we must continue to invest time as well as materials in order to continue the level of service we have promised. Operating as independent departments with differing sets of goals as well as expectations does not do us or our customers a damn bit of good.
   - I would like to see us become more proactive to change as opposed to simply watching

it take place and then scrambling to try to react to it. We need to focus attention on our customers' needs and try to predict what our customers will expect from us in the future. We need to stop focusing on the politics of the office and set a clearer direction for all employees to follow.

- I would like to see us emerge as a true team complete with the attitudes and the resources necessary to make this company the best. It is as simple as that.
- I would like to see a reorganization come out of all of this with increased accountability that would make it difficult to point fingers when something goes wrong. With a system like this, we could pinpoint problems and solve them a lot quicker.
- I would think that a natural outcome from the assessment would be senior management team building first—to set the pace and direction—and then middle-management team building to follow.
- A better way of setting policy and direction.
- Increased communication and a better sense of "all of us" instead of "us and them."
- I would like to see more efficient state-of-the-art communication systems and increased cooperation.
- I think senior management must recognize that we are not a startup company anymore. We have to start acting like a corporation. We have to develop more integrated strategies so we can proactively understand how to offset our competitors. We need to be cognizant of warning signs in the marketplace and our intelligence about what other companies are doing needs to be improved. Finally, we need to be able to better disseminate this information internally so that everyone understands what the stakes are. I think this is the most important outcome of the assessment.
- Get rid of the departmentalization that has taken root. We must collectively work to reduce administrative bottlenecks, improve our customer service systems, and eliminate redundancies. We have to focus not only on selling but also on keeping customers.
- I would like to see better communication between departments so that each recognizes that their output is another's input. A clearly defined set of goals that focuses on the customer.
- We need to reduce interdepartmental conflict. I do not know how, exactly, but just the fact that you people are here doing this project is encouraging.
- An improvement in real cooperation and communication between departments.
- I would like for us to implement some change rather than just talk about it. We need to improve our flexibility in how we attract, service, and hold on to our customers.
- I would like to see a system where all individuals realize that mistakes happen and that it does not do any good to "hang" the one who committed the error. Rather, we need to work collectively to try to make certain that the same mistakes do not happen over and over again.
- I think that an increased sense of trust and cohesiveness among the president's staff has to result from this—especially if they are permitted to read the actual comments that their employees have provided. I do not know what you have collected up to now, but I can tell you two things for certain: When you are finished, you will have a lot of people talking about getting rid of the turf battles and improving inter- as well as intradepartmental communication.
- I think that the best outcome would be increased communication and a sharing of creativity between all employees.
- One outcome I would like to see is for top management to act on the recommendations

of this report. I would also like to see a more unified approach to solving problems with decisions being made for the overall good of the company and not tailored to fit the needs of a select few.

- More cohesive and flexible teams.
- A philosophical agreement between upper managers to focus on the customer and not on cover-up activities.
- A more effective distribution of the work load.
- Faster response to customer needs. I think that another outcome would be to explore the allocation of resources as they are now and channel much needed resources where they will do the most good—in direct service to the customer to handle the customer's problems and not be distracted by our own—most of which are minor and are caused by too much in-fighting.
- As a middle manager yearning for guidance, I hope that the outcome of this project identifies and promotes corporate-wide goal setting and the mobilization of resources to attain those goals. I would also like to see progress in interdepartmental cooperation. I realize that any company needs a system of checks and balances, but all we have are the checks. This kills corporate momentum and eats up valuable time and resources toward no common end.
- I would like everyone to catch the vision of teamwork to improve interpersonal relations. To achieve this, organizational secrecy and imaginary boundaries must be eliminated. Internal communications must be improved. Also, I would expect everyone to have a better sense of work prioritization. Constant fire fighting will diminish productivity and decreases our potential to compete on an equal footing. Corporate objectives must be defined to clearly focus on the customer as the priority and in-fighting must end.
- Better teamwork between departments. Teamwork in which the entire team and not just one group or department benefits. Also, I would like to see increased efforts by the officers of the company to improve the quality of work life. This would decrease stress levels and produce a balance in the work outputs.
- A concerted effort on the part of top management to set an example of true company *"esprit de corps"* and to discourage policies or practices which benefit individual departments to the detriment of the company as a whole. Top management must seriously review the demands placed on middle managers with the overall objective of improving the quality of work.

## ANALYSIS

### Major Issues Identified by the Survey Questionnaires and the Individual Interviews

The following is a summary of the issues that were derived from an analysis of the aggregate data sets.

There is widespread perception by most middle managers that an atmosphere of internal competition for resources has resulted in a major struggle between the three primary departmental units: Marketing, Finance and Administration, and Operations. Managers believe that this has further produced an aggressive and combative problem-solving style which has filtered down and permeated their respective units. The outcome has divided the organization into territorial units, each having very real and distinct authority boundaries. The theme of Marketing against Finance and Administration, Finance against Operations, and Marketing against Operations is continual and one that was repeated over and over again.

Rapid growth may well be the prevailing factor which has fostered this environment and created the present climate of internalized competition. There is a widespread belief among middle managers that one must first be loyal to one's own department and then to the company. This has resulted in a diversion of the organization's talent and energies into "departmentalized" units, which has established a territorial "turf" system. This has been a major factor in deflecting or otherwise blocking the establishment of effective horizontal (inter- as well as intradepartmental) channels of communication. Likewise, cooperation between the departments has suffered.

There is also a perception that the structure of the company, the delegation of responsibilities, and the scope of activities in which each department is engaged is counterproductive to the overall success of the company. This is a direct product of the turf system that has materialized out of the departmentalization process. Many managers have apparently reached out to their counterparts in other departments. Yet, because of the deep-seated distrust the exists at the upper levels (e.g., the vice presidential levels), it is practically impossible for them to come together to focus on the causes and, further, on the intent of the problems that are affecting each department. Clearly, there is a lack of understanding of how decisions and outputs in one department affect and otherwise impact another department until such a time when a major problem (termed by some as a "fire") erupts and then all energies are concentrated on solving it. However, the process used to address the problem is left relatively undefined. The net result is that many middle managers are left with a sense of isolation brought on by internal conflicts that have deflected many managers' attention away from focusing on the customer. There is a widespread consensus that the organization must find a way to end departmentalization and the mindset that accompanies it. Problems which occur across departmental lines must be solved by the organization through clear communications and a sharing of the corporate vision. This allows everyone to benefit.

### Related Issues

The following issues surfaced through an intensive analysis of the data. These reflect on organizational policy, structure, practices, and operations.

1. *Where is the company now? What are our long-term objectives? What is our mission?* There appears to be broad consensus that the long-term goals and objectives of the company are not clear. For example, when considering a related question—What is our major product?—it is apparent that there is a lack of a uniform sense of corporate direction. This has caused confusion and has, in our belief, contributed to many managers expressing concern that the company is focused more inwardly than on attracting and serving customers. This problem is indicative of deep-rooted communication and corporate identity problems.

2. *Should temporary positions be turned into permanent ones?* There was relative agreement that increases in the work load have produced a situation where more administrative support is required. It is some managers' belief that although tempo-

rary help somewhat relieves the administrative burden, temporaries do not have any financial or career-related stake in the company and, therefore, do not perform at consistently higher levels. Many managers have suggested turning temporary positions into permanent ones.

3. *Should some of the internal functions we now do ourselves (e.g., customer account billing) be outsourced?* Many of the managers believe that, although many of these functions are central and directly contributes to the long-term financial health of the company, senior management should be encouraged to investigate the possibility of having accounts receivable handled by an independent contractor. This would free up some internal staff to concentrate on building a stronger service–culture base within the company.

## RECOMMENDATIONS

The following recommendations address the major issues defined in the assessment. Because these issues are closely related, these recommendations were developed in a macro format—meaning that any related and concurrent actions or interventions taken would, in our opinion, adequately address these issues providing for a more targeted and objective approach. Each of the recommendations is summarized with an explanation as to why this particular procedure or course of action is recommended. In addition, all of the recommended actions and interventions are recommended based on the following requirements:

1. That any recommendations should not contribute, in any manner, to the disruption of the conduct of the organization's day-to-day business operations
2. That all recommendations should not focus attention to altering the organization's structure through dismissal of personnel, through major policy changes, or deviate significantly from the adopted and accepted methods of conducting business
3. That each recommendation should have the potential for implementation in a minimal amount of time and with a minimal amount of effort
4. That each recommendation produce the maximum amount of positive return where appropriate and positive change where necessary
5. That each recommendation should be cost-effective and measurable

### Framework

The following recommendations are made with the understanding that concurrent events are likely to simultaneously occur throughout various segments of the organization.

1. Initially we recommend that a hybrid system of job rotation be designed and put into place, especially for managers at pay grade levels of 4 and possibly 5. The purpose here is to provide each individual with a comprehensive view of the company, particularly with the practices and problems of their contemporaries and counterparts in other areas of the organization. Typically the advantages in adopting this approach are as follows:
   a. Each manager will gain more insight into the operations and procedures of which they may be currently unaware and which vary significantly from what they are normally accustomed to.

b. Each manager will experience, firsthand, the impact that each department and each decision made in each department has on the others.

c. Each manager will develop an acute appreciation for problems in other areas of the organization. They will also gain a broader understanding of how these problems transcend departmental boundaries and how they affect the efficiency of the company's operations as a whole.

d. Taking this approach will help to dismantle communication barriers which would provide a more positive department-to-department cross-flow of ideas and information and promote a team-oriented approach to identifying and solving both routine and nonroutine problems.

e. Adopting the job-rotation suggestion will provide a more solidified infrastructure and consolidate *individual* efforts into *organizational* efforts.

f. By enacting a job-rotation program, problem areas (as well as potential problem areas) can be highlighted and solutions developed inter- as well as intradepartmentally. This will facilitate team development by providing a network where problem identification and resolution will make a positive contribution to both tactical as well as long-range planning efforts.

g. The job-rotation system will promote curiosity outside of a manager's typical operational environment and extend his or her interest more toward the *organizational* level. An extra by-product of this type of system is that it builds external departmental networks, which can be useful in defusing potential interdepartmental conflicts.

h. Such a system would positively promote the overall concept of organizational team development.

i. If successful at this level, the rotational system could be implemented throughout all management levels.

Individuals can be scheduled for rotation on a short-term basis. For example, a manager in one area could conceivably move to one of their counterparts' positions (and vice versa) for a five- to ten-day period. Since it would not be logical or in anyone's best interest to permit the rotated managers' comprehensive decision-making responsibility or authority while in their temporary assignments, authority should be retained by the most senior department or unit manager who would serve as a mentor to his or her colleague. We further recommend that a voluntary system of participation be enacted in place of a compulsory one. Individuals should self-elect to participate.

2. We further recommend that the company give earnest consideration to establishing a focus group comprised of volunteers whose task would be to identify managerial, procedural, and/or operational problems that currently exist or have the potential to exist at some future point in time.

Typically these groups should contain between six and perhaps eight members with representation coming from all three major divisions (e.g., Marketing, Finance and Administration, and Operations). Building a focus group in this manner presents a more balanced and directive-oriented approach. Because the potential for confrontation between members from various departments is significant, the group should be facilitated and moderated by an individual from outside of the organization whose role would be to maintain the group's focus on problematic issues and to prevent deviations or personality clashes.

Internal focus groups are time-tested techniques that have significant advantages:

1. Focus groups can identify problems that are cross-departmental in nature and can form, analyze, test, and implement alternate solutions.
2. Research has shown that, through voluntary input and participation, focus groups promote individual as well as team initiative.
3. Interdepartment communications become more open with information shared on a more consistent and collaborative basis.
4. Problems affecting productivity and organizational performance can be routinely addressed and equitably solved without a major investment of time or material.

To ensure that the concept of the focus group is successful, recommendations made by the group must receive support from the senior management levels. This is imperative because it reinforces the positive impact the group can have on the organization as a whole. Group structure, agendas, schedules, and so on should be accomplished through the support staff in the HR department. Alternatively, group suggestions regarding problem resolution should be addressed through the facilitator who should serve as liaison to the company's senior officers.

Optimally, volunteers in the job-rotation effort could serve as the nucleus of the initial focus group(s).

3. We recommend that the senior management (e.g., the president and the vice presidents for Marketing, Finance and Administration, and Operations) establish a clearly defined corporate mission and review the current operational policies.

This recommendation represents an opportunity to clarify overlapping lines of authority and responsibility. The intent is to clarify operational objectives and to promote a broader sense of solidarity and cooperation at the company's most senior level. We recommend that this action be undertaken with the help and guidance of a facilitator who is experienced in working on policy-related issues at a more general level. This individual should have no subjective interest in the company.

In particular, the goals of this recommendation would be to examine the roles of the company's senior managers and how these roles are appropriated. The outcome is designed to increase the efficiency of the company's operations. The fact that individual differences can positively contribute to improving interpersonal relationships is many times overlooked in favor of a less confrontational approach. Through this process, sensitivity to individual problems that affect the entire company can be increased.

In this context, the moderator assumes the role of information flow–group facilitator and attempts to bridge the gap between sides who have conflicting points of view. Research has shown that more resolute and equitable solutions can be reached by examining all sides affecting the dispute as long as each individual's needs are not permitted to overshadow those of the others.

In order for this recommendation to be effective, building sensitivity to each person's needs, ego, and attitudes will be of primary concern. As problems and resolutions at the senior level become more obvious and as relations become more productive, the outcome will filter down through the organizational structure which establishes a "role model" for subordinate managers to pattern and implement.

## SUMMARY

While the scope of this assessment has tended to focus on the more negative aspects of conditions as they currently exist with the company, there are also many positive attributes in place as well. Most notable of these is the sense of dedication and loyalty exhibited by the staff. In lieu of current times and when compared to other organizations we have been associated with, this is quite exemplary. Also, the openness with which individuals responded during the interview process denotes an air of confidence equally in themselves, in the product and service they provide, and, most important, in the future of the company itself. Add to this the degree of cooperation and hospitality provided while we conducted this assessment; it was, overall, an enjoyable and learning experience.

The company is facing exciting yet relatively uncharted times. In its present condition there is no precedent activities or histories to draw upon for purposes of comparison. This being so, the case for the need to improve interdepartmental, intradepartmental, and organization-wide communication and team effectiveness is clear. Without these changes, the company runs the risk of losing its competitive advantage. It is our concerted opinion that, should the company respond positively and react to the issues outlined herein, it will remain competitive and at the forefront of its market.

Unfortunately, there are no short-term cures. To adequately address the issues outlined in this report will require time, patience, and commitment. It will also require a substantial amount of trial and error. Overall, we believe that the implementation of these recommendations are germane to the company's continued success.

# Bibliography


Aguilar, J. *General Managers in Action*. New York: Oxford University Press, 1988.

*ASTD Buyer's Guide and Consultant Directory*, 1994.

Berry, J. "Linking Management Development to Business Strategies." *Training and Development Journal*, Vol. 44, No. 8, pp. 20–22.

Bixler, S. *Professional Presence*. New York: Perigee Books, 1992.

Borg, W., and M. Gall. *Educational Research: An Introduction*. 4th ed. New York: Longman, 1983.

Bowers, D., and L. Stambaugh. "Making Organizational Surveys Pay Off." In *Organizational Development: Targeting Change*, edited by C. Jackson, pp. 41–54. Alexandria, Va.: American Society for Training and Development, 1986.

Box, G., W. Hunter, and J. Hunter. *Statistics for Experimenters: An Introduction to Design, Data Analysis, and Model Building*. New York: Wiley & Sons, 1978.

Bradburn, N., and S. Sudman. *Polls and Surveys: Understanding What They Tell Us*. San Francisco: Jossey-Bass, 1988.

Bramley, P. *Evaluating Training Effectiveness*. New York: McGraw-Hill, 1991.

Brightman, H. *Group Problem Solving: An Improved Managerial Approach*. Atlanta: Business Press, Georgia State University, 1988.

Brown, A. "TQM: Implications for Training." *Industrial and Commercial Training*, Vol. 25, No. 1, pp. 20–26.

Bureau of Business Practice. *BPP Training Director's Handbook*. Waterford, Conn.: Prentice Hall, 1989.

Cafferella, R. *Program Development and Evaluation Resource Book for Trainers*. New York: Wiley & Sons, 1988.

Cannes, W. *Effective Meetings for Busy People*. New York: McGraw-Hill, 1980.

Champion, D., D. Kiel, and J. McLendon. "Choosing A Consulting Role." *Training and Development Journal*, Vol. 44, No. 2, pp. 66–69.

Coleman, G., and E. Van Aken. "Applying Small Group Behavior Dynamics to Improve Action-Team Performance." *Employment Relations Today*, Vol. 18, No. 3, pp. 343–353.

Cooper, H. "The Integrative Research Review/A Systematic Approach." *Applied Social Research Methods Series*. Beverly Hills, Calif.: Sage Publications, 1984.

Croft, R. "How to Minimize the Problem of Untruthful Response." *Business Marketing Digest*, Vol. 17, No. 3, pp. 17–23.

Dangot-Simpkin, G. "How Come Nothing Changed?" *HR Magazine*, Vol. 36, No. 11, pp. 66–68.

Dunnington, R. "New Methods and Technologies." In *Improving Organizational Surveys: New Directions and Methods*, edited by P. Rosenfeld, J. Edwards, and M. Thomas. *American Behavioral Scientist*, Vol. 36, No. 4, pp. 512–530.

Dyer, S. "Kirkpatrick's Mirror." *Journal of European Industrial Training*, Vol. 18, No. 5, pp. 31–32.

Edwards, J., and M. Thomas. "The Organizational Survey Process." In *Improving Organizational Surveys: New Directions and Methods*, edited by P. Rosenfeld, J. Edwards, and M. Thomas. *American Behavioral Scientist*, Vol. 36, No. 4, pp. 419–442.

Erkut, S., and J. Fields. "Focus Groups to the Rescue." *Training and Development Journal*, Vol. 41, No. 10, pp. 74–76.

Fisher, S. "Cutting Costs or Rebuilding Business?" *European Management Journal*, Vol. 11, No. 1, pp. 74–79.

Flamholtz, E. *Human Resource Accounting*. 2nd ed. San Francisco: Jossey-Bass, 1985.

Ford, D. "Benchmarking HRD." *Training and Development*, Vol. 47, No. 6, pp. 37–41.

Fowler, F. "How Unclear Terms Affect Survey Data." *Public Opinion Quarterly*, Vol. 56, No. 2, pp. 360–370.

Fowler, F. *Survey Research Methods*. Newbury Park, Calif.: Sage Publications, 1988.

French, W. "The Emergence and Early History of Organization Development with Reference to Influences upon and Interactions among Some of the Key Actors." In *Contemporary Organization Development*, edited by D. Warrick, pp. 18-19. Glenview, Ill.: Scott, Foresman, 1985.

Fulmer, R., and K. Graham. "A New Era of Management Education." *Journal of Management Development*, Vol. 12, No. 3, pp. 30–38.

Gagne, R., and L. Briggs. *Principles of Instructional Design*. New York: Holt, Rinehart, & Winston, 1979.

Gayeski, D., L. Wood, and J. Ford. "Getting Inside an Expert's Brain." *Training and Development*, Vol. 48, No. 8, pp. 106–110.

Geer, J. "Do Open-Ended Questions Measure 'Salient' Issues?" *Public Opinion Quarterly*, Vol. 55, No. 3, pp. 360–370.

Gibson, J., J. Ivancevich, and J. Donnelly, Jr. *Organizations: Behavior, Structure, Processes*. 6th ed. Plano, Tex.: Business Publications, Inc., 1988.

Gilbert, T. "Measuring Performance at Work." In *Assessment for Decision*, edited by D. Peterson and D. Fishman. New Brunswick, N.J.: Rutgers University Press, 1987.

Goldberg, C. "TQM: At the Crossroads." *Workforce Training News*, Vol. 2, No. 8, pp. 16–19.

Goldstein, I. *Training in Organizations: Needs Assessment, Development, and Evaluation*. Monterey, Calif.: Brooks/Cole, 1986.

Grant, R., R. Shani, and R. Krishnan. "TQM's Challenge to Management Theory and Practice." *Sloan Management Review*, Vol. 35, No. 2, pp. 25–35.

Greenbaum, T. "Do You Have the Right Moderator for Your Focus Groups?" *Bank Marketing*, Vol. 23, No. 1, p. 43.

Greenbaum, T. "Outside Moderators Maximize Focus Group Results." *Public Relations Journal*, Vol. 47, No. 9, pp. 31–32.

Greenbaum, T. *The Practical Handbook and Guide to Focus Group Research.* New York: The Free Press, 1990.

Griffin, R., and G. Moorhead. *Organizational Behavior.* Boston: Houghton Mifflin, 1986.

Gropper, G., and P. Ross. "Instructional Design." In *Training and Development Handbook.* 3rd ed., edited by R. Craig, pp. 195–216. New York: McGraw-Hill, 1987.

Hannum, W., and C. Hansen. *Instructional Systems Development in Large Organizations.* Englewood Cliffs, N.J.: Educational Technology Publications, 1989.

Hawthorne, E. *Evaluating Employee Training Programs: A Research-based Guide for Human Resource Managers.* Westport, Conn.: Quorum Books, 1987.

Henry, G. *Practical Sampling.* Newbury Park, Calif.: Sage Publications, 1990.

Hines, W., and D. Montgomery. *Probability and Statistics in Engineering and Management Science.* New York: Wiley & Sons, 1980.

Hon, D. *Meetings that Matter.* New York: Wiley & Sons, 1980.

Hussey, D. "Implementing Corporate Strategy: Using Management Education and Training." *Long Range Planning*, Vol. 18, No. 5, pp. 28–37.

Iman, R., and W. Conover. *Modern Business Statistics.* New York: Wiley & Sons, 1983.

James, L., S. Muliak, and J. Brett. *Causal Analysis: Assumptions, Models, and Data.* Newbury Park, Calif.: Sage Publications, 1982.

Jeffries, J., and J. Botes. *The Executive's Guide to Meetings, Conferences, and Audio-Visual Presentations.* New York: McGraw-Hill, 1983.

Karl, K., and J. Kopf. "Guidelines for Using Videotaped Feedback Effectively." *Human Resource Development Quarterly*, Vol. 4, No. 3, pp. 303–310.

Kaufman, R. "Auditing Your Needs Assessments." *Training and Development*, Vol. 48, No. 2, pp. 22–23.

Kenny, M. *Presenting Yourself.* New York: Wiley & Sons, 1982.

Kirkpatrick, D. "Riding the Winds of Change." *Training and Development*, Vol. 47, No. 2, pp. 29–32.

Kirkpatrick, D. "Techniques for Evaluating Training Programs." *Journal of the American Society of Training Directors*, Vol. 13, pp. 3–9, 21–26; Vol. 14, pp. 13–18, 28–32.

Knowles, M. *The Adult Learner: A Neglected Species.* Houston: Gulf Publishing, 1973.

Koontz, H., and C. O'Donnell. *Principles of Management: An Analysis of Managerial Functions.* 4th ed. New York: McGraw-Hill, 1968.

Kosecoff, J., and A. Fink. *Evaluation Basics: A Practitioner's Manual.* Beverly Hills, Calif.: Sage Publications, 1982.

Laird, D. *Approaches to Training and Development.* 2nd ed. Reading, Mass.: Addison-Wesley, 1985.

Langdon, D. "The Individual Management Development Program." *Training and Development Journal*, Vol. 36, No. 3, pp. 78–82.

Lawler, E. "Total Quality Management and Employee Involvement: Are They Compatible?" *Academy of Management Executives*, Vol. 8, No. 1, pp. 68–76.

Lessler, J., and W. Kalsbeek. *Nonsampling Error in Surveys.* New York: Wiley & Sons, 1992.

Lewin, K. *Field Theory in Social Sciences.* New York: Harper & Row, 1951.

Lewis, P. "Eight Steps to the Successful Appointment of a Training Consultant." *Journal of European Industrial Training*, Vol. 15, No. 7, pp. 25–29.

Likert, R. *New Patterns of Management*. New York: McGraw-Hill, 1961.

Little, R., and D. Rubin. *Statistical Analysis with Missing Data*. New York: Wiley & Sons, 1983.

London, M., and R. Wueste. *Human Resource Development in Changing Organizations*. Westport, Conn.: Quorum Books, 1992.

Long, L. "Surveys from Start to Finish." In *Info-Line*, edited by G. Spruell. Alexandria, Va.: American Society for Training and Development, 1986.

Ludeman, K. "Measuring Skills and Behavior." *Training and Development*, Vol. 45, No. 11, pp. 61–66.

Mager, R. *Preparing Instructional Objectives*. Belmont, Calif.: Fearon, 1962.

Marguiles, N., and A. Raia. *Conceptual Foundations of Organizational Behavior*. New York: McGraw-Hill, 1978.

Martell, R., and R. Guzzo. "The Dynamics of Implicit Group Performance: When and How Do They Operate?" *Organizational Behavior and Human Decision Processes*, Vol. 50, No. 1, pp. 51–74.

McClelland, S. "Gaining Competitive Advantage through Strategic Management Development." *Journal of Management Development*, Vol. 13, No. 5, pp. 4–13.

McClelland, S. "A Model for Designing Objective-Oriented Training Evaluations." *Industrial and Commercial Training*, Vol. 26, No. 1, pp. 3–9.

McClelland, S. "Performance and Productivity Improvement: Applying a Time-to-Progress Model." *Industrial Management*, Vol. 29, No. 4, pp. 10–14.

McClelland, S. "A Systems Approach to Needs Assessment." *Training and Development*, Vol. 46, No. 8, pp. 51–53.

McClelland, S. "Training Needs Assessment: An 'Open-Systems' Application." *Journal of European Industrial Training*, Vol. 17, No. 1, pp. 12–17.

McClelland, S. "Training Needs Assessment Data-Gathering Methods—Part I: Survey Questionnaires." *Journal of European Industrial Training*, Vol. 18, No. 1, pp. 22–26.

McClelland, S. "Training Needs Assessment Data-Gathering Methods—Part II: Individual Interviews." *Journal of European Industrial Training*, Vol. 18, No. 2, pp. 27–31.

McClelland, S., N. Harbaugh, and S. Hammond. "Improving Individual and Group Effectiveness." *Journal of Management Development*, Vol. 12, No. 3, pp. 48–58.

McGehee, W., and P. Thayer. *Training in Business and Industry*. New York: Wiley & Sons, 1961.

McGregor, D. *The Human Side of Enterprise*. New York: McGraw-Hill, 1960.

Miller, D. *Handbook of Research Design and Social Measurement*. 5th ed. Newbury Park, Calif.: Sage Publications, 1991.

Miller, R. "The Design and Implementation of Employee Opinion Surveys." *Employment Relations Today*, Vol. 16, No. 4, pp. 315–319.

Miller, V. "The History of Training." In *Training and Development Handbook: A Guide to Human Resource Development*. 3rd ed., edited by R. Craig, pp. 3–18. New York: McGraw-Hill, 1987.

Miriampolski, H. "Focus Groups on Sensitive Topics: How to Get Subjects to Open Up and Feel Good about Telling the Truth." *Applied Marketing Research*, Vol. 29, No. 1, pp. 6–11.

Miribile, R. "A Simple Approach to Skills Assessment." *Training and Development*, Vol. 45, No. 12, pp. 19–22.

Moore, M., and P. Dutton. "Training Needs Analysis: Review and Critique." *Academy of Management Review*, Vol. 3, No. 3, pp. 532–545.

Morris, L. "Organizational Culture and TQM Implementation." *Training and Development*, Vol. 48, No. 4, pp. 69–71.

Nadler, L. *Designing Training Programs: The Critical Events Model*. Reading, Mass.: Addison-Wesley, 1982.

Naisbitt, J. *Megatrends: Ten New Directions Transforming Our Lives*. New York: Warner Books, 1982.

Neelankavil, J. "Corporate America's Quest for an Ideal MBA." *Journal of Management Development*, Vol. 13, No. 5, pp. 38–52.

Nich, D. "Inquiry and Observation—Effective Internal Auditing Techniques." *Internal Auditing*, Vol. 3, No. 2, pp. 11–17.

O'Muircheartaigh, C. "Simple Response: Estimation and Determinants." In *Measurement Errors in Surveys*, edited by P. Biemar, et al., pp. 551–574. New York: Wiley & Sons, 1991.

Ostroff, C., and J. Ford. "Assessing Training Needs: Critical Levels of Analysis." In *Training and Development in Organizations*, edited by I. Goldstein, p. 55. San Francisco: Jossey-Bass, 1989.

Park, H., and J. Harrison. "Enhancing Managerial Cross-Cultural Awareness and Sensitivity: Transactional Analysis Revisited." *Journal of Management Development*, Vol. 12, No. 3, pp. 20–29.

Parry, S., and W. Ouweneel. "Consultants." In *Training and Development Handbook: A Guide to Human Resource Development*. 3rd ed., edited by R. Craig, p. 813. New York: McGraw-Hill, 1987.

Patel, A. "Total Quality Management (TQM): Paving the Way for Future Training?" *Industrial and Commercial Training*, Vol. 25, No. 2, pp. 23–32.

Pearson, E., and H. Hartley. *Biometrika Tables for Statisticians*. Vol. 1. 3rd ed. Cambridge: Cambridge University Press, 1966.

Phillips, J. *Handbook of Training Evaluation and Measurement Methods*. 2nd ed. Houston: Gulf Publishing, 1991.

Potts, D. "Bias Lurks in All Phases of Qualitative Research." *Marketing News*, Vol. 24, No. 18, pp. 12–13.

Reith, J. "Meetings, Workshops, Seminars, and Conferences." In *Training and Development Handbook: A Guide to Human Resource Development*. 3rd ed., edited by R. Craig, pp. 398–413. New York: McGraw-Hill, 1987.

Ripley, R., and M. Ripley. "Empowerment: The Cornerstone of Quality." *Management Decision*, Vol. 30, No. 4, pp. 20–43.

Rosenfeld, P., S. Booth-Kewley, and J. Edwards. "Computer Administered Surveys in Organizations." In *Improving Organizational Surveys: New Directions and Methods*, edited by P. Rosenfeld, J. Edwards, and M. Thomas. *American Behavioral Scientist*, Vol. 36, No. 4, pp. 485–511.

Rotondi, T. "The Annonymity Factor in Questionnaire Surveys." *Personnel Journal*, Vol. 68, No. 2, pp. 92–101.

Rue, L., and L. Byars. *Management: Theory and Application*, rev. ed. Homewood, Ill.: Richard D. Irwin, 1980.

Rummler, G. "Determining Needs." In *Training and Development Handbook: A Guide to Human Resource Development*, edited by R. Craig, pp. 217–247. New York: McGraw-Hill, 1987.

Sahl, R. "Company Specific Employee Attitude Surveys." *Personnel Journal*, Vol. 69, No. 5, pp. 46–51.

Schuman, H., and S. Presser. *Questions and Answers in Attitude Surveys: Experiments on Question Form, Wording, and Context*. New York: Academic Press, 1981.

Scrivens, M. "The Methodology of Evaluation." In *Curriculum Evaluation*, edited by R. Stake. American Educational Research Association Monograph Series on Evaluation, No. 1. Chicago: Rand McNally, 1967.

Senge, P. *The Fifth Discipline: The Art and Practice of the Learning Organization*. New York: Doubleday/Currency, 1993.

Sheatsley, P. "Questionnaire Construction and Item Writing." In *Handbook of Survey Research*, edited by P. Rossi, J. Wright, and A. Anderson, pp. 195-230. Orlando, Fla.: Academic Press, 1983.

Shelton, S., and G. Alliger. "Who's Afraid of Level 4 Evaluations?" *Training and Development*, Vol. 47, No. 6, pp. 43–46.

Shenson, H. *How to Select and Manage Consultants*. Lexington, Mass.: Lexington Books, 1990.

Sink, D. "Focus Groups as an Approach to Outcomes Assessment." *American Review of Public Administration*, Vol. 21, No. 3, pp. 197–204.

Smith, E. *The Productivity Manual*. Houston: Gulf Publishing, 1990.

Smits, S., and L. Pace. *The Investment Approach to Employee Assistance Programs*. Westport, Conn.: Quorum Books, 1992.

Stoneall, L. "Inquiring Trainers Want to Know: What Kinds of Questions Should Trainers Ask?" *Training and Development Journal*, Vol. 45, No. 11, pp. 31–39.

Sweets, C. "Role of Employment Communications." In *ASPA Handbook of Personnel and Industrial Relations*, edited by D. Yoder and H. Heneman, Jr., pp. 395–396. Washington, D.C.: Bureau of National Affairs, 1979.

Taylor, F. *The Principles of Scientific Management*. New York: Harper and Row, 1911.

Tedlow, R. "Glossary of Marketing Terms." In *Marketing Management: Texts and Cases*, edited by J. Quelch, R. Dolan, and T. Kosnik. Homewood, Ill.: Richard D. Irwin, 1993.

Thompson, C. "Project Management: A Guide." In *Infoline*, edited by B. Darraugh. Alexandria, Va.: American Society for Training and Development, 1990.

Tracey, W. *Designing Training and Development Systems*, rev. ed. New York: AMACOM, 1984.

*Training Magazine*, Vol. 30, No. 10, pp. 29–34.

Vroom, V. *Work and Motivation*. New York: Wiley & Sons, 1964.

Walton, M. *The Deming Management Method*. New York: Perigee Books, 1986.

Westgaard, O. "Measuring Performance." *Performance and Instruction Journal*, June/July, 1986, pp. 10–11.

Wiggerhorn, W. "Motorola U: When Training Becomes an Education." *Harvard Business Review*, Vol. 68, No. 4, pp. 71–83.

Wircenski, J., and R. Sullivan. "Make Every Presentation a Winner." In *Infoline*, edited by M. Callahan. Alexandria, Va.: American Society for Training and Development, 1986.

Wymer, W., and J. Carsten. "Alternative Ways to Gather Opinion." *HR Magazine*, Vol. 37, No. 4, pp. 66–71.

Zemke, R., and T. Kramlinger. *Figuring Things Out: A Trainer's Guide to Needs and Task Analysis*. Reading, Mass.: Addison-Wesley, 1984.

# Index

## ABOUT THE AUTHOR

**SAMUEL B. McCLELLAND** was Program Director in the Center for Executive Education in the College of Business Administration at Georgia State University in Atlanta. He worked for over fifteen years in the design and administration of needs assessment systems for public- and private-sector organizations. He was the author of numerous articles on the subject of management development, needs assessments, and evaluation systems.